More Praise for *When*

"Stuart Albert has given us an important, witty, and, yes, timely book about the role of timing in our decision-making. He helps us see that the timing of decisions lies within our control and that doing a timing analysis and having a 'temporal design' remains key to the success of any new venture. With examples not only from the business world, but also from politics and the arts, Albert reveals the fascinating complexity of something that we all engage in and yet rarely think about. What St. Augustine said about time applies as well to timing: 'If no one asks, I know what it is. If I wish to explain it ... I do not know.' This book does a fabulous job of explaining timing; read it and you will know."

—**Thomas Fisher,** dean, College of Design,
University of Minnesota

"Stuart Albert takes us to a whole new level of understanding of the role of time. We learn how to see windows of opportunity, identify when risks materialize, and map rhythms, rates, sequences, and intervals so as to be able to see their patterns and act in the right moment. *When* is a gift to those wanting to learn not just what to do but when to do it, as we attempt to lead in a dynamic, unfolding world."

—**Deborah Ancona,** Seley Distinguished Professor of Management
and professor of organization studies, MIT, and director, MIT
Leadership Center

when

The Art of Perfect Timing

Stuart Albert

JB·JOSSEY-BASS™
A Wiley Brand

Published by Jossey-Bass
A Wiley Brand
One Montgomery Street, Suite 1200, San Francisco, CA
94104-4594—www.josseybass.com

Jossey-Bass books and products are available through most bookstores. To
contact Jossey-Bass directly call our Customer Care Department within the U.S.
at 800-956-7739, outside the U.S. at 317-572-3986, or fax 317-572-4002.

Wiley publishes in a variety of print and electronic formats and by print-on-demand.
Some material included with standard print versions of this book may not be
included in e-books or in print-on-demand. If this book refers to media such as a CD
or DVD that is not included in the version you purchased, you may download this
material at **http://booksupport.wiley.com**. For more information about Wiley
products, visit **www.wiley.com**.

Library of Congress Cataloging-in-Publication Data

Albert, Stuart, 1941-

   When : the art of perfect timing / Stuart Albert. — 1 Edition.
      pages cm
   Includes index.
    ISBN 978-1-118-22611-7 (hardback), 978-1-118-41950-2 (ePDF),
    978-1-118-42109-3 (ePUB)
  1. Time management. I. Title.
  HD69.T54A43 2013
  650.1'1 — dc23

                      2013020215

Printed in the United States of America
FIRST EDITION
HB Printing   10 9 8 7 6 5 4 3 2 1

This book is for Rosita

contents

preface

Conventional wisdom suggests that any attempt to understand timing is futile. No one, it is said, can time the market or credibly predict the future. The world is too complex. There are too many unknowns. Every situation is different in some important way that makes past experience an imperfect guide. Moreover, sometimes getting the timing right is just a matter of luck, being in the right place at the right time with the right product or service. There is an element of truth in all of these observations. But the view that we cannot acquire skill in matters of timing is not only overly pessimistic; it is simply not true. With the right tools, we can be far better at managing and deciding issues of timing than conventional wisdom suggests. This book describes the nature of those tools and how to apply them.

For me, the key insight into issues of timing came in 2004. I was working in a makeshift office in my mother-in-law's apartment in São Paulo, Brazil. My wife and I were staying there as Dona Ella fought her final battle with cancer. A life was ending, and time was on my mind. Each morning, the cold winter sun would brighten the dark rosewood wall in our bedroom, and I would listen for the sound of the rooster that had always been present in past visits. But this year the rooster was silent. The last sounds of the city's rural past had vanished. In this apartment, where we had stayed during summers and Christmas vacations for more than thirty years, I discovered the concept of temporal architecture that forms the heart of this book. Although I didn't quite realize it at the time, this concept opened up a new way to approach the challenge of timing.

When I first began the study of timing in the spring of 1991, I made an explicit decision not to follow the norms of my profession. I am a professor in a business school, trained in the hard and social sciences. In contrast to the work of my colleagues, there was no "hypothesis" or explanation of "the facts" that I needed to test, no controlled experiments to run or large-scale surveys to administer. I didn't need a computer to "analyze the data" or build mathematical models. I didn't need statistics because there was nothing to count or measure. In short, I didn't need any of the sophisticated tools of modern social science. Instead, I went back to the time before they were invented. I became a hunter-gatherer.

I read the *New York Times*, the *Wall Street Journal*, and the *Economist* cover to cover and clipped out every article, regardless of subject matter, that had anything to do with timing. I paid particular attention to timing errors: an action begun too soon or too late, a project unexpectedly delayed, and a sound business that, to everyone's surprise, collapsed overnight. In each case, I tried to determine how better timing could have improved the outcome.

I slowly began to create a classification system to keep track of the clippings I was acquiring, now over two thousand. This was not just an academic exercise. One reason we fail to see timing issues in advance is that we don't have a practical way to search for them. The best way to find anything is to give it a name and address within a known structure. That is what this book will do: give you a way to find, name, and address timing issues anywhere in your work and life.

While I was organizing this material, I began working with a number of companies. The issues were diverse. A business venture based on a new technology failed, and timing was clearly part of the reason. A company ended up in court over a broken contract, and, in my judgment, a better understanding of timing would have produced a different outcome. I worked with the owner of a company who was trying to decide whether to match the price structure of a competing firm. A timing analysis revealed that no action was needed: the problem would solve itself because of rapid changes in the industry.

Now that I could see how deeply timing was involved in so many aspects of business, I had to pause. The topic of timing seemed boundless. It had no center, no obvious beginning or end. It was also complex, because sometimes *timing doesn't matter.* Some things will succeed or fail regardless of when we act. So, for the first ten years, I wrote largely for myself. I put what became almost eight hundred pages of notes and analysis into a folder on my computer and labeled it *A Book for My Own Use.* In the course of writing those notes, I discovered that timing errors weren't random and that, because they weren't random, at least some of them could be prevented. As I got deeper into the subject, I discovered processes and phenomena that I hadn't seen before. In my work with companies, I found that the approach I was developing had immediate practical application.

Later, as I sat down to write what I discovered, I found myself facing the great irony of our time: no time. Busy people rarely have the time to read a book of any length or complexity, so I've condensed, cut, shortened. If you start this book as you board a transatlantic flight, you will have a good idea of what a timing analysis consists of by the time you land. And if your flight is delayed (as so often occurs), then you will have ample time to finish it. What better way to kill time than to read a book on timing?[1]

introduction

Timing matters. And it matters in every aspect of business: from the launch of a new product to decisions about when to change strategic direction, spin off part of a company, accept a counteroffer, or invest in new equipment. History is full of innovative products and services that failed because they were too early. The market wasn't ready. The technology had too many bugs. Supporting infrastructure didn't exist. More commonly, in a world racing on steroids, the fatal flaw is being late. We should have moved more quickly. Our strategy would have worked, *if only* we had executed earlier. Unfortunately, as Homer said, *it is the height of folly to be wise too late.*

I've written *When* for executives in all fields and for people at every level of an organization where it is important to get the timing right. Most individuals and organizations already have some way of taking timing into account. For the individual, it may be to rely on the feeling in your gut or on what you have done in the past; for the organization, there may be a formal planning process or sophisticated models or algorithms. Whatever the approach, timing errors are common.

Some timing issues are easily identified. We know about them in advance: When is the right time to launch a product or a new business, for example? Is it too early or too late? When will a window of opportunity open, and when will it close? What time-related risks am I running? Will my industry change overnight? How should I proceed: incrementally with caution or as quickly as possible? But some timing issues are not so easy to identify, and missing them can have tragic consequences. Suppose, for example, that your job was to oversee the launch of the 2010 Winter Olympics in Vancouver, Canada. Clearly, the key issue, as far as timing was concerned, would be to make sure that the venues were ready and that all construction was completed in time for the games to begin. To do that, you would employ the sophisticated tools of project management. Your focus would be on logistics and scheduling. If things were running late, you would look for ways to speed them up, and so on. The last thing you would be prepared for would be a tragic accident just before the opening ceremony. And, yet, that is what happened when twenty-one-year-old Georgian Nodar Kumaritashvili died in a high-speed crash on the luge during his final training run. Could you—or should you—have seen this catastrophe coming? An accident is terrible whenever it occurs, but the timing of a fatal accident, just at the start of the games, could not have been worse.

If you were to look back to see how timing contributed to this accident, here is what you would see:

- There would be training runs before the start of the Olympics; in short, there was a known *sequence*: first training, then the real thing.
- The highest speeds on the track would occur at the end of training and right before the official start of the games; in short, you could predict how individuals training for speed events would increase their *rate* of speed. They wouldn't go all out in the beginning, while they are still learning the track.
- There was a clear demarcation between the end of training runs and the official start of the games—that is, a clear

punctuation mark, with little time (a short *interval*) between them.

- Beginning and endings have special emotions associated with them. An accident at the beginning casts a pall over everything that follows; an accident at the end remains in memory and darkens what came before, no matter how positive. So we know when the timing of a fatal accident would be most distressing.
- Why was the track so dangerous? In part, because the site on which it was built—selected to be a commercial success once the games were over—happened to have a topography that made for a particularly steep and twisting track. So part of the reason the track was dangerous was the result of planning that took into account its *future* use. There were two *windows of opportunity*, one during the games and one after. The latter increased the risks associated with the former.
- Finally, all these factors came together to create a condition of *synchronous risk*, the risk that two actions or events (the greatest speed on the track and the beginning of the games) would occur in close proximity with potentially serious consequences.

Would you have been in a position to highlight events that posed this kind of timing risk, and asked those building the venues to double down on safety? Or would the elements and clues you needed to arrive at that decision remain in the background, not something you were looking for or paying attention to? One objective of this book is to help you surface these kinds of timing risks in advance while there is still time to do something about them.

WHY DOES TIMING ELUDE US?

We miss timing issues, or make wrong decisions about them, not simply because our world is complex and uncertain, but because the way we describe the world and the tasks we must accomplish omit the kinds of facts we need. I call these fragmentary descriptions *time impoverished* because they fail to include all the sequences, rates, shapes, punctuation marks, intervals, leads, lags, overlaps, and other time-related characteristics that are part of the temporal structure of everything that happens, every action that is taken, every plan that is implemented.

It is not simply that we fail to include these time-based characteristics when we plan events. We routinely omit them from our everyday thinking. Consider the familiar concept of incentives in business. We normally ask whether all parties have the same incentives, whether they are the right ones, and whether they are powerful enough to produce the desired outcome. From a timing perspective, however, that is not enough. We also need to know whether all the relevant incentives will be present *at the same time*. When different incentives are present, which will dominate? Will one fade, just as another surfaces? It is not enough to blame a bad outcome on the *wrong* incentives. We need to know why those incentives became important *at that particular time*.

When I explain the concept of time-impoverished description to a college audience, the example I use is a kiss. I tell students that a kiss that lasts a fraction of a second is a peck; one that lasts a minute is a proposition; and one that lasts five minutes is an act of resuscitation. In short, we need to know how long a kiss lasts in order to know what it means. Similarly, a hug, if executed with less intensity but longer duration, is no longer a hug, but holding, the purpose of which may be constraint. Time, therefore, is not a container for our actions, but a *constituent* of them. Everything that happens in the world happens in a particular order, takes a certain amount of time, begins or ends at a specific moment, and so on. When these characteristics are left unspecified, we can easily miss or misread what is going on.

What I like to say is that *you can't solve for* t *if* T *is not in the equation*. You can't time events and decide when to act, or even know what someone else's action means, if your understanding of the world omits the **T**otality of time-relevant characteristics (sequences, rates, duration, beginnings, endings, and so on) on which timing depends. If you don't look for and note these temporal characteristics, you won't have the information you need to make good decisions about timing.

There are many reasons why our descriptions and explanations of the world tend to be time impoverished. First, as real estate agents are fond of telling us, location is everything. Our own location in time is described by a single word: *now*. *Now* is where we live, our immediate and concrete reality. We can't live in the past, except metaphorically, or in the future, except in our imagination. Although we are told to remember the lessons of history and to think long term, we will always remain closely tethered to the present moment. *Now* is the only place in time where we are truly alive.

Another source of our myopia, ironically, is the power of vision. We focus on what we can see. As a result, we forget to take time, which is invisible, into account. Consider the design of the human hand. Our thumbs are opposable—positioned opposite four other fingers—which makes it possible to grasp and hold objects. That makes the hand extremely useful. But what is missing from every account of the opposable thumb I have read is the need for synchronization. The thumb and the fingers must arrive at the same point *at the same time*. If the thumb had to wait minutes for the other fingers to arrive, or vice versa, a lot would slip through our fingers. The human hand would not function as the superb tool that it is. A spatial arrangement gets the credit, but timing does the work!

Another reason we miss the information we need to make timing decisions, besides the tendency to focus on what we can see, has to do with what our brain can and can't do.

A simple thought experiment illustrates what I mean. Imagine inserting a key into your front door. Do you have that image clearly in mind? Fine. Now notice what you omitted. You left out all the steps along the path from where you are reading this book to your front door. As you skipped over them, your brain did not remind you that these steps were being left out—that you had to walk out of a building and drive your car through heavy traffic to get there, for example. No warning bell went off. Nor did your mind fast-forward though a detailed film that included all those steps. You simply imagined inserting the key into the lock. Neuroscience calls this phenomenon time travel. I like to think of it as the brain's quantum, or Q, capacity. We are not only able to think about the distant past or future but also able to do so without imagining the path through time needed to get there. The fact that we can bypass all intermediate steps is an enormous advantage. We could not survive as a species without this Q capacity. We'd be paralyzed—slowed down by a brain that would take an hour to think about any action requiring an hour to accomplish. The result is a paradox of competence. What our brain does well is also part of the reason we fare poorly when it comes to making decisions about timing. Our ability to jump from one point in time to another makes it easy to miss sequences, intervals, pauses, and other temporal elements that truly matter.[1]

There is another feature of our brain that makes it difficult to get the information we need to make good timing decisions. In this case, I'm not talking about what we our brain does with ease, but what it cannot do, which is to image and explore the patterns that form when many actions and events go on at the same time. I call this limitation *Copland's Constraint*, after the composer Aaron Copland, who pointed out that when we listen to music, it is difficult to listen to more than four melodies at once. With four or five melodies playing at the same time, the composition becomes a blur of sound. Its internal pattern of organization is lost. The same happens with events. At any given moment, there are hundreds of thousands of events and processes going on at the same time. We can easily miss the patterns they form. To anticipate the risk of a perfect storm, for example, we would need to monitor and make sense of large numbers of synchronous processes, sequences, actions, and events. That is not something we can do in our head. In a sense, we are poorly adapted to our environment. We are serial creatures: when we speak, we say one word after another; when we walk, we place one foot in front of the next; when we plan or reason, we think about what follows what. But we live in a massively parallel world. As a result, we miss many of the future implications of all the events that are happening now because we lack the peripheral vision to encompass and understand them.

These two characteristics, the brain's Q capacity and Copland's Constraint, mean that it is easy to miss the information we need for deciding questions of timing. It should therefore come as no surprise that mathematical models that take time-impoverished descriptions of the world as their input, won't—indeed, can't—tell us *when* bubbles will form or *when* we will face a liquidity crisis or what the devastating effects of perfect storm may be. The information (**T**) that we need to anticipate such conditions isn't in the models.

That is equally true of the stories we read or hear in the news. Every article we read online or hear on the radio will be incomplete. It will omit information about the temporal characteristics that are needed to understand why events happened when they did, and what we can expect in the future. The reason these stories omit information we need—the enormity of what is left out will become apparent by the end of this book—is not a lack of space or faulty editorial judgment. The problem is that all the temporal characteristics that influence the timing of events never entered the mind of the reporter who wrote the story, the editor who reviewed it, or the reader who read it. We often talk about systemic risk, connecting the dots. But before we can connect the dots, we need to find them. As we saw in the case of the fatal accident at the 2010 Winter Olympics, this is not easy. The solution therefore is not data mining, bringing millions of scattered bits and pieces of information together, and then connecting the dots.

No matter how large the database or how sophisticated the search algorithms, one cannot retrieve what has not been deposited.

When we include all the intervals, rhythms, sequences, and so on that are associated with real-world events, we will find ourselves better able to predict not only what might happen but *when*. The Arab Spring provides an example of what a "time-rich" description can look like. As you recall, the start of the Arab Spring, which now seems so long ago, began when a street peddler in Tunisia was humiliated by police and set himself on fire. His death led to protests that forced the resignation of Tunisia's president. At that point, the question on everyone's mind was, What would happen next? Would protests spread to Egypt? No one knew. To see how timing is involved, let's look at the chronology of events.

Fall 2010—Parliamentary elections were held Egypt. These elections were widely viewed as fraudulent.

December 17—A Tunisian peddler, Mohamed Bouazizi, set himself on fire, and on December 18, protests began in his hometown.

January 4, 2011—Bouazizi died in a hospital shortly after receiving a visit by Tunisia's president that was deemed too little, too late. Violent protests broke out due to public outrage over Bouazizi's death as well as the high unemployment that continued to surge.

January 14—Protests forced Tunisia's President Ben Ali from office.

January 25—Demonstrations in Egypt, planned months in advance to protest police brutality, began and quickly escalated.

February 11—Egypt's President Mubarak was forced to resign.

To underscore how the timing of the events contributed to Mubarak's resignation, let's change them. First, let's assume that the events in Tunisia occurred *five months later* than they did.

That adjustment would have two consequences. First, it would *distance* them from the mid-autumn elections in Egypt. Anger can more easily build when the instigating events are close in time. Second, it would also put them after January 25, the date demonstrations were planned to protest police brutality. That would mean that the protesters on January 25 wouldn't be able to use Tunisia as a model because the events in Tunisia had not yet occurred.

Next, let's keep the chronology intact, but assume that there had been no day set aside to protest police brutality. Tension might rise in Egypt following the events in Tunisia, but it would have no planned point of release. Protests are more likely to erupt when there is a single point in time where they can be concentrated. (Pressure = Force/Area, for those who remember their high school physics.)

Finally, let's assume that the protests in Tunisia had a different trajectory. Instead of *building quickly* and leading *immediately* to the ouster of President Ben Ali, they *grew slowly*, and it took *months* rather than *weeks* to force him from office. As a general rule, physical causes are perceived as more potent when their effects are *immediate*. So, too, for human actions. Individuals experience a sense of efficacy when they achieve a difficult objective *quickly*. So, what made the events in Tunisia a powerful model to be imitated was not simply *what* the Tunisian protesters achieved but the *speed* with which they achieved it.

Change the timing of events, and Mubarak might still be in power. We can't know, of course. Demonstrations might still have forced him out. But when we include these temporal elements—the time-shape of the protests, how quickly they emerged and grew, the date of a planned protest against the police, its location relative to other events, and so on—we gain a much better understanding of what happened and when. Include them in our thinking and monitor them in real time, and we will be better prepared for what the future holds. Our assessment of risk will be more accurate.

GETTING BEYOND THE USUAL SUSPECTS

I've noticed that when I mention I've written a book on timing, people make a number of assumptions. So it's important to tell you what this book is *not* about. At the end of the film *Casablanca*, the chief of police turns to a subordinate and utters the now famous line: "Round up the usual suspects." Here are the usual suspects. This book is not about any of them.

It's not about speed, strictly, or how to be fast and flexible—the personal and organizational capacity to turn on a dime. It is not about efficiency, how to do more in less time. This is not a book on timing the stock market; I won't tell you when to buy or sell. It's not a book about not having enough time to do what we need to do. It's not about setting priorities. It's not about time management or project management or about becoming better organized. It is not intended to help you streamline operations, for example, to make sure that the right part or resource is available just when it is needed. Nor will I discuss scenario planning, trend analysis, or how to predict the future. In short, it is *not* about the usual suspects.

Instead, it will develop your ability to manage four critical timing-related issues. All groups and organizations face them. We also routinely confront them in our personal and professional lives. They are

1. Knowing when to act
2. Managing timing risk
3. Discovering that timing matters
4. Choosing the right temporal design

Let's look at each of these in turn.

Knowing When to Act
The first issue can be summarized in a one-word question, *When?* When is the right time to launch a new product, enter or exit

a market, acquire another firm, restructure one's organization, invest in new technology, or implement or deviate from a strategic plan? When is the right time to act?[2]

Conductor Leonard Bernstein describes what it feels like when the moment is right:

> There is only one possible fraction of a second that feels exactly right for starting. There is a wait while the orchestra readies itself and collects its powers; while the conductor concentrates his whole will and force toward the work in hand; while the audience quiets down, and the last cough has died away. There is no slight rustle of a program book; the instruments are poised and—bang! That's it. One second later, it is too late.[3]

Bernstein gets the timing right because he is acutely aware of a temporal pattern—in this case, the rise in tension associated with beginning a concert, an increase in tension that demands release at exactly the right moment.

For many executives, the conventional response to the question of timing is *speed*—taking swift action in order to beat the competition. Being first is usually considered to be advantageous—and it is if

- The image of *being a pioneer* is important.
- *Learning and experience* are important and will be difficult to imitate.
- *Customer loyalty matters.* Once customers have made a choice, they may not pay attention to or be interested in alternatives.
- You can *preempt scarce resources* or completely occupy a market niche.
- *Starting early means that you can develop a track record with suppliers and distributors* that will secure cost advantages or priority treatment.

- *Early, large, and irreversible commitments will deter others* from entering the same market.
- *Buyer switching costs are high.* Once a firm has invested in adapting to a seller's product, that firm can become locked in.
- *Being first ends the game*—that is, there is mutual agreement among competitors that whoever first secures the prize removes it from competition because to continue the fight would damage everyone.[4]

Yet waiting for someone else to be first can be the better strategy if

- *You can catch up.* A firm may have special strengths in manufacturing, marketing, or distribution that make it possible to recover lost ground quickly. It can afford to let other firms educate the customers and make the mistakes, and then quickly imitate what works.
- *There is a high degree of market uncertainty.* Sometimes it is wise to wait until standards emerge and risks are clarified. An early mover may build the wrong skills, invest in the wrong technology, and face high costs of replacing them as circumstances change.

Being first is a disadvantage, as well, if others aren't ready to follow your lead. The most dramatic example I know occurred in the Soviet Union around the time of the Great Purge. At the end of a Communist Party conference, a tribute to Stalin was announced. Everyone rose to his feet and promptly erupted into applause. The clapping continued for several minutes. As the seconds ticked by, the mood became slightly tentative and then somewhat strained. Who would be the first to stop clapping? Not the secretary on the podium—his predecessor had recently been arrested, and the secret police were present at this event. Finally, after eleven minutes, the director of a paper factory, among those on the platform, was the first to stop his applause and take his seat. Relieved, the crowd followed his lead. That night, the man was arrested. After being told by his interrogator to "never be the first to stop applauding," he was given ten years in prison.[5]

This story is darkly amusing—in part because it happened a long time ago and didn't happen to us. But it does underline the point: first is not always best, and "When?" is not an easy question to answer.

Managing Timing Risk

The second timing issue is *risk*. We inevitably run into timing risks that we did not anticipate—and wish we had, as was the case at the 2010 Olympics. Financial writer Mark Ingebretsen, in his book *Why Companies Fail*, describes a typical example. A major U.S. food producer built a pineapple-processing facility located upstream from where the pineapples actually grew. When it was time to harvest the pineapples, a barge was to carry them to the cannery. Unfortunately, *at that time of year*, the river current was so strong that the barge couldn't make it. I wasn't present when the company's profits floated away with the rushing river. But it is not hard to imagine the scene: angry voices, finger-pointing, perhaps someone's job threatened. Understandable, and perhaps fair. The people in charge *should* have known. Their mistake was not taking timing into account.[6]

When we think about risk, we usually think about *type*: What *kind* of risk am I facing? Will new competitors enter the market niche I currently dominate? Will new legislation limit my ability to innovate? Will new advances in science and technology make my products or services obsolete? Then we think about *magnitude*: How serious is this risk? What would happen if it materialized? But there is another consideration—namely, timing: *When* might a risk, such as the risk of a perfect storm, materialize, and how much advance warning will I have?

Discovering That Timing Matters

Steven Ballmer, CEO of Microsoft, was asked in 2009 what he considered the most challenging part of his job. What made him frustrated, he said, was "when progress runs up against issues that should have been anticipated, or that simply couldn't have been foreseen."[7]

Not all timing issues are obvious. For example, perhaps you knew that you needed to make decisions about hiring or firing, but you didn't realize that the window for making them was rapidly closing. You might be concerned about how competitors would respond to your new product line, but you didn't think through how the timing of their response would affect your marketing plan. You might know in your gut that the project you are leading will take longer than planned for, but you didn't realize what you needed to do immediately to protect your people and resources from the consequences of a delay. In any complex business, there are a host of timing issues that you need to be aware of. This book will help you surface them so that you are not blindsided when they arise. .

Choosing the Right Temporal Design

Sometimes it is possible to take a single action at a single point in time. A colleague resigns suddenly from a technical position that requires specific skills and training; you need someone to step in promptly to fill the slot. Therefore, you immediately hire the one person in your trusted network who has the right experience.

More often, we pursue a time-extended course of action. In order to ensure proper succession planning, a board of directors and the current CEO may spend several years considering suitable chief executive replacement prospects. They interview a range of candidates, bring them on as key lieutenants, and put together an action plan for how and when the sitting CEO will retire at a defined moment in the future. The timing is carefully orchestrated.

Choosing the right *temporal design* requires deliberation: What should be done first? Should I proceed incrementally, develop a prototype, and then test the waters? Should I pause, or would it be better to move as fast as possible? Each approach has its place, depending on the larger context. This book will help you choose the best temporal design—that is, the right sequence, rate, rhythm, and so on for what you need and what to do. George Mitchell—who won the Nobel Peace Prize for his efforts in Northern Ireland—provides a good example of effective temporal design when he describes planning a meeting between the United Kingdom's Prime Minister Tony Blair and Ireland's Prime Minister Bertie Ahern:

> When we start on Thursday morning, it has to be clear to everyone that we'll continue until we finish, one way or the other. There can be no discussion of a pause or break. I intend to tell the parties that I won't even consider such a request. If someone says to me, "We're nearly there but we're all tired, let's break until next week," I'm going to say, "That's completely out of the question. There's not going to be a break, not for a week, not for a day, not for an hour. We're here until we finish. We'll either get an agreement or we'll fail to get an agreement. Then we'll all go out together and explain to the press and the waiting world how we succeeded or why we failed."[8]

This account contains two critical decisions. The first was about temporal punctuation (discussed in Chapter Three). Mitchell demanded a continuous rather than a discontinuous process. There would be no gaps, no time-outs, no pauses, just one long effort to reach an agreement. The second decision was about *when* this particular design was needed. Having gained the respect of both parties, Mitchell had the power to choose. Of equal importance, however, is that he realized that he had a choice and that one design was likely to be more effective than another *at this particular moment*.

A TIMING ANALYSIS

A timing analysis is a structured method for finding the facts you need to make better timing decisions in any situation. At the most fundamental level, it consists of three steps: (1) finding patterns in your work and in your environment, (2) analyzing them, and (3) using the information they contain to make decisions.

The heart of a timing analysis is the search for patterns—but not just any pattern. The patterns that matter for answering questions of timing have two characteristics. First, they are composed of six elements, which I will name in a moment. Second, they have a particular structure that can be illustrated using a familiar image: a musical score. For those of you who don't happen to be musicians, I have reproduced part of the score from Beethoven's Fifth Symphony in Figure I.1.

Don't worry about the complexity of this particular score. No musical knowledge is required. It is the overall structure of a musical score that is important.

As you can see, a musical score has a vertical and horizontal dimension. Different instruments (arrayed vertically) play different parts. The notes making up the parts are played in sequence, from left to right on or between sets of horizontal lines. Notes played at the same time create chords or harmonies or, in some music, dissonance. Notes played one after another create melodies. The relationships among the notes constituting the horizontal and vertical dimensions define and create the composition.

If you think for a moment about your own work, the analogy to a musical score will become clear. Every situation in which timing is important has a lot of moving parts. Many things are going on simultaneously (the vertical dimension). One firm may be doing one thing; another firm may be doing something else. Every individual or group will be playing its own tune—or at least trying to (the horizontal dimension). Each tune (a set of

Figure I.1 Part of the Score from Beethoven's Fifth Symphony[9]

actions) will have its own sequence, pace, and rhythm. The way these different and overlapping tunes play out together—whether they are in harmony, create dissonance, or just produce noise or chaos—will determine when conditions are right for certain kinds of actions.

If you look closely at what is going on in any business environment, you will see that it is composed of six elements. The first five—*sequence, punctuation, interval, rate,* and *shape*—define and describe the *horizontal* dimension of the score. The sixth adds multiple layers and hence the *vertical* dimension. I'm going to borrow the musical term *polyphony* (many voices or sounds) for this final element. Let me briefly define each element.

- **Sequence**. This element refers to the order of events, like the notes in a melody. In any situation where timing matters, it is useful and often essential to have a sense of what follows what. First you manufacture something and then you sell it, or perhaps the reverse: first you sell it, and then you build or manufacture it.
- **Temporal punctuation**. This element refers to times when events or processes begin, pause, or come to an end. Temporal punctuation functions like linguistic punctuation, inserting commas, periods, and so on into what would otherwise be a continuous stream of action or events. Every business has deadlines; every plan or process has a start date.
- **Interval and duration**. This element indicates how much time elapses between events (the length of the interval) and how long each event lasts or will take (its duration). Everything in business, as in life, takes time.
- **Rate**. This element refers to how quickly events are happening. Some things develop quickly, others more slowly. Who hasn't had a project run over time and over budget, or been surprised by how quickly business conditions can change?
- **Shape**. This element describes rhythms and other patterns of movement, such as cycles, feedback loops, and peaks and valleys. For example, will a market bottom look like a V, a W, or something else?
- **Polyphony**. In any pattern, many things may be going on simultaneously, each with its own trajectory. Polyphony raises the

question of their interrelationship. A slowdown in China, combined with a crisis in the EU, can affect economic conditions in the United States.

What makes a firm work is the way its parts are organized. The same is true of the six elements. It is the way they come together musically to form vertically and horizontally organized patterns that gives us insight into timing. For example, a window may open when a particular chord sounds—that is, when certain conditions are present at the same time (a market exists, your product is ready, and your competitor is years behind). When different conditions are present, the result can be a perfect storm or a tragic accident. What I like to say is that if you want to get the timing right, you need to know the score![10]

I will refer to the patterns we need to find as *temporal architecture* because of the way they are built and structured, the uses to which they are put, and because, like spatial architecture, they have an esthetic or emotional quality. They feel right or wrong, good or bad for the task at hand. (A more detailed discussion of temporal architecture can be found in the Appendix.) As you find and examine the patterns of temporal architecture, you will discover that you know much more about timing and how a situation is likely to develop than you thought. What seemed unknown or uncertain will appear less so.

A timing analysis does not attempt to predict the future. Rather it is a way to work with patterns that are already present, simply unseen or unexamined. Neither is it the application of an abstract model, framework, or set of research findings. What works in the laboratory, for one company, in one industry, or at one time in history may not apply to the challenges you face. Instead, a timing analysis is best thought of as a set of *diagnostic and analytic* tools for working with the idiosyncratic, complex, messy, real-world situations that you actually face—with, as they say, conditions on the ground.

A timing analysis has multiple uses. It will *complement* and *extend* the way you and your organization currently manage and decide issues of timing and, when necessary, *critique* and *correct* them. It will also provide a common language for discussing timing. A common language makes it easier for different parts of an organization, each speaking its own dialect (the language of finance, economics, software engineering, marketing, and so on) to talk and work with each other. Timing solutions developed in one department or division can be shared as well as codeveloped with others. The result will be a more coordinated timing strategy for the firm as whole.

THE STRUCTURE OF THE BOOK

In order to see patterns, we need to find their component elements. That is the task of the first six chapters. Each chapter describes one element. Think of each chapter as a lens (a set of examples, illustrations, places to look, and knowledge of what to look for) that helps you search for and examine that particular element in detail.

We have all heard the saying, Give a man a fish and you feed him for a day; teach a man to fish and you feed him for a lifetime. You will find many places in this book where a specific example, tool, or technique will have immediate application in your business. It solves a particular problem, helps you make a difficult decision, and so on. That's the first part of the proverb. But the reason I use the lens metaphor is that the chapters in this book serve a broader function. They will teach you to *see* and *analyze* timing issues in *any situation*, in the same way that you can use binoculars to view any object and find details not previously visible. That's the second part of the proverb, and to my mind, the deeper and more important takeaway from each chapter.

Each of the first six chapters begins with an example or two. The examples will orient you and help you see the element in context. I also describe the characteristics of that element in detail. There are usually no more than half a dozen characteristics, depending on the element. These characteristics are important because they are a source of timing-related risks. You can use the information about risk in two ways: to prepare for what you might encounter in the future, and, retrospectively, to understand how timing-related mistakes might have caused a plan or project to fall short of expectations. The section on risk in each chapter is usually followed by one on options and opportunities. These describe ways to use that element to make your work more effective and profitable. The last part of each chapter is titled "The Temporal Imagination." This short concluding section describes something that I found particularly intriguing. I think of this section as dessert after the main course. It is intended to be light and frothy—although I must admit I occasionally include one that could be a meal in itself.

I also include a chapter summary at the end of each of the lens chapters to highlight the main ideas.

The seventh chapter—The Timing of Dissent—brings all the elements together to demonstrate how the six timing lenses apply in a common business situation—a meeting where a CEO and his colleagues are discussing whether or not to launch a new product. The chapter illustrates how to use each of the elements to make one's comments timely and effective.

Finally, the last chapter of the book provides a set of steps and general guidelines for conducting a timing analysis. This chapter builds on the foundation laid in the previous chapters.

As you train your eye to find the elements of temporal architecture and the patterns they form, you will discover a richer and more complex world. That is always the case when you look beneath any surface, examine the infrastructure of a building, or take an MRI of the brain. The goal of a timing analysis, however, is not to *add* complexity but to *restore* it, to bring back what our eye doesn't see and our mind doesn't consider. The good news is that a timing analysis provides a way to organize this complexity. That is what makes it powerful.

Another source of the power of a timing analysis is that it applies in nearly every situation an executive is likely to face. One reason is that barriers which prevent us from getting the timing right are not limited to a specific setting, organization, or role: we bring them with us in the form of Copland's Constraint and the brain's Q capacity, among others. The second reason is that the tools and techniques of a timing analysis are highly general. Indeed, it would be inefficient and counterproductive to treat the world as a set of silos where we must think one way in one situation and a different way in another. We need tools that work in multiple settings.

In a complex world, there is always a combination of factors—financial, legal, economic, organizational, competitive, strategic, political, and psychological aspects, among others—for leaders and executives to consider. For this reason, this book contains a diversity of examples. Leaders and executives need to think broadly, to explore all the different facets of an issue before making a decision about timing, particularly if a lot is at stake. Furthermore, to develop skill in matters of timing requires that we learn to look beneath the surface of an issue to its underlying temporal design or architecture, and the best way to do that is to see the same timing principle at work in different contexts.

The examples that fill each chapter fall into two basic categories. Some describe conditions in the world, what is going on in a particular setting or environment. Others describe actions that you or others might undertake. These categories reflect the dual use of a timing analysis, which is to understand your environment so that you know when to act and then to design a time-extended course of action that is effective in that context.

THE ART OF TIMING

Although I will provide you with practical tools to solve timing problems, I think it is fair to recognize that skill in matters of timing is an art. It is not something we can automate or do "by the numbers." I can think of no better illustration of the art of timing than a description of a rehearsal by Peter Brook, one of the legendary theater directors (italics mine).

> *Sometimes* all attention must be given to one actor; *at other times* the collective process demands a halt to the individual's work. Not every facet can be explored. To discuss every possible way with everyone can be just too slow and so it can be destructive to the whole. Here the director has to have *a sense of time*: it is for him to feel the *rhythm* of the process and observe its divisions. *There is a time* for discussing the broad lines of a play, *there is a time* for forgetting them, for discovering what can only be found through joy, extravagance, irresponsibility. *There is a time* when no one must worry himself about the results of his efforts. . . There is *another point* the director must sense. *He must sense the time when* a group of actors intoxicated by their own talent and the excitement of the work loses sight of the play. *Suddenly one morning* the work must change: the result must become all-important. Jokes and embroideries are then ruthlessly pared away and all the attention put on to the function of the evening, on the narrating, the presenting, the technique, the audibility, the communicating to the audience. So it is foolish for a director to take a doctrinaire view; either talking technical language about pace, volume, etc.—or avoiding one because it is inartistic. It is woefully easy for a director to get stuck in a method.[11]

We know from this description that Brook is a master. He is reading his environment perfectly. He knows what issues he will face, and when, and how his actions at those precise moments will determine the success or failure of the rehearsal. His focus is not just on the play or on the skills of the actors but on the *temporal design* of the rehearsal. He listens for the rhythm of what is going on, for its moments of tension or release, for moments when he must pause and change direction. There is a sense in which this quotation captures what timing expertise is like in any domain.

You cannot acquire overnight the level of skill that Brook demonstrates. But time spent building your timing skill is well spent if you and your organization want to spot opportunities first, execute on them well, and avoid costly mistakes. When you are done reading this book, you will have a powerful new way to look at what you do every day. Your actions and activities will be better timed and hence more likely to succeed.

o n e

Sequence

Time is nature's way of keeping everything from happening
at once.

—*John Wheeler*[1]

Picture yourself pouring water through a funnel. If all the water
tried to escape the small end of the funnel at the same time,
the result would be chaos, like a crush of people trying to exit a
movie theater after someone yells "Fire!" A funnel works because
gravity and other forces gently encourage the water molecules to
get in line, a line that becomes a fast-moving spiral. When we look
at a funnel we see its shape, and we understand its function. What
we don't think about is the underlying, and often invisible, timing
mechanism that makes it work: sequence.

In business, as in life more generally, we control and manipulate most easily what we can see and touch: we replace one
technology with another; we redesign the packaging of our products. Sequences, in contrast, are abstract and intangible, and they
are therefore easy to miss. But it is important to find them. Modify
a sequence—produce a product *before* the demand is apparent,
as opposed to *after*—and your risk and opportunity profile looks

very different. Modify or redescribe a sequence, and it can change how a product is perceived, which can affect its sales. Is the secondhand Jaguar you are about to buy "pre-owned"—owned by someone else *before* you purchased it, or "used"—purchased *after* someone else has driven it?

Finding or noting the presence of a sequence can be the key to deciding when to act. For example, knowing the steps a country needs to go through to produce a nuclear weapon is critical in determining when, if ever, you should take steps to prevent it. That's why we need to train our eyes to look for the sequences in our environment; they provide clues about timing. They can also help us understand why something is delayed. For example, if there is no clear sequence of steps allowing a country to exit the EU without putting itself (and the remaining countries) at risk, then expect a decision to start down that path to be postponed—perhaps indefinitely.

THE CHARACTERISTICS OF SEQUENCES

When you find a series of events that form a sequence, like the water molecules exiting a funnel, zoom in and look more closely. Sequences are not just about what follows what. Sequences have a number of important characteristics, which I describe in this section.

1. **Order**. What follows what, and why? Is there some reason why A is followed by B, and B by C? Is this order required? Would it be better to do something in a different order?
2. **Punctuation**. Are there recognizable steps or stages? Can one be skipped, and can you come (loop) back and finish it later?
3. **Interval and duration**. How long will each step or stage take, and how much time will elapse between steps?
4. **Shape**. Will there be bottlenecks or other shapes (I'll describe one in a moment) that will make progress slow or difficult?

5. **Location**. A sequence defines a series of locations. Does an event occur early in a sequence, in the middle, or perhaps at the end, and does its location matter?

6. **Extension**. How long is the sequence? When does it begin and end?

Take a moment to find some of these characteristics, illustrated in Figure 1.1, a close-up view of a sequence.

Let's move on and consider each characteristic in more detail.

Order

The *order* in which an event or action occurs is the primary property of any sequence. A is followed by B, B by C, and so on.

In creating a new flavor of coffee, you would take certain steps before announcing the product: agree on the formula, name the flavor, market-test the taste, iterate the ingredients to adjust the taste, market-test again, and so on. Once you observe or identify a particular order in your activities, such as the one in this coffee example, the next question to ask is whether it can be changed. Could one step come before another, or could two steps be inverted? And would a change in order benefit your business? Suppose you waited to name the coffee flavor until after the market test, for example—would that change how customers react? Or could a step be omitted? What if you omitted the second market test—how might that impact your budget? Everything

Figure 1.1 A Close-Up View of a Sequence

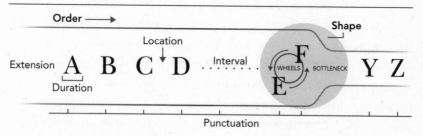

we do has a particular order. Sometimes it is useful to pause and consider alternatives, particularly if you have been doing things in the same order for years.

When the order of a sequence can't be changed (one step must follow another, and no step can be skipped), it can cause problems. Let's use the launch of Dean Kamen's Segway as an example that illustrates what I call *strict serial constraints.*

You may have seen someone riding the original Segway PT (personal transporter) when the machine was first introduced in 2001. At the time, it probably looked like it would tip over, passenger and all. But that didn't happen because the Segway is self-balancing—that's what makes it breakthrough. Still, you would be skeptical about safety and ease until you rode one for yourself. So, with that in mind, when would you buy one? Probably not until you had a test ride. And when is that? Not until distributors carried it. But distributors didn't carry it for quite some time because laws in most states prohibited the use of Segways on sidewalks. Therefore, you wouldn't have been able to purchase a Segway until state laws were changed. The company lost five-plus years of sales because it introduced the product before it could be widely used.

Segway found itself caught in a *vicious cycle*: distributors wouldn't carry its product until they knew there was a market, but they couldn't know about the market until customers tried the product, and customers couldn't try it because distributors didn't carry it. Due to its revolutionary nature, the Segway was developed in secret, which meant that work on downstream tasks, such as lobbying municipalities to allow the device to be used on sidewalks, could not start until the product was unveiled. Did the Segway's developers identify possible routes to faster state approval or decide on a later launch? Did they anticipate the vicious cycle involving distributors? I don't know the answers to these questions, but in a certain sense, for our purposes, they are immaterial. What matters is that you learn to ask sequence-related questions in your own business so that you can better anticipate the difficulties you might encounter.

Notice in the case of the Segway that all of the timing risks related to order could have been identified at the outset if someone had been looking. But the company's timing strategy appears to have been typical: the focus was on speed, getting the product to market as soon as possible. The theme of this book is that there is a lot more you can see if you know how and where to look.

Like Dean Kamen, Saul Griffith needed to recognize the steps needed to make his invention successful. In 2004, when Griffith was a PhD student at MIT, he invented a way to custom manufacture low-cost eyeglasses for people in the developing world.[2] The problem, as he understood it then, was manufacturing lenses without having to build an expensive factory, which poor countries couldn't afford. Griffith's solution was a technology to shape a fast-drying liquid into any lens.

Technically, his invention was a great success. He received a $30,000 award from MIT and a $500,000 "genius grant" from the MacArthur Foundation. Unfortunately, Griffith didn't have a *timing lens* in his tool kit, one that would help him see the sequence on which the success of his invention depended.

As Griffith put it, "The real problem with eyeglasses in the developing world isn't making lenses . . . it's testing eyes and writing prescriptions for people with little or no access to medical care—a matter of politics and economics rather than technology."[3] He missed the steps individuals needed to take before they could use his technology; as a result, his invention never found a market. But Griffith also misdiagnosed the problem. He saw it as one of politics and economics, which it undoubtedly was. But it was also a sequence problem.

Sequences, of course, have other characteristics besides order that are relevant in business. I'll mention them briefly, as they will be covered in greater detail in later chapters.

Punctuation

Sequences use steps and stages as a way to break a continuous process into parts in the same way commas and semicolons divide a sentence, and additional white space separates paragraphs. Usually, we think of condensing a process and eliminating steps as a time-saving perk for customers using products. But eliminating steps and inserting a period sooner is not always the answer. For instance, a freeze-dried egg could have easily been included as part of the ingredients in pancake mix. All a consumer would have to do, then, was add water, mix, and cook. But manufacturers believed that women at the time would feel guilty about a process so simple and devoid of fresh ingredients—so they added the extra step of asking women to add the egg themselves.

It is not always possible to skip to the end without inserting a pause or another punctuation mark. In the first Gulf War, for example, allied troops rushed to Baghdad, detouring around a number of smaller cities on route. This allowed them to reach the capital sooner, but it meant that they had to go back later to deal with security issues that had grown more serious in the interim. When there is an emphasis on speed, be prepared for skipped steps and the timing issues they raise. Ask yourself: *When will a return be possible, and what will I find when I get there?*

Skipping ahead can even be illegal, as in "front-running" in finance. Front-running occurs when a trader receives an order from an investor to buy a stock and the trader steps in ahead of that order, which he knows will raise the price of the stock, to buy it for the house account. He then sells what he has bought to the investor at the higher price and locks in a profit.

If you don't take all the steps in a sequence into account, you can make an error. As an example, let's take something that is fundamental to any business: the price of a commodity on which the business depends. Increase the supply of this commodity, and the price should fall. Increase demand, and the price should rise. But things are not so simple in the real world. The price of natural gas, for example, will not to rise or fall based on how much is produced and the overall level of demand, because natural gas does not go directly from well to consumer. There is an intermediate step. Natural gas can be stored. When storage capacity rises, excess supply can be kept off the market until prices recover. If you forget about this step in the sequence, like the omission of a comma or period that makes a sentence difficult to read, you will not understand why an abundance of natural gas (what is coming out of the well) does not always result in lower prices for consumers.

Interval and Duration

When we look at a sequence, we need to notice how much time elapses between steps (interval) and how long each step or stage takes (duration).

After a start-up company receives financing, for example, investors prefer profitability to happen sooner rather than later—they want the shortest possible time between these two steps. There are many instances when a short interval between steps or stages is preferable. In fall 2010, for example, European regulators met to consider reducing the time between when a transaction is completed and when securities are exchanged for cash. A shorter interval would reduce the risk that an unexpected event, like a default, might occur in the interim.

We customarily divide the week into a series of days that form two large groups, the five-day workweek and the two-day weekend. I wonder whether the outcome would have been different in the case of the financial crisis affecting Lehman Brothers in 2008 if the weekend were five days long and the workweek two. That would have given the government more time to think things through and perhaps find a solution that would have saved Lehman.

Shape

When we think about a sequence, we generally think of one thing logically following the next. The simplest visual representation is a series of points on a line in which A is followed by B, B is followed by C, and so on. To get a new product to market, for example, we have to go through A (the product has to be invented), B (it has to be manufactured), and C (it has to be marketed). But there are two shapes that can get in the way in this or any sequence of events: wheels and bottlenecks. As you can see in Figure 1.1, if we visualize these two shapes, neither looks like a straight line.

Wheels represent a classic catch-22 situation. For example, the Segway was so novel that customers wouldn't buy them until they could try them out, but distributors wouldn't carry the product until they knew there was a market, which wouldn't happen until customers tried the product.

Bottlenecks slow things down. In the summer of 2006, for example, the Centers for Disease Control proposed new guidelines that urged primary care doctors to test everyone for HIV regardless of his or her risk factors. AIDS activists were alarmed because expanding testing without expanding access to care would leave many patients without adequate treatment. Upstream solutions run the risk of creating downstream bottlenecks. To increase speed effectively, one must modify the entire sequence in order to avoid bottlenecks. In the case of HIV care, patients who are symptomatic or at high risk of infection should be put at the front of the line for testing and care.

We will examine a variety of shapes in more detail in Chapter Five.

Location

We expect some steps or stages in a sequence to be shorter or longer than others—and it is important in business to be aware of these expectations. When a sequence has a clear beginning, middle, and end, we usually expect the beginning and ending stages to be relatively short. Flying, for example, can be tedious. We prepare for long security lines prior to boarding. But after we are seated and poised for takeoff, any delay can be painful.

Whereas a fifteen-minute delay in midflight will hardly be noticed, passengers will become extremely frustrated if the same fifteen-minute delay occurs when the aircraft is parked at the gate and they can't deplane. When we are ready to exit the plane, we don't want anything to stand in our way. Thus *when* a delay occurs can be as important as *how long* the delay lasts.

Extension

By extension I mean the length of a sequence from beginning to end. We rarely consider the full length of many sequences, and that oversight can lead to problems. We think that a sequence is over when it is not. Or we may forget how early the sequence begins, as Saul Griffith discovered. As a result, we may be surprised by events we could have foreseen.

In 2007, a large number of toys manufactured in China were recalled. The headline in the *New York Times* read, "The Recalls' Aftershocks," implying that the recall was not a single event but a series of "shocks" in which downstream events played an important part.[4] "The first step is the product is recalled," said Rachel Weintraub, director of product safety at the Consumer Federation of America, who was quoted in the article. "The second step is the manufacturer gets some of the product back. And the third step is: what happens next?" No one knew the next step in the sequence. The article went on to say that as many as 80 percent of recalled products are not returned to manufacturers. Even if companies know where these products are, they are under no legal obligation to do anything about them. Furthermore, manufacturers are permitted to resell recalled products abroad if the recall was voluntary.

The long sequence of events surrounding a recall was not expected. As a result, tainted products found their way back into the hands of children.

As you become aware of sequences in your business environment, always look for the *longest relevant sequence*—sometimes it spans decades. Make sure that the sequences you are looking at stretch far enough back into the past and far enough forward into the future to capture everything that is important.

■ ■ ■

When we fail to consider the full extension of a sequence, or miss another timing characteristic that is relevant in a given case, we also may miss important risks and opportunities that are associated with the sequence.

SEQUENCE-RELATED RISKS

If identified in advance, many of the risks associated with sequences can be avoided. But even if you can't avoid them, you will be better prepared to deal with them. Here are some of the most common sequence-related risks.

Missing a Sequence

The most common risk is failing to recognize that a sequence is present at all, that A must precede B, for example, as was the case for Saul Griffith. Consider the credit crisis of 2008–2009, a series of interrelated events that happened in the banking sector, as another example. National debt explodes. The housing bubble bursts. Subprime mortgages hit crisis mode. Many financial professionals recognized isolated issues and troubling problems, but they failed to see how one thing would lead to the next, and how quickly. They didn't connect the dots. But the problem was not just connecting the dots, as if the dots were visible and ready to be connected. The problem was that the dots themselves were caused by chains of action: if A did x, then B would do y, and once that happened, A would respond with z—and do so quickly. Then C would enter the fray, and so on. People and institutions became locked into chains of action they did not foresee and from which they could not free themselves. As we have seen, finding a remedy in this situation is difficult.

If sequences are so important, then why (beyond the fact that they are abstract) do we miss them? One reason is what I call *cat-point thinking*. When we engage in cat-point thinking, we first decide on a category of action. *I'm going to open a wine and dessert bar in Cannes.* Then, separately, we decide when: *on my fiftieth birthday.* Cat-point thinking focuses our attention on a single *point* in time. The more we dwell on that single point, the more likely we are to miss the sequences that determine what will happen before that moment and what is likely to happen after.

In order to avoid the risks associated with missing a key sequence, remember to ask yourself, *Have I identified the order of events related to a given process or situation?* Keep in mind that there may be several sequences that overlap.

Inverting a Sequence Unwittingly

A sequence inversion occurs when the order of two steps is changed. Instead of A then B, B comes first, followed by A. A *Pepper ... and Salt* cartoon in the *Wall Street Journal* illustrates an amusing sequence inversion. A person is interviewing a job candidate. The caption reads, "You came to the job interview before scheduling it—I like your initiative."[5] Although inverting the normal sequence seems to have worked in this case, mistakes happen if you put the cart before the horse—committing funds for a project before you have budget approval, for example.

In many cases, getting the order right can be a complex endeavor. When an economy with a large deficit is faltering, for example, what should you do first? Should you cut spending and then wait to see if additional stimulation is needed, or should you first stimulate the economy and then cut back? Which is the right sequence? A mistake can result in a depression or an economy that struggles for years. Of course, not all sequence inversions (assuming that there is a "right" order) are tragic. For instance, according to the *New York Times*, the day before Kristen Gesswein and Stephen Fealty were to be married, on January 15, 2000, they called off the wedding. They decided, however, to go ahead with the reception. The next day, the couple went on their honeymoon to Mexico, where, a few days later, they were married in a civil ceremony on the beach.[6]

The questions to ask: *Have I gotten the order right? Is there a chance that one or more steps or events are in the wrong position in a sequence? If I adjust the order of events in a sequence, will it lead to better results?*

Failing to Look Downstream

Often it is the last few steps in a sequence that are the most difficult to envision—because they are so far downstream we don't see them. Yet it is important to anticipate how a sequence of events will end or terminate. It is easy to create a profile on Facebook, for example, but difficult to quickly and completely delete it.

"Be first, be early" is presumed to be a sufficient rule for competitive success. Unfortunately, it is not. (Remember the Segway.) The result of our overreliance on speed is that we do not look downstream to consider future steps or stages. That limits our understanding of what is going on and can expose us to risks we should have seen coming. Each element of a sequence has its own risks and opportunities. Even a decision to act first should take into account what is likely to happen over the long term and what the ending phase will look like.

Questions to ask: *Have I looked far enough into the future to anticipate downstream events? Am I aware of how a particular sequence might end? What does each potential ending scenario tell me about how to sequence my actions today?*

SEQUENCE OPTIONS AND OPPORTUNITIES

Sequences and their characteristics can be a source of opportunities and not just risks. For example, you can sometimes secure an advantage by inverting the normal order in which something is done, or by creating a sequence where none existed. Each sequence characteristic provides an opportunity to create a new product, process, or service, or to improve one that already exists. Here are some examples.

Deliberately Invert a Sequence

A salesman in Brazil told me that his firm makes technology that enables retailers in certain countries to electronically deposit money into a bank the moment the consumer cashes out at the register. A few days later, an armored truck arrives to transport the actual cash to the bank. The usual sequence requires that the merchant deposit the cash *before* he could begin to earn interest, but by using the company's technology, he can start earning interest days earlier, an advantage that results from inverting the usual sequence: first deposit the cash, then earn interest. According to the salesman, his company's technology wasn't commercialized sooner because retailers believed that credit cards would replace cash entirely, leaving little need to better manage cash transactions. In fact, as we know, this hasn't happened.

Thinking about business processes as sequences can lead to new insights, opportunities, and business models. Consider prepaid phone cards. Instead of receiving a bill after you use a service, you pay in advance.

In the medical field, modifying the order of activities has saved lives. A 2006 study found that administering chemotherapy both before and after surgery for stomach cancer improves the chances of survival for many patients. Chemotherapy administered only after surgery, which had been the traditional practice, had little or no effect.[7] In a fast-moving world, an action that is early, decisive, and precise (surgery) will be chosen before one that is late, slow, and diffuse (chemotherapy). That is the normal sequence. But in this case, a counterintuitive move—inverting the sequence—saves lives.

Choose the Right Duration

To succeed, it's not enough to do things in the right order; you must also pay attention to how long each step or stage takes relative to others. Consider the advice of Joan Vickers, the Canadian professor of kinesiology, for sinking a putt (italics mine): "when you are ready to putt, gaze calmly and steadily at the hole (or target spot) for about *three* counts, bring your eyes back to the ball in *one* count, and fix your eyes on the back (or top) of the ball for *two counts*. Then make the stroke and continue to gaze at the ground, where the ball was, for at least *one* more count."[8]

The choice of how long to let a step or stage continue is important in many contexts. How long to test a product prototype or to allow a project to fail before cancelling it are common examples. If a consumer products company takes the time and energy to first develop a brand, its next product will be in a better position to succeed when it arrives in the market.

Create a Sequence

Suppose you are planning a twenty-four-hour fundraising drive for a public television station. You consult the calendar and debate the pros and cons of various dates. Finally, you decide on a day in mid-May. Unfortunately, when that day comes, a freak ice storm downs the power lines and plunges the city into twenty-four hours of darkness. No one is prepared, and it takes almost a week to recover. The fundraising event is cancelled. Your station needs to cover news of the storm and its aftermath. The decision to a choose a single date for the drive—as per cat-point thinking—left you at the mercy of unforeseen events.

When you look at the fundraising drive through a sequence lens, you see that by focusing on a specific day to hold the event, you missed a sequence strategy. You could have divided the drive into two parts, separated by an interval of time. The station could offer listeners a choice: if the station met its goal during the first part of the drive, the second part would be cancelled. A sequence solution, which many fundraising drives have adopted, has two benefits. First, having the event span an extended period of time diminishes the risk of selecting the wrong day to hold it.

Second, no one likes fundraising drives. A sequence solution gives viewers control over how long the drive lasts. This approach still requires decisions about timing—the choice of starting date and the length and separation of each phase. But it gives the station more flexibility and a way to minimize the risk of a single-point solution.

Choose a Different Location

Changing the location of a decision or action and moving it to a later step or stage of a process can be an advantage. For example, in the case of patents, the United States recently changed its patent filing process recognizing "first to file," which was the international standard, rather than the earlier requirement, "first to invent." It moved the process downstream. For the patent office, it didn't matter when you invented something, only when you filed the patent application. There were two reasons this was desirable: it encouraged "greater co-operation and efficiency in patent examinations globally,"[9] and—what big companies liked—it prevented someone showing up later and claiming that he had previously invented the core of the company's patent.

Skip a Step

Skipping steps creates new business opportunities. Fifteen years ago, for example, we took a snapshot and then went to the local drugstore to have it developed. This was the sequence: click the shutter and then, maybe a week or so later, see the picture. With digital photography, we click the shutter and see the picture immediately. Digital photography allows us to skip two steps: the need for film and the need for printing. The ability to skip those two steps created a new industry, at the same time that it effectively forced Kodak, whose profits were based on sales of film, into bankruptcy.

Sometimes skipping a step can close a deal, as in the case of the sales technique called the "presumptive close."[10] Instead of asking whether you are ready to buy shares or invest in a particular company, the salesperson will ask whether you want to buy one hundred or three hundred shares—which presupposes that you have already made a decision. This is a marketing gimmick, of course, but it may give you an idea of how you can approach a well-established process differently by skipping a step.

Give People a Choice

Does your product or service mandate a particular sequence of steps that can't be altered? (Again, I call this a *strict serial constraint.*) In some cases, a given order is necessary. If not, it can be useful to offer consumers a choice. That is what the writer Julio Cortázar did in his novel *Hopscotch.* As the title implies, the structure of the book encourages readers to skip around as opposed to reading in a linear fashion. In fact, the author's note suggests that the reader can proceed in one of two possible ways, either progressively from chapters 1 to 56 or by "hopscotching" through the larger set of 155 chapters according to a "table of instructions" created by the author. Cortázar also leaves the reader the third option of choosing his or her own unique path through the book.

Remember Cortázar's strategy, and you will always ask an important question: *Is there advantage in changing the order of a sequence, including giving customers or other stakeholders a choice?*

■ ■ ■

As a starting point for discovering sequence-related opportunities, list all the sequences on which your work or personal success depends. Then ask, "What if?" What if any one of these sequences were modified by you or someone else? How would that affect your performance, profit, reputation, future plans, and so on? This is not something you can do overnight, but it should become an integral part of every strategic planning exercise.

THE S4 FRAMEWORK: WHEN IS SEQUENCE THE ANSWER?

Beyond the risks and opportunities associated with any given sequence, there is also a larger question: When is sequential ordering (doing things one step after another) the right way to proceed? The purpose of the S4 framework described here is to help you decide among several options.

Singularity. You can attempt to do everything in a single step at a single point in time—this is cat-point thinking. You decide what to do and then select a single point in time to accomplish it. An investigative journalist, for example, researches his subject and, when he is ready, writes a lengthy article about it. The risk is that the article comes out at the wrong time. An unexpected crisis captures the reader's attention and overshadows the piece. Alternately, the article may be too early (there is no interest in the topic) or too late (another reporter has scooped him). Darwin had to rush his masterpiece on the origin of species into print for fear that his peer, the British naturalist Alfred Russel Wallace, would beat him to it. If time is short and you won't have another chance, then seize the moment. But as a general rule, trying to accomplish everything at a single stroke is not only impossible but also undesirable. The risks of choosing the wrong moment are too great.

Sequence. This, of course, is the subject of this chapter. You can proceed in a step-by-step sequence, or you can invert the typical sequence. This requires a decision about which sequence characteristics (order, number of steps, spacing, and so on) matter in a given situation. There are many advantages and risks associated with the use of any step-by-step procedure. The most salient disadvantage is that, compared with the next option, proceeding step-by-step is slow.

Simultaneity. The advantage of simultaneous action is speed.

One of the most dramatic examples of a choice between a sequence and a simultaneous strategy was the decision by the German high command at the beginning of World War I. The plan was to fight on two fronts by attacking both France and Russia simultaneously. Worried that he was making a decision that could cost him the war, William II, the emperor of Germany (Kaiser), suggested that they switch their plans to a sequential approach, thereby focusing all of their might on defeating one adversary at a time. His chief of staff, General Helmuth von Moltke, disagreed, saying that "once settled, [the plan] cannot be altered."[a]

As Professor Allen Bluedorn of the University of Missouri has pointed out, because "the cold war took its origins from World War II, which took it origins from the outcome of the First World War, whose outcome was intimately linked to the Kaiser's decision . . . in a very real sense the entire direction of twentieth-century history turned on that strategic decision."[b] Simultaneity carried the day, and the rest is history.

Silence. The final alternative is silence. You take no action—at least for the moment. A newspaper may decide *not* to publish a story, or postpone publication for national security or other reasons. As Mark Twain said, "The right word may be effective, but no word was ever as effective as a rightly timed pause."[c]

a. B. Tuchman, *The Guns of August* (London: Macmillan, 1962), 100, cited in A. C. Bluedorn, *The Human Organization of Time: Temporal Realities and Experience* (Stanford, CA: Stanford University Press, 2002).

b. Bluedorn, *The Human Organization of Time*, 1–2.

c. "Pause Quotes," *BrainyQuote*, http://www.brainyquote.com/quotes/keywords /pause.html#gSCFwO8VlkHdALLY.99I've.

Keep in mind that each timing element, including sequence, is only one piece of the puzzle. Events in the world are multidimensional. So too are issues of timing. Although your ability to see and use each element is important, if you want to address timing issues in the real world, you will need to find all six elements and the patterns they form with each other. We are just getting started. When we are done, you will have a powerful new way to look at what you do every day. Your actions and activities will be better timed and hence more likely to proceed according to plan.

THE TEMPORAL IMAGINATION

Look at the photographs of these two products: an upside-down bottle of Hunt's ketchup and a package of Rogaine.

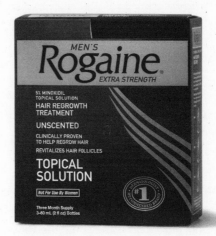

Now ask yourself: How are they similar? They appear to have little in common. Rogaine was first marketed as a possible cure for baldness. Later the company decided to also market it as prevention, something to use before your hair starts falling out. Still puzzled about what is similar? Think about the old-style ketchup bottle. You had to turn it over and bang on the bottom to get the catsup to come out. The upside-down bottle moved *downstream* to the next step in the sequence of use, just as the change in the patent law moved from "first to invent" to "first to file." Rogaine did the opposite: it moved *upstream* in the sequence of use. Ads now talked about prevention and not just cure, the same upstream move as occurred in the medical example in which chemotherapy was administered before surgery and not just after. It is common to focus on "things"—objects or products that we can see in front of us—not on the temporal sequence that defines their use. The latter focus requires an act of temporal imagination, the result of which can be the discovery of new ways to improve a product or process.

SEQUENCE: IN BRIEF

Characteristics of sequences:

Order. Which event follows the next in a series?

Punctuation. Where does the sequence begin, pause, or stop? How is it punctuated into steps and stages?

Interval and duration. How long do steps or stages take or last, and how much time elapses between them?

Shape. Is the sequence linear, looping, or cyclical?

Location. At what point within a sequence does an event take place?

Extension. How long is the complete sequence from beginning to end?

Risks associated with sequence include

- *Missing a sequence*: not understanding until it's too late how one event is likely to follow another (the creation and popularity of mortgage-based collateralized debt obligations and the housing boom)
- *Unwittingly inverting a sequence*: doing B before A, when A needs to happen first for B to succeed (failing to get budget approval before committing funds)
- *Failing to look downstream*: not accounting for how a sequence will play out (posting a personal video on the Web without realizing it cannot be removed)
- *Missing a step or stage*: not realizing that a step or stage is necessary (before individuals can purchase prescription eye glasses, they need access to a doctor who can write a prescription)
- *Failing to take location into account*: where an event happens within a sequence can determine how it is perceived (A plane lands, but there is a 10-minute delay before a gate becomes available. The same 10-minute delay during the flight would hardly be noticed)
- *Not anticipating a change in shape*: (failing to anticipate a bottleneck or a catch-22 situation)

Opportunities associated with sequence can stem from

- *Deliberately inverting a sequence*: finding benefit in reversing the usual order (selling first and then manufacturing)
- *Choosing the right duration*: understanding how the length of an event can affect the larger plan (knowing how long a kiss should last to signal affection—or desire)
- *Creating a sequence*: designing a sequence or series of actions so as to minimize risk and maximize flexibility (designing a fundraising drive as a sequence of actions rather than as a one-time event)
- *Changing location*: doing something last that's usually done first, or vice versa (paying the toll for the person behind you in line)
- *Deliberately skipping a step*: pruning steps from the usual ways of doing business (allowing borrowers to prequalify for a loan before applying)
- *Giving people a choice*: adjusting sequences to optimize the customer experience (letting them either register for your site or proceed directly to checkout)

t w o

Temporal Punctuation

"The reason he [Jared L. Loughner, who shot Representative Gabrielle Giffords] was able to be tackled was he had to *pause* to reload," said Dennis Henigan, vice president of the Brady Center to Prevent Gun Violence.... "The problem is, he didn't have to *pause* to reload until he'd already expended 30 rounds." [italics mine]

—*Jo Becker and Michael Luo*[1]

Temporal punctuation refers to how we divide the continuous flow of time into separate units by creating steps, stages, beginnings, endings, midpoints, and deadlines. Similar to the commas and periods in a sentence, these marks of temporal punctuation tell us where we are and when to start, stop, or pause. For example, a company will use the end of the calendar or fiscal year to time the beginning and end of its strategic planning process. Every industry has an annual trade show or an important convention or sales meeting, which affects when new products are introduced. Money managers who are sitting on cash may be required by their funds to be fully invested, so they will jump back into the market by the end of the quarter.

Examples of temporal punctuation are everywhere, part of everyday life. Think of that special interval we call "now," which perpetually separates past from future. The numbered dials on our watch and the dates on our calendar are marks of punctuation. So are the moments of sunrise and sunset that mark the beginning of the day and night, or the fleeting expression of fatigue in a host's face that tells us it is time to leave. Individual marks of temporal punctuation are important because they can tell us a lot about timing. The trouble is, we often don't notice them.

Here's an example. A young man working as a grocery clerk was interested in advancing his career. He was able to secure a new job at a high-tech company by promising not to cash any of his paychecks until he had proven that he was the best keypunch repairer in the business. If we ask ourselves *when* he would be able to prove he was best, most of us would throw up our hands and say that it's impossible to know. As it turned out, the young man got the job, worked hard, and, as he promised, didn't cash his paychecks. But when the accounting department tried to close its books for the quarter, it found it couldn't because of all the uncashed checks. At that point, the branch manager, who had forgotten the deal he had made, released the young man from his promise.

That is how James Cannavino, the chief strategist at IBM, who retired in 1995 after thirty-two years with the company, got his first job with Big Blue.[2] Neither the branch manager who hired him nor Mr. Cannavino himself thought about the punctuation mark (quarter-end) when the accounting department would need to close its books.

There are two reasons why punctuation marks supply useful clues in matters of timing. First, many actions are coordinated with specific times and dates on the calendar. We know, for example, that there will be a party on New Year's Eve. Other events will only happen *after* a known punctuation mark. When would President Obama have flexibility in negotiating a reduction in nuclear missiles with Russia? We know the answer because an open mike picked up part of his conversation with Prime Minister Medvedev of Russia on March 26, 2012. He told Medvedev that he could be more flexible after his reelection. Presumably, concessions before then would be used against him: his opponents would portray him as weak. The second reason is that people like to appear rational. They want to be able to give objective reasons why they acted when they did. Rather than admit they did something on a whim or for emotional reasons, they will point to a mark of punctuation. They will say, for example, *I chose that time because it was*

- *Before* something that just started or ended
- *After* something that just started or ended
- *In between* two recognized points in time
- *During a pause* in the action

We all need to be able to explain (to our boss, the board, an external stakeholder, and even to ourselves) why we chose one time over another. And that is not always easy. This is particularly true when a decision is based on what I call a *magnitude rule*. A magnitude rule is one in which the timing of an action is triggered whenever a state or process reaches a certain magnitude or threshold. "I'll do that when costs are too high, when the market is too small, or when my patience runs out." A timing rule like that is difficult to implement, except arbitrarily. After all, how high is *too* high, how small is *too* small, and how long is *too* long? It is often impossible to tell. Therefore, people use temporal punctuation marks to decide when to act: We will look at costs *at the end of the quarter*, they say. We'll judge whether a market is too small *after we have one full year of sales*, and so on. Because we know that others will use punctuation marks to time and justify their actions, we can use that knowledge to predict when they will act, and hence better time our own actions.

Punctuation marks can also explain why an action *wasn't* taken at a particular time, because punctuation marks keep together whatever is between them. For example, a meeting begins and ends. Those two punctuation marks separate the events of the meeting from what went on before and after. But they also group, and therefore bind together, the events that constitute the meeting. Leaving in the middle of a meeting feels disruptive. When there is no pause, no beginning or ending, then there is no easy way in or out. The converse is also true: punctuation makes entrances and exits possible. Television programs tend to begin and end on the hour or half hour, not a few minutes before or after.

John Goode, a portfolio manager at Smith Barney, carried out a research project in early 2000 with analysts at Sanford C. Bernstein. The project involved a specific temporal punctuation mark. Using publicly available data for the year, they looked at the amount of money raised in initial public offerings and calculated how much stock owned by insiders might be coming into the market once the "lockups" (the amount of time officers must hold their stock) expired. They determined that as much as $150 billion in insider shares could be freed up from March 30 to June 30 of 2000.

Goode received that report on March 16, a week before the NASDAQ hit what would prove to be its all-time high. The findings—what Goode felt represented a tsunami of stocks available to come to market—were all that he needed to put his fund on what he calls a "technology-free diet." Most of us who were in the market at the beginning of January 2000 weren't thinking about how beginnings or endings would affect stock prices. By examining a punctuation mark (lockup expirations), Goode was able to avoid the bloodbath that ensued.

"It was basic Economics 101," he says.[3]

Actually, it wasn't basic economics. You won't find an explicit discussion of temporal punctuation or, for that matter, many references to the term *lockup period* in most beginning texts on economics. Like their linguistic counterparts, marks of temporal punctuation can easily get lost amid other concerns. But putting them to use can make a big difference. When we know the location of punctuation marks, we can use them to make predictions and decisions.

CHARACTERISTICS OF TEMPORAL PUNCTUATION

As with all of the timing elements, using temporal punctuation to make decisions about timing begins with knowing what to look for. Here are eight characteristics that are important.

1. **Type**. There are many kinds of punctuation marks.
2. **Strength**. Some are strong; others are weak.
3. **Objective or subjective**. When something *is* over in reality and when it is *perceived* to be over need not be the same.
4. **Meaning**. What does a given mark of temporal punctuation mean? How do different stakeholders interpret it?
5. **Location**. Where a punctuation mark is placed within a process matters.
6. **Number**. There is often more than one.
7. **Spacing**. How much time separates them?
8. **Alignment**. Which ones occur at the same time?

Type

Specific times and dates can serve as punctuation marks. To find them, look at different calendars. Most of us in business watch the *economic* calendar, when the Federal Reserve will meet to determine interest rates, for instance. But we also need to think about other time lines—the *political* calendar, for example, when an election will occur that could alter the balance of power at the state or federal level. When we are planning a product launch, we need to consider *religious and secular holidays*, such as Christmas, New Year's Day, and July 4. We need to think about the *legislative* calendar, when bills affecting our business may be acted on.

We also need to pay attention to *internal* and *external* punctuation. The schedules and timetables associated with projects inside our own organization are right there in front of us. But we need to be aware that external stakeholders will have their own deadlines and sense of when to begin or postpone an activity. We also need to know when events in the wider world are beginning or ending. Are we at the dawn of a recession? If so, then it's probably not the right time to expand payroll.

We can't spend every moment monitoring time lines and temporal punctuation (football coaches sometimes assign a specific person to keep track of the clock and help make decisions about time-outs), but remember that there are many types of time lines, each with its own punctuation.

Strength

Punctuation marks can differ in terms of function or strength.

The Period

Of all the types of temporal punctuation, periods have the most power. In most hierarchical organizations, we can debate, ponder alternatives, and even object to a course of action. But once our boss has made a decision, the moment for debate and deliberation is over. To continue to argue beyond that point is risky. Like running a stop sign, it can put your life (within that organization) in jeopardy.

An important decision can function as a period. Whereas the *logical function* of a decision is to choose among alternatives, the *temporal function* of a decision is to separate the present from the past. There is a time before the decision, and a time after. That is one reason we value decisiveness. Decisions free the future from the grip of the past in the same way that a period at the end of a sentence prevents the old sentence from running on. In addition, by stopping the past, a period creates space for something new to begin.

The Comma

NATO was fifty years old in April 1999. The Soviet Union, one of the main reasons NATO existed, had collapsed. Still, as events all around the world continue to show, the alliance is not going out of business just yet. Alexander M. Haig Jr., a former NATO commander, treated the anniversary more as a comma than a period. In a speech, he described the moment as a time to reflect on the past and envision the future. His choice of comments made it clear that NATO was not at an end, but instead was at an inflection point.

All of us, managers included, have choices to make about punctuation. Whenever a mark of punctuation is called for, we can decide whether the time is right to declare an end, to permanently terminate what has been going on, or simply insert a comma, a brief pause to evaluate the immediate past and plan for the future.

Some punctuation marks are perceived as more significant than others—the "big Five-O" for baby boomers, for example. The end of the fiscal year is usually more important than the end of the second quarter, and so on. When a deadline is imposed, we need to know whether it is a hard or soft deadline. Must it be met, or can it be treated as just another step along the way, more of a comma than a period?

Objective or Subjective

It is important to look for *subjective* as well as *objective* punctuation. Objective punctuation refers to events in the real world, the time when a contract expires or a website goes live. There is no debate over objective punctuation. Subjective punctuation, by contrast, is, well, subjective. We feel that something is over or is beginning, regardless of the objective facts. Everyone may know that a project or business relationship is over before it is officially declared dead. Similarly, an activity may seem like a "new beginning" without anyone making a formal announcement to that effect.

Meaning

The question of whether a punctuation mark is objective or subjective is closely tied to the question of meaning. Do different stakeholders interpret the same mark in the same way? One person's comma, or pause, can be another person's period, and vice versa. If someone doesn't respond to your email for a certain period of time, does that mean that he or she wants to end the relationship?

Location

Exactly where a punctuation mark is inserted into an ongoing process or sequence of events is critical.

A punctuation mark can be inserted too early. When a person has just hit his thumb with a hammer, what should he do? We know the answer: put ice on it. But using ice to treat bumps and bruises was not something earlier generations would have done. They would have said that healing requires heat. But they were making a timing error. Just because the hammer is no longer in contact with the person's thumb does not mean that the injury is over; it is not. It continues, and ice slows its progress. After that, heat can be applied.

One reason that we declare something (such as a recession) over is that we want to distance ourselves from the pain it has caused. But there is another reason: we need the past to be over to create the possibility of a new and better future.

A punctuation mark can also be inserted too late. Consider an old police interrogation tactic. Here's how it worked before the Supreme Court declared it unconstitutional. The police first questioned a suspect without telling him that he had the right to remain silent and consult a lawyer. The police were aware that they couldn't use what the suspect said in court. After a break, the police came back and then read the subject his rights. Suspects usually simply repeated what they said earlier.[4] The punctuation mark in this case (the Miranda warning) was inserted late on purpose to make the suspect feel that it was *too late* to take back what he or she said. The Supreme Court subsequently invalidated the general use of this tactic.

Number

Pay attention to the number of punctuation marks that are or will be present in any time-extended process. An excessive number can slow things down. We have all been on a short flight, only to find that the drive home—exiting the parking ramp, pausing at stop signs, halting for traffic lights, and getting on the highway—took longer than the flight itself. We underestimate how long a task will take to accomplish because we fail to consider all of the punctuation marks, the various borders and boundaries that we will have to cross en route, even though we know about most of them in advance. That is why it is so important to include them in our planning.

There are a number of reasons why we don't. First, some punctuation marks, such as an unexpected delay, can't be predicted. Second, some are unpleasant. We want the drive home from the airport to be short and sweet. Punctuation marks slow us down. Third, when there are a lot of punctuation marks, it is not easy to keep them all in mind. For example, when you drive home from the airport, think about how many stops and starts you have to make—and that's the point. You have to stop and think. We are not used to taking punctuation into account.

Neither IBM's Cannavino nor his boss were thinking about punctuation—namely, that by the end of the quarter all those uncashed checks would pose a problem for the accounting department. If it's easy to ignore a single punctuation mark, what should we do when there are dozens of beginnings, endings, pauses, and stops and starts, as in most projects? One of the difficulties in dealing with large numbers of punctuation marks is that we don't have a place to put them, so that when we need to find them, we don't know where to look. One solution is to think of the future as a set of parallel lines or tracks, one line for each event, process, or course of action. We could then, for example, put all the times and dates of the legislative calendar that affect our business on one line, all the dates of important industry events on another, the times and dates of our company's strategic planning process on another, and so on. That way we could keep track of all the punctuation marks that matter.

Spacing

Spacing, the time between punctuation marks, allows us to predict events that would otherwise be unpredictable. As an example, let's consider Attorney General Janet Reno's decision to storm the compound of the Branch Davidians on April 19, 1993. Located in Waco, Texas, the compound had been under siege for over a month. The standoff began February 28, when agents of the Bureau of Alcohol, Tobacco, and Firearms attempted to serve David Koresh, the religious head of the Branch Davidians, with a warrant. Heavily armed Davidians fired on federal agents, killing four officers and wounding sixteen. The government began negotiating with Koresh in an attempt to convince him to surrender. Koresh had twice indicated that he would leave the compound, but reneged each time. Finally, after weeks went by, Koresh said that he would exit the compound at the end of Easter/Passover. When that date came and went and Koresh did not surrender, the government made its move. The timing rule they followed was the same as in the first Gulf War: when negotiation fails, use force.

Punctuation entered into the government's decision in two ways. First, Koresh was a religious figure, and the selection of a religious date for a resolution of the crisis had a certain rationality to it (an action was *aligned* with a punctuation mark of the same "type"). But when he failed to come out at Easter/Passover as promised, the government lost hope, hope that had been raised precisely because the time of exit seemed understandable in a situation ruled by unpredictability and violence. When a time that appeared to be rational did not produce the desired result, the government lost hope of a reasonable outcome, and so acted with force.

There is another way timing came into play. The next time the crisis might be resolved by using a major religious holiday was Christmas, but Christmas was still eight months away. If Christmas were celebrated in May rather than December, the government might have paused. Its negotiators could have tried to build a story around Christmas as a "logical" time when the crisis could be resolved. Only an accident of the calendar (the long interval between Easter/Passover and Christmas) prevented it. That is one reason we sometimes say that timing is a matter of luck; but this is exactly the wrong conclusion. The fact that Christmas is celebrated in December rather than May is precisely what we needed to know to predict when the government would act. The spacing of these two punctuation marks decided the question of timing.[5]

The Waco example introduces an important principle: *the more it seems impossible to predict when an event will occur or a decision will be made, the more its timing will be determined by the location of temporal punctuation.* When will David Koresh promise to leave the compound? Answer: at the end of Easter/Passover. Koresh was a religious figure, and the selection of a religious date had a certain logic to it. When will the State of Minnesota Supreme Court decide the contested senate race between Norm Coleman and Al Franken in 2009? Answer: right before the Fourth of July weekend so that the results of the election wouldn't be left hanging and prove an embarrassment during the Fourth of July parade. When will Cannavino prove that he is the best keypunch repairer? Answer: at the end of the quarter. When will most people start an exercise program? Answer: right after New Year's. So if we can determine which punctuation marks are salient for decision makers, we have found an important clue about the timing of their actions, especially when it appears that they have no other grounds on which to make a decision.

Alignment

When a number of similar punctuation marks occur at the same time, our sense of a border or boundary is strengthened. The power to change an organization is strongest, for example, when a new leader arrives, because two punctuation marks are aligned: a new leader and a new direction. They occur at the same time.

One particular alignment of temporal punctuation is so common it deserves a name. I call it the *no gap, no overlap rule.* This rule suggests that the next step or stage should begin immediately after the cessation of the previous one, with no gap or overlap between them—the termination of an existing product with the launch of its replacement, for example, or the resignation of a key leader with the appointment of his or her successor. The rule—expressing a kind of temporal agoraphobia—requires that there be no empty or "dead" space between the end of one event and the beginning of another. The rule also requires that two processes or events not overlap, which might cause one to compete or interfere with the other, such as when one product cannibalizes another. The exception to the no-overlap component arises when continuity is important. For example, a company might ask a retiring employee to train her successor.

We generally think that alignment is good, and misalignment bad, but not always. Looking as old as we are or feel may or may not be a good thing. The ability to intentionally align (or misalign) one's *actual* age with one's *psychological* age and the age that one *presents to the world* is what keeps the health and beauty industry alive and profitable. The ability to align the outcome of a project with the time when it will be evaluated turns out to be a powerful motivator.

In general, misalignment raises questions. Regularly scheduled meetings act as a form of punctuation. When a decision comes at a different time, we wonder why. In October 1998, for example, the Federal Reserve cut two key interest rates. The market soared, but because the move occurred in between regularly scheduled Fed meetings, it "served to make already-battered bond investors more nervous than ever."[6] Bystanders wondered whether the timing of the action was a signal that the looming recession was closer than anticipated. As this example illustrates, misalignment can have unintended consequences.

TEMPORAL PUNCTUATION RISKS

There are a number of risks associated with missing or misreading this element of timing.

Missing Punctuation

Perhaps the greatest risk is failing to note that an ongoing activity will have punctuation marks. Their presence and location can have a major impact on a decision. For example, researchers followed eight Israeli judges for ten months, making note of their rulings on the one thousand prisoners who applied for parole during that time. What they found was that prisoners were far more likely to be granted parole if their applications crossed the judges' desks at the beginning of the day. As the hours passed, however, fewer and fewer requests were granted. The number rose significantly again following two daily breaks, during which the judges stopped for food. But then, as the day wore on, the approvals once again plummeted.[7] So if you want to get out of jail, make sure your application is considered early in the day. Knowing where a punctuation mark is placed and understanding its effect can provide important information about timing.

A similar lesson can be drawn from the Dow's thousand-point plunge and subsequent recovery in May 2010, in what was known as the Flash Crash. One primary cause of the plunge was a computerized trading glitch that prompted a sale of $4.1 billion in shares. The algorithm responsible was designed to execute a trade regardless of price or time, which meant that it continued to sell even as prices dropped sharply.[8] The unintended consequence of automatic, high-frequency trades placed at the wrong moment can be a market downdraft or plunge. After the Flash Crash, part of the solution by regulators was to expand trading curbs (or circuit breakers). They essentially inserted punctuation where it was missing, so that stock trading is halted for five minutes if the price moves by 10 percent or more in a five-minute period.

Fortunately, the temporal punctuation lens is one of the easiest to use because it involves looking for familiar categories: beginnings, pauses, midpoints, endings, known dates on the calendar, and so on. As I indicated earlier, we simply need a place to put the marks so that we can keep them in mind and use the information they contain to make better decisions.

Questions to ask: *Have I anticipated all the steps and stages, stops, starts, and pauses that will punctuate an event or situation? What impact will each have on my progress and final results?*

Conflicting Interests

Mistakes and oversights occur when we feel obliged to focus on one kind of punctuation and then forget or downplay another as a result. For example, all executives live with inherent conflicts between the realities of the financial calendar—Wall Street's focus on results and measurement—and the need for projects to develop at their own pace if they are to be successful. As a result, projects may be rushed or cut short to meet immediate needs, such as quarter-end accounting and earnings reports.

Question to ask: *If a situation has multiple punctuation marks, which will take precedence, and why?*

Misreading Temporal Punctuation

Problems arise when we mistake a comma for a period: we thought that something was over when it was not, or vice versa. Misreading temporal punctuation happens all the time. In November 2007, for example, Tom Lauricella wrote in the *Wall Street Journal* that "after successfully dodging the bond market storm earlier this year, several big mutual funds *thought the worst was over*. It was a bad call, and now they're feeling the pain."[9]

Questions to ask: *Have I correctly interpreted temporal punctuation? Is it possible that what I think is a full stop is really just a brief pause?*

Disregarding Temporal Punctuation (and Whether It Can Be Changed)

The present, which separates past from future, is a punctuation mark. We hope we can change the future, and we know we can't change the past. The practice of "backdating," however, disregards this fundamental idea. In backdating, a company pretends that the options it gave executives had been issued at an earlier date when the stock price was lower, which ensures that the person receiving them makes a profit. If we fail to pay attention to where and when things start or stop, and whether anything about those facts can be changed or seen differently, we may find ourselves facing risks we didn't anticipate. Although backdating is not in and of itself illegal, the SEC found some cases of backdating to be fraudulent when they were in violation of tax rules.

Questions to ask: *Am I ignoring or disregarding temporal punctuation for convenience's sake? If so, what might be the effect?*

Simultaneous Punctuation

Mistakes occur when we don't consider what will happen if punctuation marks coincide. Pharmaceutical companies, for example, must plan for the times when patents on multiple drugs expire simultaneously, or pay a high price for that oversight. They need to be ready with new drugs to fill the revenue gap, or have a brand strategy that allows them to rise above the flood of competition. Likewise, if all the bonds in a portfolio mature at the same time, we have to hope that interest rates and our need for cash are exactly what we thought they would be when we bought the bonds. To avoid that risk, financial advisers often recommend a bond ladder, in which different bonds mature at different times, thus minimizing the risk of a forecasting error. The classic solution to synchronous risk, the risk that several events will occur at the same time, is an asynchronous strategy, a plan to keep them apart.

Questions to ask: *Are several punctuation marks, such as deadlines, occurring simultaneously? If so, do I have a plan to manage their co-occurrence?*

Inserting a Period Too Soon

Similar to using heat instead of ice on a wound, a common timing error is to be too quick to insert a period—concluding erroneously that something is over when it is not. President Bush's "Mission Accomplished" banner during the Iraq War is one example. The tendency to treat an event as concluded when it is not is quite common. In January 2007, it looked as if the housing market might be recovering from its slump, but financial writer Daniel Gross added a cautionary note having to do with how the Census Bureau calculates the supply and demand for housing. He noted that a percentage of the home sales finalized in December are in fact cancelled in early January. Yet the number is never right-sized, and the December figures are reported without correction.[10]

A sale isn't a sale if it is cancelled, but the Census Bureau still counts it. The mistake is to think of a sale as a single event, when it is really a time-extended sequence.

Question to ask: *Is this really an ending, or is the event still under way?*

Spacing Risks

Spacing risks occur when we fail to measure or account for the time in between punctuation marks. For example, if a family had a dozen children in as many years, I think it is safe to say that we would find the parents physically exhausted, not to mention financially stressed. Paying attention to starts and stops allows one to better allocate one's resources.

Question to ask: *Have I built enough time in between events to prepare for what comes next?*

Pattern Risks

Pattern risks arise when we fail to anticipate the shapes and patterns that are predictably associated with a punctuation mark—for example, the hockey stick jump in effort that occurs right before a deadline, as everyone works around the clock to meet it, or the lowering of expectations right before quarterly earnings are made public, so that the company can beat them. There are often patterns surrounding punctuation marks. We need to plan for them.

Question to ask: *What predictable patterns of behavior are associated with different marks of punctuation, and have I taken these patterns into account?*

Misinterpreting Temporal Punctuation

There is always a risk that someone may misinterpret a mark of punctuation. In a business negotiation, for example, one side may pause for what seems a very long time. Does the length of the pause suggest a lack of interest, or does it simply reflect the time the other side needs to resolve internal differences?

In 2008, Michael Gordon, writing in the *New York Times*, wondered how the U.S. exit from Iraq would be interpreted. "If the Iraqis know that American forces are on their way out, regardless of what they do, would they be more likely to respond by overcoming their differences or by preparing for the sectarian bloodbath that might follow?"[11] Different parties can interpret a mark of punctuation differently.

Likewise, when a traffic light (the punctuation mark) turns yellow, drivers respond in varying ways. A study of fifteen hundred drivers in Ohio found that "truckers tend to speed through, as do cars travelling in the right-hand lanes."[12] In this case, different interpretations of a punctuation mark can literally cause accidents.

Questions to ask: *Can a mark of temporal punctuation be interpreted in more than one way? Is there a right interpretation or a reasonable difference of opinion?*

TEMPORAL PUNCTUATION OPTIONS AND OPPORTUNITIES

There are many opportunities to use temporal punctuation in our own lives and work. We can use a pause or a period to start a new relationship or introduce a different idea, terminate a project that has gone on for too long, create or diminish a sense of urgency, and perform a wide variety of other actions for which temporal punctuation is the right tool. Often it is not merely what we do but how we do it that determines success or failure. The greatest opportunity to use punctuation in business occurs in managing change, particularly the timing of entrances and exits (inserting a period).

Create Exit Strategies

Creating an exit strategy is essentially the same as adding a period. Let's assume that we are in the midst of a particular course of action—funding a research project, developing a business, or maintaining a long-term relationship. It could be anything. Now assume that things are not working, and we know that it is time to end our present commitment. Every situation is unique, of course, and there are always a multitude of factors to consider. But what is important for our purposes is how questions of time and timing enter into planning an exit strategy.

Unfortunately, unless it is a major undertaking, and even then, exit strategies are rarely discussed *before* a project or activity is begun. Doing so would be perceived as a lack of confidence in the new venture. It is hard to think about an exit when one is getting ready to launch a project. One solution is to make the discussion of exit strategies, and their timing, into a ritual. Rituals have the right temporal properties: they are *time limited*, so they won't interrupt the launch, and they are safe because they *are* rituals, as opposed to the real thing. And they can be practiced, and thus performed flawlessly even under stress. Because of these characteristics, rituals can be inserted into any activity at *almost any time* to achieve what would otherwise be time consuming or difficult.

These are some of the factors to take into account when considering an exit:

1. *Permanence and reversibility.* Is the situation that raises the question of an exit permanent or temporary, and would additional resources turn the situation around within a reasonable period of time?

2. *The timing of alternatives.* When will alternative opportunities be available? It is not uncommon to delay an exit until a viable alternative is present—even when it is obvious that continuing the present course of action makes no sense. If a project is evaluated solely against a set of internal benchmarks, a timely exit is unlikely. Someone must be given the task of identifying alternative opportunities and monitoring when the window opens and closes for pursuing them.

3. *The timing of costs and benefits.* When we talk about the costs and benefits of an exit, we usually think in terms of type and size. What costs or benefits do we anticipate? Will they be large or small? A timing analysis adds a third consideration: *When* will they occur? When most of the costs of a project are incurred at the *beginning* and most of the benefits are expected to come only at the *end*, a timely exit will prove difficult. Managers will be tempted to wait for the benefits, if only to justify the costs that have already been incurred. An obvious solution, when feasible, is to structure the project so that benefits track costs.

Most discussions surrounding an exit also include closing costs (as if that phrase somehow takes timing into account). We need to remember to ask how large closing costs will be *at each point in the future,* and how those costs will be evaluated when they are incurred. Costs that are acceptable when times are good may look excessive when times are tough.[13]

4. *The temporal pattern of success and failure.* Might a project show initial signs of success, but then seem to stall? If so, it is

easy to become trapped. The British philosopher and social critic Bertrand Russell once remarked that the importance of early religious experience is not that it is religious but that it is early. The same is true of early success. Early success has the power to draw us in, to keep us committed until, like a gambler at a slot machine, we have lost everything. Managers should forecast the *shape* of possible *time-extended patterns of success and failure* that are associated with their projects and discuss how each might result in a timing error. These discussions should take place early, *before* problems emerge.

5.   *A shift in motivation over time.* Over time, there can be a shift in motivation from seeking gain to avoiding loss, as illustrated in the box "The Dollar Auction."

THE DOLLAR AUCTION

Hold up a dollar bill. Announce that you will auction it off to the highest bidder. The only thing, you add, is that the loser will also have to pay. The bidding will start with a dime. OK, you say, in your best imitation of auctioneer, who will give a dime for dollar. Dime for a dollar?

What will happen—if someone is foolish enough to begin and another person is even more foolish to raise the bid—is that bids will ramp up rather nicely. As the bidding gets closer to a dollar, the loser will realize that if she doesn't raise her bid, she will lose more than she thought and will have gained nothing. At that point, the motive to maximize gain is replaced by a motive to avoid loss. And so, to avoid the latter, she raises her bid. The result is that bids often exceed one dollar, sometimes by a substantial amount.

Note: The dollar auction was invented by Allan I. Teger and is described in his book, *Too Much Invested to Quit* (New York: Pergamon Press, 1980).

If you think about it, many business situations have this dynamic in fast-moving markets and highly competitive industries where events change quickly. We invest in real estate hoping to make a profit, but then the bubble bursts, and our only concern is how to avoid a complete loss.

6. *Blame and responsibility.* How will blame be assigned if the decision is to exit at a given time? The natural question to ask is, Who will be held accountable? But it is not merely *who* will bear the responsibility, but what that individual's world will be like at the time an exit is required. If everything else is going well, it will be easier to take responsibility for what isn't working. But if times are bad, we can expect those in charge to delay an exit in the hope that the situation will improve. Hence we need to anticipate the context in which an exit decision is required, or we will find ourselves surprised that it was made too early or, more likely, too late.

7. *Identity, status, and reputation.* The more an individual's or firm's identity, reputation, or status is closely linked to a project or activity, the more the decision to exit will be postponed, particularly if the same group who began the project is responsible for ending it.[14]

8. *Language and culture.* Timing an exit is influenced by an organization's culture.[15] Some organizations prize persistence, staying the course. Others value speed. The former will be late; the latter will jump the gun. One clue to an organization's culture is how it views costs and benefits. If a cost is considered an investment rather than an expense, questionable returns will be viewed with less alarm. The firm will be slow to exit from an unprofitable venture. Attitudes and expectations about measurement are another clue. If an organization places a high value on quantification, anything that cannot be counted will be suspect. The firm will delay its decision to exit while waiting for greater precision and proof, which may be impossible to obtain. Many economic indicators are revised months or even years later. If we need to wait for perfect data before making a decision, we might have to wait a very long time.

9. *Prior commitments.* The greater one's prior commitment to a project, the more difficult it will be to exit. In other words, we need to know what relationships or interests will be threatened

if the project is terminated. The more numerous and important they are, the more an exit will be delayed.

10.   *The multidimensionality of endings.* Endings are difficult in complex situations because the right time to exit on one dimension may not be the right time on another. Think of the war in Afghanistan, or any war for that matter. When will the various missions be accomplished (nation building, defeating the Taliban, securing key parts of the country, and so on)? When can troops be withdrawn safely? When will our obligations to others be discharged? When will we know that past achievements will be sustained? And how do the answers to these questions depend on eroding popular support for the war?

Bioethicist Daniel Callahan illustrates the many dimensions of an ending in the way he defined natural death:

> [It occurs at a] point in a life span when (a) one's life work has been accomplished; (b) one's moral obligations to those for whom one has had responsibility have been discharged; (c) one's death will not seem to others [as] an offense to sense or sensibility, or tempt others to despair and rage at human existence; and finally, (d) one's process of dying is not marked by unbearable and degrading pain.[16]

Because exits involve many dimensions, it is important to explore the conflicts that arise among them. What would be too early on one dimension might be too late on another. Because these are difficult conflicts to resolve, it is best to identify them in advance and leave enough time to think them through.

■ ■ ■

Successful exit strategies are complex achievements. The ten issues I've discussed here, merely a starting point, should help you think through some of the timing issues involved. If we decide that an exit is needed, the next question is how to do it.

CREATE CLOSURE: THE DELETE DESIGN MODEL

An ending is not simply an objective fact—it is also a psychological process. And it is a process that needs to be well managed. Endings can be painful, and, as any attorney will tell you, lawsuits are caused as much by the feeling of injury as by the objective facts. With that in mind, I will describe the five steps in what I call the *Delete Design Model*, which can be used to create the feeling of closure; they are a way to insert a psychological period. Closure is important in managing change because groups will not take full advantage of new opportunities if they remain tethered to the past and are not ready to move on. What is distinctive about this model, and why I am presenting it here, is that the steps of the model take timing into account.

1. *Summarize the past (S)*. A summary is an abbreviated history of the past. To create a sense of closure, a summary must capture the full meaning of what has occurred. It must include not only the objective facts but also the hopes and dreams of the people involved, their feeling of accomplishment, their celebrations. The summary should present a view of history that leads to the conclusion that the present moment is the right time to act. That often requires going far back in time to the conditions that led to the project or business in the first place, and observing how they have changed.

2. *Justify the change (J)*. Find reasons why change is necessary and desirable, such as the successful attainment of a goal, an instance of failure that cannot be repaired, a loss that cannot be recovered except by moving on, and so on. One must justify why change is not only necessary and desirable but also necessary and desirable *now*.

3. *Make positive statements (P)*. Eulogize the past and honor it. One cannot leave a valued course of action *without* acknowledging, expressing, and celebrating the worth of what is being left. We cannot put the past to bed without a bedtime ritual.

4. *Create continuity between past and future (C)*. It is important to acknowledge the loss, emotional or otherwise, of what does not continue. It is never sufficient to deal with change by simply stating its necessity or arguing that there was nothing of value in what is being eliminated. Change, especially that which is radical in nature, will always be met with resistance. But something as simple as the promise that some valued elements of the past will be preserved and even strengthened in the new arrangement will ease the transition. That is what Alexander Haig did in his NATO speech, mentioned earlier.

5. *End with well wishing (W)*. Express hope for the future. We create closure by finding a new task or purpose that becomes a source of hope. To exit on time, we must have something to exit to, something that pulls us into the future.

You will find this framework, the sequence SJPCW (the letter that defines each step), to be effective in a variety of settings: a child's bedtime ritual, a graduation speech, a retirement dinner, the end of a business partnership, or any occasion where *timely* closure matters.

Note: This discussion follows closely S. Albert, "A Delete Design Model for Successful Transitions," in *Managing Organizational Transitions*, ed. J. Kimberly and R. Quinn (Homewood, IL: Irwin, 1984), 169–191.

Speeding the Pace of Change: Subtract a Period

Thus far we have discussed adding a mark of punctuation, in this case a period. But, put, a, comma, after, every, word, in, this, sentence, and, reading, it, will, feel, like, swimming, against, a, choppy, sea. Exhausting. So sometimes the task is not to add a period but to subtract one—or at least improve the flow by replacing a period with a comma.

The end of a television show, for example, can be construed as either a period or a comma. The network, of course, prefers the comma. It wants viewers to stay tuned for the next program. There was a time in fall 1994 when every network except Fox tried to completely eliminate punctuation in between shows.[17] Instead of appearing between shows, the commercials were to be moved into the body of the programs. Eliminating a period between the end of one program and the beginning of another was intended to keep interest high. The same reasoning was applied to yacht racing. Larry Ellison, head of BMW Oracle Racing, and Ernesto Bertarelli, head of the Alinghi syndicate, made sure that there would be races every summer in the years between formal cup races.[18]

One way to increase productivity is to eliminate interruptions —that is, remove unnecessary punctuation. In 2007, *Wall Street Journal* columnist Sue Shellenbarger noted that Dow Corning had a "no-meeting week" once a quarter, calling a halt on all nonessential internal meetings. This allowed employees to reduce travel and to work without interruption. Similarly, IBM rolled out company-wide "Think Fridays," a block of Friday afternoon time free of nonessential meetings and interruptions.[19]

Choose the Right Location

Where we place a period or comma can make all the difference. Consider a team that has been working on a new product for many years. Pressure is growing to bring the product to market; as a result, the group may be tempted to jump the gun and rush to launch before either the product or the market is ready. To prevent that error, the group needs to find a way to counter the pressure it is feeling. Placing a punctuation mark in the right place can help.

Most of us think of the world as being composed of three separate time periods arranged in a sequence: the past, the present, and the future.

There are two ways we can punctuate this sequence. We can put an imaginary period *after* the present, which groups (brackets) it with the past, like this:

[PAST PRESENT]. FUTURE

Or we can put a period *before* the present, which makes the present the first step of a new future, like this:

PAST. [PRESENT FUTURE]

If the present is grouped with the past, the past becomes the reference point. Someone will say, "This product has been under development for over a decade. When are we going to get it to market?" In contrast, if the present is grouped with the future, the future becomes the reference point. Then the need to move quickly will be tempered by the need to make sure that we create the right first impression. Someone will remind us that if the launch is botched, it can take a very long time to recover.

By changing the location of a period, one can alter the timing of a decision by making the decision appear to be urgent or one that can and should be delayed.

Postponing Punctuation—Controlling Tension

Temporal punctuation can be used to control events and situations in some interesting ways. In fact, the marketer and catchphrase specialist Arthur Schiff created a number of ingenious advertising slogans based on this principle. In his work promoting Ginsu knives, he raised doubts and expectations with hyperbole: "It's a knife that will last forever.... It's a product no kitchen should be without.... It's the most incredible knife offer ever." And then, right on cue, the memorably repetitive refrain: *But wait, there's more.* As journalist Rob Walker explained in the *New York Times*: "In addition to making the offer more desirable, Schiff builds tension by continually postponing the end of the sales pitch, tension that he hoped customers would relieve by picking up the phone and ordering the knives. Many did. "But wait, there's more," sold a lot knives."[20]

Notice the use of the same principle of tension reduction that was involved in the discussion of premature closure. We want the injury to our thumb to be over. President Bush wanted the war in Iraq to be over. Punctuation influences and is influenced by the need for release. When tension is high, we can reduce it by inserting a period, whether or not the time is right to declare an ending. The ability to see the relationship between the "Mission Accomplished" banner and an advertising pitch for a set of knives is what I mean by training our eye to look beneath the surface.

Rethink Your Use of Punctuation

By simply reimagining how we think of beginnings and endings—and how we use temporal punctuation in a business setting—we can open the door to innovating everyday processes. At the very least it helps us look at things differently. Here are a few specific ideas.

Type

There are many types of punctuation that one can choose or reference. Instead of paying attention to an external clock or calendar when setting a deadline, for example, ask a team to report back when they think they are half done, leaving the exact time up to them. That will focus their attention on time and efficiency in a way that having them report on progress after a fixed interval won't. Selecting a different external reference point to time our activities—the date of a religious holiday, such as Christmas, rather than the end of the fiscal year, for example—can provide a fresh perspective.

Strength

Choose between punctuation marks of different strengths. Replace a period with a comma, or vice versa. Deciding on a punctuation mark based on strength is one way to control the meaning of an action. Putting a project on hold instead of cancelling it, for example, sends an entirely different message.

Number

Intentionally increase or decrease the number of punctuation marks. Pause more frequently in meetings, for example, to give other people time to respond to what you are saying. Replace a timing rule based on magnitude with one based on punctuation—for example, "We will terminate the project by the end of the year if it is not successful by then," rather than "We will terminate it when costs become prohibitive." Delete a punctuation mark:

run two activities together without a break, or start an activity without formally acknowledging that something new has begun. Each of these opportunities to increase or decrease the number of punctuation marks will have a different impact on outcomes.

Location

Adjust the alignment of multiple punctuation marks. For example, make sure that all relevant events and activities start and stop at the same time, or don't stop and start at the same time. *Reposition* a punctuation mark. For example, set an early deadline or extend an existing one. Place a period before the present moment in order to define the present as the first step of a new future, rather than the last step of a long past. *Change the spacing* between punctuation marks. Decrease the time between performance evaluations, for example, in order to offer more detailed feedback.

Finally, remember that the sections on risks and opportunities that I have placed at the end of each chapter have a dual use. They can be used before you act, as part of a process of due diligence to help you identify pitfalls and choices in advance. They can also be used after the fact to learn went right or wrong, and why.

THE TEMPORAL IMAGINATION

When a period is required, timing is everything.

A performance ends, and the performer leaves the stage. The audience bursts into applause. The performer returns, bows, leaves the stage, and after an interval returns. Each time she returns, she benefits from the rise in tension that is created: Will she will come back and perform an encore? If we applaud loudly enough, the audience reasons, maybe she will. The audience is well aware that the game is drawing to an end. Everyone is standing, and some call out. Will the performer reject the audience's expression of appreciation? Will she return, but decline the request for an encore?

Uncertainty fuels the applause, which increases in intensity. But what is so intense cannot be sustained. Past a certain point, pleasure becomes pain. As a result, the number of departures and returns that applause can fuel is limited. And that limitation solves a timing problem. If the performer remained on stage until the applause died down, at what moment would she choose to leave? If she left prematurely, the audience would feel cheated. But if she waited too long, she would have overstayed her welcome. She would be demanding more than the audience was prepared to give. The invention of the curtain call, with its rhythm of departure and return, was an act of genius. It solved a difficult problem. When is enough, enough? When is the right time for an exit?

At a macro timescale, we notice only that a performance ends. But at a more micro timescale, we see the sequences, rates, intervals, and so on that are involved in creating that moment. A period seems simple, but it is really a complex achievement. That is why it is important to look at any issue that requires a period or other punctuation mark at different timescales to see the time-related processes that are required.

PUNCTUATION: IN BRIEF

Characteristics of temporal punctuation:

Type. Many kinds of dates and events can be used to divide what would otherwise be a continuous process.

Strength. Marks of temporal punctuation differ in importance.

Objective or subjective. A period can be seen as a comma, a comma as a period.

Meaning. Different stakeholders can interpret a punctuation mark differently.

Location. Where a punctuation mark is positioned or located within an ongoing process matters.

Number. There is usually more than one punctuation mark in a sequence or process.

Spacing. The time, or lack of time, between punctuation marks can be important.

Alignment. Notice which temporal punctuation marks occur at the same time, and which don't.

Risks associated with punctuation include

- *Missing punctuation.* We fail to note that an ongoing activity has punctuation marks (conducting a conference call without pausing for comments and questions).

- *Conflicting interests.* We focus on one kind of punctuation mark while ignoring another. (A product fails to meet its milestones, but we don't make that fact known until after announcing quarter-end results.)

- *Misreading temporal punctuation.* We mistake a comma for a period, or vice versa. (We thought the market hit a peak when it was still surging.)

- *Simultaneous punctuation.* We fail to plan for the times when two or more punctuation marks occur at once. (A pharmaceutical company needs to know when more than one of its patents will expire at the same time.)

- *Inserting a period too soon.* We think something is ending when it is not (counting revenue as final when the sale can still fall through).

- *Spacing risks.* We neglect to take into account the time—or lack of time—between punctuation marks. (One deadline comes right after another, and we are caught short staffed.)

- *Pattern risks.* We don't anticipate the shapes and patterns that are predictably associated with a punctuation mark (the hockey stick shape of increased effort that occurs right before a deadline).

- *Misinterpreting temporal punctuation.* We fail to consider how others might interpret punctuation. (In a negotiation, a pause by one party may be interpreted as a lack of interest by the other.)

Options and opportunities associated with punctuation include

- *Inserting a period.* We end something at exactly the right time. (An exit strategy is in place.)

- *Subtracting a period.* We speed the pace of change to better control a situation (eliminating commercials in between programming to keep viewers tuned in).

- *Postponing punctuation.* We manage stops and starts (holding a positive announcement until Monday morning so that people can ride the good news all week).
- *Rethinking the use of punctuation.* We reimagine the use of punctuation. (Counterintuitive starts, stops, and pauses can lead to creative solutions and innovative ideas.)

three

Interval and Duration

Among Chuang-tzu's many skills, he was an expert draftsman. The king asked him to draw a crab. Chuang-tzu replied that he needed five years, a country house, and twelve servants. Five years later the drawing was still not begun. "I need another five years," said Chuang-tzu. The king granted them. At the end of these ten years, Chuang-tzu took up his brush and, in an instant, with a single stroke, he drew a crab, the most perfect crab ever seen.

—Italo Calvino[1]

Despite the show of force, military officers conceded that they did not have full control of Dili (a city in East Timor) and that it would take far longer to enforce security in the rest of the territory.

"How long is a piece of string?" one colonel said when asked for a time estimate.

—Seth Mydans[2]

The king and the colonel, in the quotations above, face a common managerial problem: How long will it take to achieve a desired outcome? We see the same question arise is business.

How long will it take for a new service to gain market share, a revised policy to be successfully implemented, or, for that matter, the housing market to turn around? The usual answer is that it is hard to say. As the colonel put it, how long is a piece of sting? If we had asked Instagram founders Kevin Systrom and Mike Krieger in 2011 how long it would take for someone to offer them a billion dollars for their photo-sharing app, I'm sure they would have replied that they had no idea. (It took a year and a half.)

So, when should the king fire Chuang-tzu and hire someone else who could get the job done faster? That depends on the king's estimate of how long the job *should* take. And what about the colonel? Is he incompetent? That depends on how long it *should* take to enforce security. In another sense, deciding when to act depends on the length of an interval. If time is limited and a lengthy task can't be shortened (or, once begun, the remaining parts put off for another time), then it's foolish to begin. It would be like trying to force an SUV into a parking space barely big enough for a bicycle. In order to plan effectively, we need to be able to estimate know how long something will take and how long events or conditions in the environment will last—what will persist for a long time and what will be over quickly.

The ability to estimate the length of intervals is at the heart of the question of timing. Yet before we can estimate an interval of time, we need to recognize that an interval is present. We can't make a prediction about something we don't know exists. This becomes even more complex because the way we describe the world often omits intervals that matter. An article published in the *Wall Street Journal* about how and when to end an alliance exemplifies this point:

> Not clearly stating *when* an alliance should end can be lethal, even when partners have agreed on *how* the alliance should end. Partners' perspectives on the timing of dissolution can differ, leading to lengthy and expensive haggling [italics in original].

This is why the first step in devising a successful exit strategy is to have clear trigger provisions. *Triggers may consist of such contingencies as the inability of the alliance to meet certain milestones, performance metrics or service-level agreements; breaches of contact terms; or the insolvency or change in control of one of the partners* [italics mine]. When pharmaceutical and biotech companies team up to bring an experimental drug to market, the partners often use milestones as exit triggers, such as whether the drug reaches a particular stage of a clinical trial.[3]

Although the article focuses on *when* to end an alliance (punctuation), it nonetheless neglects to factor in other relevant *intervals* of time. As a result, the actual triggers for ending the alliance are left ambiguous. Here are the intervals that the description omits and that are frequently overlooked in discussions of milestones, performance metrics, or service-level agreements. Each can be critical.

- How should key milestones be defined: by the *time until* a specific event or condition or by the *time until* a specific date (five thousand miles or three months, whichever comes first)?
- How *long until* a milestone should be reconsidered or revised?
- Does it matter if one party to an agreement misses a milestone by a *small amount* of time? And what is a small amount? Two weeks may be critical for one company, but may not matter for another.
- *How long before* a deadline arrives does a company realize that it cannot meet it? When does a company discover that it cannot meet a deadline or that it will miss a milestone?
- *How long* will it take to catch up or repair the damage caused by being late? When can this interval be estimated with any degree of certainty?
- Once the answers to these questions are known, *how long will it be* before this information is communicated to all relevant

parties? Will everyone be told at the same time? If not, how will the gap between the first and last to be notified be managed?

* Do the answers to the previous six questions depend on *how long* the parties have known each other?

These intervals clearly matter. I don't think they were omitted because they weren't important. I think they were omitted because it's easy to leave them out. Recall the "key in the door" experiment I described in the Introduction. Our mind can jump gaps in time without noticing that it has done so. Another reason we tend to omit critical intervals from our thinking is our assumption that high speed is an advantage.

For example, researchers believed until recently that using CT scans sooner and more often to detect early-stage lung cancer would save many more lives. But that is not what studies showed. To understand why CT scans didn't improve survival rates, we have to look at the problem more closely. According to the *New York Times*, more cancers were found and treated as a result of CT scans, "but the death rate was the same ... [because] screening led to detection and treatment of cancers that did not need to be treated—they would not have grown enough in the person's lifetime to cause any harm. And many of the deadly cancers that were treated still ended up killing patients."[4] In this case, research found that the extra surgeries, prompted by additional screening, sometimes caused complications, such as blood clots or pneumonia, that were life threatening or fatal.

These results contradicted prior advice that suggested that "more than 80 percent of lung cancer deaths could be prevented with CT scans."[5] That analysis—in assuming that anyone with lung cancer would die of it without treatment—failed to take into account three intervals:

Interval 1: How long a patient would live despite the fact that he or she had cancer.

Interval 2: How long it would take the cancer to kill a patient if it were left untreated. Maybe the person would die of other causes before that happened (per Interval 1).

Interval 3: How long a patient with cancer would live if the cancer were treated. Some treatments are lethal.

The initial research, which justified additional CT scans, uses the traditional perspective on timing—earlier is better. This is a variation on the "first-mover advantage" theme discussed in Chapter One. As we've seen, that predisposition has significant limitations. If the benefits of a technology have to do with timing—in this case, the assumed benefit is early detection—then it is essential to know how timing enters into the problem your technology is trying to solve. In this example, that means taking into account the three intervals I just described.

THE CHARACTERISTICS OF INTERVALS

I have presented the six timing lenses in a particular order because the use of one lens facilitates the use of the next. The sequence lens directs your attention to steps and stages; the punctuation lens to beginnings, endings, pauses, specific dates on the calendar, and so on. All of these marks in time can help you find intervals that you might otherwise overlook. There are, of course, an infinite number of intervals in any given situation—and only you can decide which ones matter. However, let me offer some suggestions about what to look for, beginning with the following list of interval characteristics:

1. **Type**. What kind of interval is it? There are four kinds. Make sure you look for and find all four.
2. **Size—the Interval Envelope**. Look for very long and very short intervals. Understand the minimum and maximum length of each.

3. **Objective or subjective**. There may be a difference between the objective length of an interval and how it is experienced: a second can be an eternity.

4. **Contents**. Look inside. Is an interval transparent? Do you know what is going on during that time period? If not, what should you assume?

5. **Meaning**. An interval can mean different things to different people. What kinds of interpretations are possible?

6. **Number**. Look for multiple intervals. As the aforementioned illustrations (triggers for disengagement and CT scans) suggest, there are more than you think.

These six characteristics are organized in a particular order. First, we need to know what we are looking for, hence the discussion of type. Then we consider the size, how big or small. Is the size fixed, and if not, how big or small could it become? When you consider size, ask yourself what matters: how long an interval is or how long it *seems*—that is, consider the objective and subjective size of the interval. Next, look inside: What is going on during that time period (contents), keeping in mind that different stakeholders might interpret the contents of a interval differently (meaning)? Finally, always look for more than one interval (number).

Type

There are four types of intervals. Before you decide to act, make sure you have found at least one example of each. If you haven't, you are probably missing something important that will affect the timing of your actions.

1. *Time in between*. How much time will elapse between event A and event B? When the twin towers of the World Trade Center were hit on 9/11, for example, one of the questions the insurance company faced was whether to consider the attack one occurrence or two in terms of coverage. For the purposes

of designing an insurance policy, this highlights the importance of defining the parameters of coverage keeping "time in
between" intervals in mind.

2. *Time since.* How much time has elapsed since event A has
    occurred? A common question of international diplomacy, as
    well as modern warfare, is how long to wait before responding
    to an attack or provocation. If a village is shelled, leaving
    hundreds dead, can you wait a year to respond? The same issue
    comes up in business all the time. A competitor has introduced
    a new product. How much time can you let go by before you
    counter with a new product of your own?

3. *Time until.* A deadline is coming up. Is there enough time
    to complete the work? How much time before a new rule or
    government regulation goes into effect? What do you need to
    do before that happens?

4. *Duration* measures how long something continues. When
    will the recession be over? Should you sign an office lease
    that will commit you for three years or five years? How long
    will a bottle of milk last before it goes bad?

Different parties may view the same interval differently, which
is why it is important to be aware of these four types. For example,
are we out of danger because a number of years have passed since
9/11 (time since)? If we think that another attack is inevitable,
then the "time until" the next attack must be shrinking, as the
bombing at the Boston Marathon demonstrated, so our prepared-
ness must increase proportionately.

Size—the Interval Envelope

The Interval Envelope refers to the *minimum* and *maximum* length
of the *longest* and *shortest* intervals that are important for your
business. That sentence is a bit of a mouthful, so let's proceed step-
by-step. First, look for extremes: intervals so small or so large that
you might miss them. Then, think about how small or large these
intervals could become under different circumstances, and

then whether that expansion or contraction would cause problems.

Look for Extremes

Always look for the longest and shortest intervals that are present in the situation you need to manage. Short intervals are easy to miss. According to the *Wall Street Journal*, nine months before the massive March 2011 earthquake and tsunami cut off power to the Fukushima Daiichi nuclear plant, one of its reactors lost power after a subcontractor "inadvertently bumped into an auxiliary relay with his elbow. That led to a 'momentary' flutter that was *long enough* to trip a circuit breaker, shutting off the reactor's main power supply, but was *too short* to trigger the normal backup power supply"[6] (italics mine). The problem might have been serious except for quick-thinking control room personnel who activated a backup generator. There was no contingency in the system that accounted for this brief interval in time.

Some intervals must remain short; therefore, we need to ask about the *maximum length of the shortest interval.* The implications will depend on the situation. For example, Western Staff Services, a temporary help firm, says that holiday Santas need to work short shifts, four to five hours, because "it's impossible to stay joyful" for longer.[7] That obviously has implications for seasonal staffing in retail and entertainment venues.

In some situations, a very short time period can make an occasion more memorable. In his address to a graduating class at Penn State, the biologist Edward O. Wilson cited Salvador Dali as giving the shortest speech on record: "He said, 'I will be so brief I have already finished,' and he sat down."[8] A close second is Don DeLillo's speech upon winning the National Book Award in 1985. At the ceremony, DeLillo stood up and said, "'I'm sorry I couldn't be here tonight, but I thank you all for coming,' and abruptly sat down."[9] Of course, short can be too short. (What is the *minimum length of the shortest interval?*) As Leonardo da Vinci cautioned, "He who wishes to be rich in a day, will be hanged in a year."[10]

In some cases, the shortest interval can be extremely short. During the summer of 2011, for example, Congress was never in recess. In fact, one day, the Senate met for a total of fifty-nine seconds. The reason was that if Congress adjourned, which it can't do for more than three days without permission from the other chamber, President Obama could make recess appointments of nominees blocked by the Senate Republicans.[11] With Congress always in pro forma session, Obama was unable to act.

The companion question is, what is the *maximum length of the longest interval?* In a situation I read about in the *New York Times,* a gentleman believed he was making a wise business decision, but he was surprised when a relevant interval went on far longer than he had anticipated.

> André François Raffray thought he had a great deal 30 years ago: He would pay a 90-year old woman 2,500 francs (about $500) a month until she died, then move into her grand apartment . . .

> But this Christmas, Mr. Raffray died at age 77, having laid out the equivalent of more than $184,000 for an apartment he never got to live in.

> On the same day, Jeanne Calment, now listed in the Guinness Book of Records as the world's oldest person at 120, dined on foie gras, duck thighs, cheese, and chocolate cake at her nursing home near the sought after apartment in Arles.[12]

When I think about the *minimum length of the longest interval,* I think about the interrelated economic crises that have erupted across the globe in the last decade. Some crises come and go relatively quickly, but is that really a good thing? In some cases, I find myself hoping that a crisis will last long enough for a solution to be devised. In 1999, Jeffrey Garten, then dean of Yale School of Management, published an op-ed in the *New York Times* that made this point. He said that the global economic crisis of 1998, marked by the bailout of Long-Term Capital Management and the Russian credit default, caused millions of people in emerging markets to suffer terribly. Yet "the crisis wasn't long enough or deep enough to result in the kinds of corrective measures that would result in a less risky global economy. Indeed, [one year later] little of a fundamental nature has changed."[13]

What was true in 1999 is true today. If a long-term solution requires considerable time to be devised, negotiated, and then implemented, then we can only hope that the crisis lasts long enough for that to happen. The skiing and snowboarding industries rely on snowy winters. When will they be motivated to lobby for environmental reforms related to global warming? Only, I suspect, after three or four or more consecutive years of warm winters. An issue that comes and goes quickly can be ignored, particularly if it is costly to address. Hence, beware of magnitude-driven thinking: just because a problem is *serious* does not mean that it will be addressed. It won't be if the duration of the problem is shorter than the time needed to solve it.

As these examples suggest, look for the *maximum* and *minimum* size of the *longest* and *shortest* intervals that matter. I've arranged these combinations in a two-by-two table (Table 3.1). Think about each of the four cells (1–4). For example, look back at your day and consider something that seemed to occur at lightning speed. Then ask yourself how short or long that process could become under different conditions, and if it hit those extremes, would it pose a risk or an opportunity? Would it throw off your timing, or would it make no difference at all?

Table 3.1 The Interval Envelope

	Shortest Interval	Longest Interval
Minimum Length	1	2
Maximum Length	3	4

Size: Is It Fixed, or Can It Vary?

Some intervals come in fixed sizes—a year is 365 days. Others can be lengthened or shortened, expanded or compressed, depending on a host of factors.

Consider airline safety. It takes only two or three major crashes within the span of a year—the current evaluation interval—to provoke an outcry about airline safety. One could reduce the sense of crisis if one used a two-year evaluation interval rather than a one-year evaluation interval. But that is unlikely to happen, because we measure so many things on an annual basis.

Fixed intervals have known risk characteristics. A fund manager whose investments underperformed in the first half of the year, for instance, may buy riskier stocks during the second half because he must, on average, outperform the market annually. Birds face a fixed interval problem every night: how much energy to use in search of food. If they haven't gotten enough food by the end of the day, they will not survive the night, but if they expend too much energy searching, they will also die. As night approaches, birds have to make a life-and-death decision. Some birds take excessive risks and perish as a result.

What Determines Interval Size?

Every profession, organization, or institution has established norms regarding how long various activities should take. It is hard to break "habits" acquired over many years, whether they are good or bad. Legal systems and bureaucracies, for example, are notoriously slow. "Congress is an incremental institution," said Professor Julian Zelizer of Princeton University. "... That's its flaw and its virtue."[14] How long something takes is heavily influenced by tradition and culture.

Psychology is another factor that influences our expectations about interval size. If a time period is painful, we want to shorten it; if it is pleasurable, we want to extend it. Most individuals are reluctant to accept financial losses, so they take their time in doing so. The typical investor is slow to sell stocks that have lost value over time, hoping they will recover. But if a stock crashes, losing most of its value overnight, most of us want to sell immediately to avoid additional pain, thereby missing the possibility of a rebound.

When we become emotionally invested in a particular outcome, that can influence our sense of timing as well. For example, the *New York Times* cited a report that 63 percent of the doctors surveyed overestimated the amount of time their terminally ill patients would live by a factor of 5.3. In an article accompanying the original report, Dr. Julia L. Smith, medical director of a hospice in Rochester, wrote, "'Those of us who know our patients longer often become attached to them . . . We, too, hate to admit that death is near.'"[15]

Finally, if you need to guess whether an interval will shorten or lengthen, and have no other information to go on, look at how the interval begins and ends. If it starts with an important question, most of us want the answer as soon as possible. If we face a serious problem, we want it solved right away. If a crime is committed, we want the criminal caught and punished immediately, and so on. In Table 3.2, I've diagrammed the forces that cause us to act to shorten intervals.

In contrast, if an interval begins *and* ends with a problem, many of us want to delay the second problem until the first has

Table 3.2 The End Points of an Interval Attract

Problem	Solution
Question	Answer
Need	Satisfaction
Goal established	Goal attained
Crime	Punishment
Lost	Found
→>|	|<←

Time Between

been solved. Like a magnet, similar beginning and end points repel; different beginning and end points attract. No doubt there are exceptions, but this is a reasonable rule of thumb. I call it the *magnet rule of interval size.*

Objective or Subjective

Keep in mind that the length of any interval has both a subjective and an objective dimension. Sometimes time flies; sometimes it drags. It's not how long or short an interval is but how it is perceived under varying circumstances. A customer waiting in line to make an important purchase as opposed to one waiting to make a complaint will experience the same interval of time differently.

Contents

An interval can be filled with anything or nothing. Let's first consider the case of the empty interval—a time in your business, market, or industry when nothing significant seems to be going on.[16] It is important to look inside empty intervals because there is often more going on than you think, just as physicists have learned that vacuums are not really empty. Here are four reasons why an interval may appear to be empty when, in fact, it is not:

- *Early stage.* What is going on inside the interval may need time to develop. It may not be of sufficient size or strength to be detected or recognized, and when it is, it may be too late. Nokia may not have been worried when Steve Jobs first began moving from computing into mobile technology, but by the time the iPhone was released in 2009, the Finnish cellular company was too far behind the curve to easily catch up.
- *Masking.* One process or activity may mask or direct attention away from another. Firms often focus on their current customers, adding more and more sophisticated bells and whistles to existing products. When the economy is growing,

they prosper. What they do not notice is the rise of low-cost innovations developed in emerging markets that will threaten their business.

- *Inhibition.* Forces may be present that inhibit or block what is going on. A product may be extremely useful but fail to find a market because its potential customers are currently out of work and are fighting to make ends meet.
- *Missing component.* An interval may appear to be empty because its contents need a catalyst. Without those enabling conditions, nothing will happen. Mobile games require high-speed networks. No one wants to wait an hour to download a free app.

In some cases, of course, an interval may be as empty as it appears. Perhaps it is August, and everyone has "gone fishing." Some industries simply change much more slowly than others. Luggage, for example, remained almost exactly the same for decades—an interval of time when nothing was going on—until the 1970s, when Bernard Sadow invented rolling suitcases. At first, the innovation did not take off, but once it did, it was the popular choice until the sleeker design of the Travelpro Rollaboard supplanted it in the late 1980s.

What Shapes Fill an Interval?
In order to see what is going on inside an interval, we need to be aware of the shape of the processes that might be found there. We like to think in terms of straight lines and linear processes. (As Euclid told us, a straight line is the shortest distance between two points.) Straight lines are fast and predictable. But the problem, as Spanish architect Antoni Gaudí pointed out, is that there are no straight lines in nature; nature, Gaudí said, is a "symphony of forms."[17] Take the experience of waiting. Everyone knows that waiting is frustrating. But if you graph how quickly frustration builds, the result won't be a straight line. Most of us will wait quietly for a while and then, at some point, simply run out of

patience. Or think about buying a new car. As soon as you drive the car off the lot, its value drops dramatically. Economists tell us that the farther a reward is pushed into the future, the faster its value declines. Even the Swiss, masters of timing, failed to anticipate a nonlinear process. They greatly underestimated how quickly electronic watches would improve and how quickly prices would drop.[18]

Time is filled with all kinds of mathematical curves and shapes besides straight lines, bottlenecks, wheels, processes that speed up exponentially, and so on. We need to remember to look for unexpected shapes. We will examine this characteristic more closely in Chapter Five.

Meaning

How we *label* an interval can change its meaning, and hence its commercial value. The artist Christo, whose work includes wrapping the Reichstag in Berlin completely in fabric, found an interesting way to transform a means into an end. As the following passage illustrates, that shift in meaning allows Christo to better cope with the long and difficult task of gaining approval for his projects, which can take years.

> When Christo does one of his environmental installations, his "art" is not just the piece itself, but every transaction required to realize it... Christo's works are consented to by every possible affected group or authority. He secures these clearances with publicity, endless meetings, visualizations and all of his great personal charm. He even raises the money to realize the work and, vitally important, insure it against liability. Then there is the massive work of coordinating the construction: recruiting the volunteers, training them, feeding and housing them, and keeping all the workers in communication with each other. And there is the

documentation, recording the entire event—its prepara-
tions, its construction, and the experience of the work in
place.[19]

. Thus the lengthy steps before and after Christo's project
are not wasted; they are valuable in themselves. Relabeling an
interval is an underutilized strategy for solving problems and
allowing people to look at things differently. For example, if a
plane cannot take off due to bad weather, why not label the
delay a "safety hold"? It's still a delay, but passengers will be less
frustrated by the wait. In your own work, try to imagine how the
means to an end could become an end in itself. Could the process
used to create a product become a product in its own right?

Number

There is more than one interval involved in most complex situations. For example, investigators found that it took more than
an hour for the emergency alarm to sound on the ship after the
Costa Concordia hit rocks off the western coast of Italy in January
2012.[20] It is not clear why that delay occurred, but as a result,
there was not enough time between the emergency signal and the
order to abandon ship for people to react. The captain needed to
consider *two* intervals: how long to wait after the ship ran aground
to sound the emergency alarm, and then, how long after that to
give the order to abandon ship. In this particular case, those two
intervals were related: the longer the first, the shorter the second.
Obviously, the captain didn't think about this issue, or if he did,
he didn't act on that knowledge.

One reason it is important to find multiple intervals is that differences between or among them matter. The *New Yorker* magazine
referred to one of its customers, who was living in a nursing home
at the time, as "the late" reader. Still alive, "this person wrote
to the magazine demanding a correction. *The New Yorker*, in its
next issue, of course complied, inadvertently doubling the error,

because the reader died over the weekend while the magazine was being printed."[21] An interval difference: the reader's life span was shorter than the time needed to correct the error. Bad timing.

INTERVAL AND DURATION RISKS

As we have seen with the other timing elements, mistakes occur when we miss or misread them. The reasons we fail to see and understand intervals are subtle, and the list of risks I will present is far from exhaustive, but it addresses some of the barriers to finding and understanding intervals that I have seen over and over again.

Language

One reason we miss intervals is the efficiency of our language, which allows us to capture a series of actions in a single word or phrase. On February 14, 2007, for example, an ice storm hit the Northeast. Passengers spent hours stranded on a JetBlue flight in New York's JFK airport. It couldn't take off and couldn't go back to the gate (the gate was filled). David G. Neeleman, the company's CEO at the time, said he was "humiliated and mortified" by what had occurred.[22]

In order to prevent this type of occurrence, we can't simply think about canceling or not canceling *a flight* (a noun). We must think about sequences: a plane leaves the gate, taxis to the takeoff runway, then takes off—or not. Then we have to find the *intervals* within that sequence and understand the factors that influence the duration of each. The noun *flight* represents a very high level of abstraction. It does not reveal the more detailed sequence of intervals that a flight actually consists of, any one of which can cause trouble. We need the efficiency of nouns and verbs that stand for complex sequences of action—communication would be impossible without them—but what is lost is often exactly what we need to identify timing-related risks and manage them.

Question to ask: *Have I overlooked the time between steps and stages because of the shorthand language we use to describe events?*

Magnitude Thinking

If we ask someone the rate of turnover in a company, his or her answer will be a magnitude—the number of people entering and leaving within a given period of time. We have a concept, turnover, and we assign a number to it, a magnitude, and we think we are done. That number, however, will tell us nothing about *how long* those positions may be vacant, whether the company had *advance warning* that individuals would leave, and *how long* it will take to replace them. As we discussed with JetBlue's canceled flight, the concept of turnover doesn't *stop* us from asking these questions. But it doesn't call our attention to them either. The English language (and many others) makes it easy to summarize a complex process in a single word or magnitude. In fact, anytime someone talks about a *variable*, you know that there are hidden intervals involved. A variable, like turnover or the number of flights departing an airport per hour, will tell you *what* you need to take into account or measure. But if you want to know the risks associated with a variable, you need to look further. You need to find the intervals that make up the variable, and determine when they might become too long or too short.

Question to ask: *Has magnitude thinking (defining a situation based on a number that is variable) caused me to miss relevant intervals?*

Time Line Thinking

Whenever we find ourselves facing a problem, the natural next step is to search for a solution, which we hope will be found as quickly as possible. As indicated by Table 3.2, we can represent the interval between problem and solution as follows:

$$\rightarrow > |\textbf{Problem} \text{---} \textbf{Solution}| < \leftarrow$$

If the problem is a serious one, we fear that finding a solution may take a long time, which can create any number of difficulties.

Time to solution, however, is not the only interval we need to be concerned about. The way to start is to give problems and solutions their own time lines, which I illustrate here:

Problem ————————————————————————————→

Solution ————————————————————————————→

This form of visual representation accomplishes two things. First, it counteracts the unconscious gap-closing tendency that causes us to underestimate the time needed to find a solution. Second, and just as important, it reminds us that a solution can persist long after the problem that caused it is over, in which case, the *solution* may *become* the *problem*.

That is exactly what happened in the stock market in 1959. A speculative fever caused trading volume to mushroom. The market couldn't handle the spike in volume, and it took weeks for some trades to clear. Extra clerks and accountants were hired, but the system was again overwhelmed a few years later. The NYSE responded by adding computers and other automation. But by 1970, the cost of those improvements exceeded the volume needed to pay for them.[23] This example is over fifty years old, but the principle (solutions may become problems) is as valid now as it was then. Take airport security. Will our great-great-grandchildren, when they are adults, still have to take their shoes off before they board a plane? It's hard to say, but what I know with certainty is that some future problems will be the result of solutions that refused to die when their time was up.

There is another advantage to putting problems and solutions on separate lines: it allows us to think about their sequence. Logically, solutions should follow the problems they are designed to solve. But sometimes we need to begin a solution before we know that the problem exists, or risk being too late. Global warming is an example. If we could find a way to make a solution profitable in itself, perhaps we could get started before it is too late.

Question to ask: *Has my focus on "time to solution" caused me to miss other significant intervals?*

Cat-Point Thinking

We are used to thinking about performing a *category* of action at a single *point* in time. It is therefore easy to forget about the sequences of steps—and the intervals between them—that will be involved. There is a wonderful *Dilbert* cartoon that illustrates this point. Dilbert is buying a chair. After he selects one, the salesman compliments him on "an excellent choice," but tells him that his next task is to sit quietly and not ask "the one question that will kill this sale." Of course, Dilbert asks it: "Is the chair in stock?" The salesman replies that "we don't sell chairs. We sell the hope that a chair will someday be made for you." So Dilbert naturally asks, "How long will that take?" The salesman replies, "If I could answer that question, it would be the same as selling you an actual chair. How about if I tell you it will ship in two months, and you call and yell at me every three months for eternity?" Dilbert returns to his office, and in response to a question about whether he bought a chair, he replies, "There is no way to know."[24]

The point of the cartoon is profound. Actions and transactions we expect to be instantaneous, or nearly so, are in reality extended sequences filled with intervals of varying lengths. Rolled up inside the name of any activity is a set of sequences and intervals that you need to discover, like the dimensions of the world the quantum physicists tell us we don't see, if you really want to know how long something will take.

Question to ask: *Have I overlooked a series of intervals by treating a situation or action as a single event?*

THE ED2 + R SEQUENCE

There is one series of intervals that is sufficiently common that I have given it a name. I call it the *ED2 + R* sequence. In an ED2 + R sequence, a problem or issue *exists*, *E*. Some time later (interval 1) it is *detected* or *discovered*, D_1. Then, some time later (interval 2), the problem is *disclosed* and communicated to relevant stakeholders, D_2. Finally, after a long or short time (interval 3), efforts are made to *remedy* or *repair* the damage that it caused, *R*. These three intervals, the time from when a problem exists to when it is communicated to others and then finally resolved, can be critical. They are often a source of misunderstanding. "Do we agree," one party can say to the other, "that when either of us runs into a problem, we will tell the other within X days, even if we think the issue will be resolved quickly?" That kind of understanding can prevent problems down the line. By making the intervals of the ED2 + R sequence explicit, parties can be clear about what they need and expect from each other. A discussion of the ED2 + R intervals should be part of every contract negotiation.

Intervals That Are Too Long or Short

There are risks associated with intervals that are either too long or too short. One way to check for those risks is to fill in all four cells of the Interval Envelope—that is, try to estimate the *maximum* and *minimum* length of the *longest* and *shortest* intervals that are involved in the work you are doing, and identify the risks if those intervals were to occur. In the 2002 World Cup, for instance, the United States upset Portugal, 3–2. One reason Portugal's coach Antonio Oliveira gave for the defeat was that "with our players in European leagues, we only had two weeks to prepare."[25]

Be alert for *horizon errors*, which occur when you don't look far enough back into the past or far enough forward into the future. Scott McCleskey (head of compliance at Moody's from April 2006 to September 2008) noted that "once Moody's issues these ratings ['on thousands of municipal bonds'], it rarely reviews them again—leaving them fallow, sometimes *for decades*."[26] Aging financial infrastructure poses the same risk of horizon errors as aging physical infrastructure: after a while, it may not be safe.

Questions to ask: *Do the longest or shortest intervals in a series present risks? Have I considered what will happen if the shortest interval in a sequence is shorter than I anticipated, or the longest interval, longer?*

Elasticity

Is the size of an interval fixed, or can it be made longer or shorter as needed? Term limits, for example, which serve to standardize the length of an interval, help insure accountability. But they have significant risks as well—namely, the loss of expertise, which is particularly important when the issues to be decided are complicated and the consequences for mistakes long lasting. In a business situation, is a deadline a true deadline, or can it be adjusted, giving those working on a task a longer or shorter time to accomplish it?

Question to ask: *Have I considered whether an interval is fixed or elastic, and does the distinction matter?*

Norms

We often establish norms about how long an interval should last. When these norms are violated, people notice. In February 2000, for example, after just two years as president of Brown University, E. Gordon Gee surprised the Brown campus and the higher education community nationwide when he abruptly resigned to become chancellor of Vanderbilt University. "Two years is just too short, and I admit that up front," Gee said, "this is a fast-forward world we're in right now, in which there's a lot of change."[27]

When you violate a norm associated with an interval, be prepared to explain yourself or have your actions questioned. I suspect that if Gee also chose to leave his Vanderbilt job in just a year or two (he did not; he stayed until 2007), he would have difficulty repairing his reputation no matter what explanation he provided.

Question to ask: *What will happen if the length of an interval is longer or shorter than expected?*

Missing the Location of an Interval

When an interval occurs can be just as important as how long it is. For example, Tony Gwynn of the San Diego Padres made the following comments in 1999: "What if it is the last year of your contract and you feel you're not playing well? With the kind of money out there, could Creatine or Andro or steroids make a difference in your play? And if you only take them one year to prolong your career, would it really be dangerous to your health?"[28] If we know *when* a risk is present, we are more able to avoid or mitigate it. Were baseball to focus its enforcement on the times when players are most likely to use banned substances, those efforts might be more effective. *When* players begin, resume, or permanently discontinue drug use is probably not random.

Question to ask: *Have I considered where an interval occurs within the larger sequence of events?*

Content Risks

You can make an error because there is more (or less) going on during an interval than you realize. Some intervals are truly empty: nothing is going on, as was the case in the luggage industry before Sadow. But sometimes there is a lot happening, such as when banks systematically lower their debt levels right before quarterly reports, and then undo those actions at the start of the next quarter, which has led the SEC to consider new rules to deter banks from "dressing up their books."[29] It is also possible for the contents of one interval to mask the contents of another, such as when important nonpolitical news doesn't get reported during a hotly contested presidential election.

Questions to ask: *What, if anything, is truly happening within a given interval? Is it exactly what it seems or something else altogether?*

Misinterpreting Intervals

It is common to misread how others will interpret an interval. Back in 1993, for example, a federal judge awarded $11.5 million (at the time a record) to a former General Electric employee who exposed defense contract fraud at the company. GE said that the whistleblower, Chester Walsh, delayed reporting the fraud so that he could collect the large sum. Walsh countered that "he needed that much time [more than four years] to build his case against his employer."[30] After you locate an interval that is critical for the success of your work, ask yourself how others might interpret it and whether there is a risk that they could interpret it in the wrong way. According to a study by the National Marriage Project in 2001, women tend to view living together as a step toward marriage, whereas men reportedly view it as trying out a relationship.[31]

Questions to ask: *Am I interpreting the contents and meaning of an interval correctly? Might others interpret the same interval of time differently?*

INTERVAL AND DURATION OPTIONS AND OPPORTUNITIES

Paying attention to intervals—their size, sequence, and location—can enable you to design a more effective course of action. For example, NASCAR used a sequence of intervals to solve a difficult timing problem. Suspecting that various teams were modifying racecars in ways that were prohibited, NASCAR officials wanted to cut down on the cheating and faced a question of timing: When should they issue a warning? On the one hand, if the warning were issued too early, it wouldn't be taken seriously. *Why now?* someone would ask. Perhaps the threat that it warns against won't materialize. On the other hand, a warning that is issued too late is, well, too late. As conventionally understood, this is a cat-point problem. At what point in time should a warning (a category of action) be issued? But that is not how NASCAR approached the problem. Its solution was to use a *sequence of intervals.*[32]

1. NASCAR issued a warning during the *previous season* that "penalties would escalate if infractions continued."
2. *Three weeks* before teams arrived at Daytona for Speedweeks, teams were warned again.
3. The *Sunday before* the Daytona 500, scheduled for February 18, 2007, "NASCAR suspended five crew chiefs and a team vice president, and assessed fines and subtracted valuable race points from five drivers and teams before Sunday's season-opening Daytona 500."
4. The penalties were timed so that they began at the *start of the new season*, thus completing the cycle.

There were two warnings before violators were punished, and the intervals between them were of decreasing size. Warnings were issued about a year, a month, and a week in advance. Penalties were timed to coincide with the *start* of the new *season*, thereby using a punctuation mark. Thus NASCAR's solution did not rely on a single warning, because deciding how early to warn drivers and to have that warning be effective was an impossible problem to solve. It would be attempting to solve a timing problem by reference to a single magnitude—that is, using an interval of a given size. Instead, NASCAR moved from a *point* solution, selecting one point in time, to a *path* solution, one that involved a sequence of intervals.

Finding intervals leads to better solutions. For example, research shows that cancer patients don't like waiting at the hospital for blood test results in order to know whether they are strong enough to receive chemotherapy. The conventional solution would be to reduce waiting time. Can the results of the test be obtained more quickly? If not, can patients be distracted by TV or engaged in other activities?

The Cancer Center at Sloan-Kettering in New York asked the design firm IDEO to investigate. The result was to offer some patients the blood tests the day before they were scheduled for chemotherapy. The Center found that many patients actually preferred making two trips rather than having testing done at the last minute.[33] The key was where in the sequence of events (testing–results–chemo) the important waiting interval was *located*, rather than its size. Size suggests a magnitude solution: when an interval is too long, shorten it. But in this case, the better solution was to *relocate* the critical interval (the wait from test to result) to the previous day. If the results were favorable, patients wouldn't have to wait for chemotherapy when they arrived the next day. Notice that this redesign works because of what does *not* happen over time. If the patient's test results varied minute by minute, the two-trip solution would not work.

Think about what makes the NASCAR and cancer examples similar despite their obvious differences. In both cases, the solutions involved seeing a sequence of intervals, stretching over months rather than weeks for NASCAR, and days not just minutes for the Cancer Center. That is why it is important to search for intervals: they can suggest new and better solutions when conventional ones prove inadequate.

THE TEMPORAL IMAGINATION

The comedian Jonathan Winters recalls a conversation he had with a fellow tourist when he was visiting the Temple of Athena in Greece.

> "A woman asked what I thought of it," [Winters] related, "and I said that I was terribly disappointed."
>
> "Why?"
>
> "Everything is broken."
>
> "But it goes back five centuries before Christ."
>
> "Well, it should have been fixed by now."[34]

Winters reminds us to think about what we should expect with the passage of time. We expect parts to wear out, what is broken to be fixed, memories to fade, a jazzy new phrase to become a cliché, and leaders to retire or be ousted. When a process that should take a long time doesn't, we know something is wrong, as when a widow remarries the day after she buries her husband. She hasn't allowed enough time, a long enough "decent" interval, to separate these two events.

Sometimes the fact that nothing changes with the passage of time, a true empty interval, should raise a warning flag. As we know, there were not enough lifeboats on the *Titanic* when it sank. But the ship was in full compliance with all marine laws. The difficulty was that the British Board of Trade "hadn't updated its regulations for nearly 20 years," and "it had been 40 years since the last serious loss of life at sea."[35] Regulations were simply out-of-date. I suggest we time-stamp all policies, rules, and regulations related to safety, or any other critical matter, with dates of origin and expiration so that we know when they need to be revisited, revised, or revoked.

INTERVAL AND DURATION: IN BRIEF

Characteristics of intervals:

Type. There are four kinds of intervals (time in between, time since, time until, and duration). Make sure you look for them all.

Size—the Interval Envelope. Look for the longest and shortest intervals and understand the minimum and maximum length of each. Know the complications that may occur if a long or short interval becomes even longer or shorter.

Objective or subjective. Timing depends on two clocks, the external clock on the wall or on your device and the one inside your head. These two clocks may not register the same elapsed time. Everyone tells time by more than one clock.

Contents. Look inside an interval to determine what is going on during a given time period.

Meaning. An interval can mean different things to different people.

Number. Look for multiple intervals. There are always more than you think.

Risks associated with missing or misinterpreting intervals include

- *Language risk.* We miss intervals because our language allows us to capture a series of actions in a single word or phrase; that efficiency fails to reveal the sequences that are associated with those actions. (The word *flight* stands for an entire sequence of intervals that need to be managed.)

- *Magnitude thinking.* Answering a question with a single number, ratio, or percentage often hides relevant intervals. (What is the rate of employee turnover? Twelve percent. That number tells us little about how long a specific position will remain unfilled, whether the company had advance warning that those occupying it would leave, and how long it will take to replace them. Single numbers, percentages, or even variables ignore the intervals that are the constituent temporal parts of the concept being measured. We need to remember to look for them.)

- *Cat-point thinking.* When we associate an event or action with a single point in time, it is easy to forget about the sequences of steps—and the intervals between them—that will be involved. (A holiday, such as Christmas, occurs on the same day every year, yet dozens of intervals, from shopping and decorating to travel, occur before and after December 25.)

- *Intervals that are too long or short.* Misinterpreting the length of an interval can have timing consequences. (Underestimating the duration of a business cycle will affect budgets and projections.)

- *Inelasticity.* It is important to know whether the size of an interval is fixed or variable. (A year is always 365 days. A recession can last a few quarters or much longer.)

- *Norms.* We establish norms about how long an interval should last. When these norms are violated, there can be repercussions. (When we accept a job, for example, we are usually expected to remain in the position for a reasonable period of time or risk our reputation.)

- *Location risk.* When an interval occurs can be just as important as how long it lasts. (Athletes may be more inclined to take performance-enhancing drugs in the year just before they retire than at an earlier time.)

- *Content risks.* You can make an error because there is more (or less) going on during an interval than you realize. (An institution may lower its debt level in advance of quarter-end reports, and reverse the action at the start of the next quarter.) It is also common to misread how others will interpret the content of an interval. (Investors may interpret the announcement of a merger with concern or suspicion.)

- *Conflicting interests.* You may treat the same interval differently than someone else. (One stakeholder wants every potential problem disclosed immediately; the other wants to wait until it can be determined whether the problem is material.)

Finding intervals also offers options and opportunities:

- Paying attention to the size, sequence, and location of intervals can create opportunities to design a more effective course of action. Recall how NASCAR used intervals to solve the problem of teams modifying racecars in ways that were prohibited.

- Abbreviating or lengthening an established interval can improve a system or process. Perhaps combining two intervals will change a customer's perception of an event or lead to an innovation. Sloan-Kettering in New York moved an interval up sooner (a blood test) in order to improve patients' experience.

four

Rate

I know that most of what's out there in the world is occurring too quickly or too slowly for me to see.

—*Roni Horn*[1]

Fast! Last night I cut the light off in my bedroom, hit the switch, was in the bed before the room was dark.

—*Muhammad Ali*[2]

Good timing depends on understanding how the environment is changing. A new technology has emerged. Does it represent a threat to your core business? One company may respond to change by taking its time, adopting a wait-and-see attitude. Its environment has always been stable, and executives may be right in assuming that any change will be slow and incremental. In another company, the winds of change can blow at hurricane force for years at a time, and it seems as if executives need to be supermen or superwomen to keep up. This chapter will examine different rates of change and help you use their different characteristics (direction, transparency, and so on) to make better decisions about timing.

Despite the fact that change is all around us, the actual *pace* of change is easy to miss or disregard. In 1995, for example, AIDS researchers made a significant discovery that revealed they had misunderstood the rate at which the virus interacted with a victim's immune system. Prior to 1995, the spread of the HIV infection was thought to be a gradual process. In fact, research revealed that the virus and the immune system were engaged in a pitched battle from the very start of the infection. This finding had major implications for the design of drug therapies and for how the disease is treated. So why did researchers overlook this crucial fact for so long?

Dr. Simon Wain-Hobson, who directed the molecular retro virology laboratory at the Institut Pasteur in Paris, said that his first reaction was, "Why didn't I think of this—it's so obvious." He went on to say that the AIDS research field might have missed the forest for the trees in regard to rate: "we have technology that is so powerful, that is churning out so much data, so much information, that people don't take time to think," Wain-Hobson said.[3]

We all have this problem: too much information and too little time to think. But the difficulty isn't just a lack of time; it is that we make the wrong assumptions. We assume, for example, that a slow rate of change is caused by another slow rate of change. Like creates like. We've learned this equation from our experience with the physical world. Swing a bat slowly, and the ball won't go very far. Swing it faster, and the ball will fly off the bat at greater speed and land much farther away. What we forget is that a given rate of speed can be the result of multiple processes, some of which can cancel each other out, like stepping on the brake and the accelerator at the same time. As AIDS researchers discovered, we need to remember that a given rate can have many causes. We like things simple: single rate, single cause. But the world is complex.

Another reason we fail to see multiple rates is that we fixate on a single rate at the expense of others. For example, Robert J. Gordon, a Northwestern University economist, discovered in the

mid-1990s that "there has been *no* productivity growth acceleration in the 99 percent of the economy located outside the sector
which manufactures computer hardware."[4] High tech was moving
so quickly that economists missed or failed to note the lapse in
progress elsewhere. We all were distracted.

Sometimes we fail to notice a rate of change because we
simply assume that it doesn't exist. A good example involves
our understanding of fat cells. Prior to 2008, scientists believed
that individuals were predisposed, early in their lives, to develop
a certain number of fat cells, and they lived with them. The
hypothesis was that fat cells change in size but otherwise remain
as part of our makeup. Then, in May 2008, the *New York Times*
reported on Swedish researchers who discovered that "every year,
whether you are fat or thin, whether you lose weight or gain, 10
percent of your fat cells die. And every year, those cells that die
are replaced with new fat cells."[5]

The finding has major implications for weight loss. Reducing
the rate of replacement may open up a new avenue for controlling
obesity. One reason the constant turnover of fat cells wasn't
discovered sooner was that scientists had no way to measure the
life and death of fat cells. But that wasn't the only obstacle. As
science and health reporter Gina Kolata pointed out, "few even
thought to ask that question."[6]

The question you need to ask in your own work is, *What rates
of change are you not paying attention to?*

CHARACTERISTICS OF RATES

The most obvious characteristic of a rate of change is magnitude:
how fast or slow something is happening. But that is only the
starting point. There are a number of other characteristics you
need to take into account.

1. **The normal rate.** What's the normal or expected rate of change
    for a process?

2. **Size—the Rate Envelope**. What is the fastest and slowest rate of speed or change that you might encounter, and how fast or slow could that rate become?

3. **Duration**. How long will a given rate or frequency continue unchanged?

4. **Direction**. Does direction matter? If a rate changes, will it speed up or slow down?

5. **Objective or subjective**. Is there a difference between the real rate of change and the perceived rate of change?

6. **Meaning**. What does a given rate mean? How do different stakeholders interpret it?

7. **Number**. How many different rates of speed or change will you run into or have to manage?

Let's consider each of these characteristics in detail.

The Normal Rate

Different systems operate at different speeds. Although these speeds may change over time, it is important to know what the normal rate—or *N-rate*—is for a given system. The futurist and scientist Ray Kurzweil argues that progress in information technology occurs at an exponential rate—therefore, it is always accelerating. Its normal rate of change is very fast, whereas the normal or default speed of other systems can be very slow. As a general rule, technology changes more rapidly than political, legal, or cultural systems, which have different goals and requirements.

The N-rate is always contextual. When Robert Ludlum wrote the novel *The Cry of the Halidon* in 1975, he published it under the name Jonathan Ryder. When the book was republished in 1996, he used his real name. The reason, according to Ludlum, was that in 1974, an author who wrote more than one book a year would be considered a hack.[7]

There are at least two reasons why you should pay attention to the N-rate. First, systems with different N-rates can clash when they encounter one another, like two gears running at different speeds. (A familiar organizational solution is to create skunkworks to protect fast-moving innovators from the bureaucracy that would slow them down.) Second, systems running faster or slower than normal will return to their normal speed over time. Markets, for example, will seek equilibrium. Or, as statisticians say, there will be regression to the mean. So if something is running slower or faster than average, don't expect it to continue. In this case, the timing question to ask is, *When* will it return to its normal speed, and does the timing matter?

Size—the Rate Envelope

Pay attention to extreme rates of change. They can have dramatically different consequences depending on the extreme. Fire and rust, for example, are both results of oxidation; the difference is the speed with which the chemical reaction takes place. Fire is the rapid oxidation of materials. Rust results when oxidation occurs slowly. Likewise, financial markets exemplify why extreme rates of change matter: on any given day, the pace of trading can be frenetic, but markets can also freeze and stop functioning for a period of time. Both extremes have a notable impact on trading.

To find extreme rates, look for the fastest and slowest process that is important for the work you are doing. Those processes could be inside or outside your organization. Next, look for the maximum and minimum speed of each process. The result is what I call a *Rate Envelope*, defined by four combinations, or cells, as shown in Table 4.1.

Table 4.1 The Rate Envelope

	Slowest Process	Fastest Process
Minimum Speed	1	2
Maximum Speed	3	4

Let's look at each of the four cells (1–4) in some detail to see why they are significant. I'll begin with the slowest process.

The Minimum Speed of the Slowest Process

Slow can be too slow. A project risks being cancelled if it fails to show at least minimal progress over time. The slowest rate, of course, is zero. It is important to flag anything that has a zero rate of change because what cannot change, bend, or flex can simply break. And that can happen quickly. For example, if a business has high fixed but low marginal costs, once the high fixed costs are met, every sale goes directly to the bottom line. But in a declining market, companies with high fixed costs can rapidly fall to their death, which is what happened during the Internet boom and bust of 2000–2001.[8]

The Maximum Speed of the Slowest Process

An important question is how much you can speed up a process that is inherently slow. For example, after a Hollywood film is shot, there is a long period of postproduction that must be accomplished in as short a time as possible because many films need to be ready either for the summer season or for a Christmas release. But film editing, like many processes, has a maximum speed. Because film production is a job where different teams manage specific tasks—adding visual effects, correcting the color, attaching the sound track, removing dust and scratches—changes made by one team must be accommodated by the others.[9] That accommodation takes time. Even the latest technology gets you only so far where human effort and expertise are required. A recurring theme in this chapter is that we are slower than the technology we invent, which is one reason we invent it.

To identify processes in which the maximum speed of the slowest process is *too* slow, look for situations that are difficult to change or reverse, or processes that depend on precedent and continuity. Stamping out steroids in baseball takes a long time because of the confidentiality of doctor-patient relationships, "the sanctity of the clubhouse culture and union concerns about privacy rights."[10] Anything involving legal issues is likely to be slow. More than three hundred years ago, Shakespeare wrote about "the law's delay." Certain things have not changed since Shakespeare's time.

The Minimum Speed of the Fastest Process

Some processes need a minimum rate of speed to succeed. Discount stores like T.J.Maxx depend on frequent repeat visits. If there is not a constant stream of new items to be browsed, shoppers will not return. I think of this as stall speed: fly slowly enough, and you will crash. The same is true for an economy. If it does not grow, it can fall into a recession.

The Maximum Speed of the Fastest Process

As a general rule, expect to find extremely high rates of speed or change in processes that depend primarily on symbols, such as letters or equations, or words that stand for real objects. For example, we can add the word *tree* to a sentence on a page, orders of magnitude faster than it takes to grow a real one. And when symbols refer only to other symbols, the speeds can be dazzling. Think about computers that use high-speed algorithms to execute thousands of trades per second on Wall Street. The maximum speed of the fastest process (symbols referring to other symbols) is very, very fast.

The speed and complexity of symbol systems came into play during the financial crisis that swept the globe in 2008. In fact, it recalls the time one hundred years ago when Wassily Kandinsky painted the first completely abstract painting. In an abstract painting, the shapes on the canvas do not depict anything in the real world. The artwork creates its own reality: it is a closed self-referential system. The same is true of complex financial instruments. Like abstract art, the structures financial engineers build often have no *direct* connection to what we call the "real world" or the "real economy," which led the novelist Thomas Wolfe to describe stocks and bonds as "evaporated property." "People completely lose touch [with] the underlying assets. It's all paper—these esoteric devices."[11]

Abstract artists needed only canvas, brush, and paint to separate symbol from reality; the modern financial system needed the birth of computers and the Internet. To paraphrase Carl von Clausewitz, I think that the modern financial system can be viewed as the continuation of abstract painting by other means. Both speak to a deeply human need, the need to use, play, and create with symbols. In fact, I think that one could say—a bit tongue in cheek—that one of Jackson Pollock's paintings (*Autumn Rhythm*, for example) is as good a picture of the modern financial system as you are likely to find. Complex derivatives are the natural result of financial "artists" at work.

The writer Italo Calvino describes what happens in a world in which symbols refer only to other symbols. One of his characters comments,

I have built my financial empire on the very principle of kaleidoscopes and catoptric[12] instruments, multiplying, as if in a play of mirrors, companies without capital, enlarging credit, making disastrous deficits vanish in the dead corners of illusory perspectives. My secret, the secret of my uninterrupted financial victories in a period that has witnessed so many crises and market crashes and bankruptcies, has always been this: that I never thought directly of money, business, profits, but only of the angles of refraction established among shining surfaces variously inclined.[13]

The difference in speed between how quickly we can change a sign or symbol and change the material reality to which it refers is one of the most important rate differences of the modern world. The result is that we have systems that run at hyper-speed and create a level of complexity that we—even those who seek to regulate such systems—cannot easily grasp.

■ ■ ■

Use the Rate Envelope as a way to assess what you know and don't know about a given situation. If you have little information about a particular cell—perhaps you don't know the maximum speed of the fastest process—then there are risks associated with your plans and projects that you haven't discovered.

Duration

It is important to know how long a given rate may last, as an amusing story about an old poacher and a local game warden illustrates.

The game warden, it seemed, was on to the poacher, who he heard was sneaking out into the woods before dawn to hunt deer illegally. Feeling exasperated that he was unable to catch the poacher red-handed, the warden organized a 2 AM stakeout in the bushes behind the fellow's cabin. He waited in the cold and darkness for signs of life, planning to follow the poacher out and confront him. Sure enough, at about 4 AM, the lights went on in the cabin, and the warden saw some activity. He was feeling optimistic.

Then the old poacher stepped out onto his back porch and called out into the darkness: "Mr. Warden," he said, "no sense of you layin' out there gettin' all cold and damp in them bushes. Come on in here and get yourself a nice cup of coffee."

The warden, seeing that his cover was blown, got up and went into the cabin to warm up. But he went back for another try a few weeks later. Again, he snuck into the bushes behind the poacher's cabin at 2 AM in the freezing cold. Finally, a light went on in the cabin. Again, there were signs of activity. The poacher came out on his porch.

"Hey, Mr. Warden," he yelled. "Don't go catching cold out there in them bushes. You come in here, have some coffee and get warm." So the warden, very embarrassed, went in and had a cup of coffee with the old poacher.

This went on for some time, and the warden was unable to catch the poacher. Some time later, he heard that the poacher was in the hospital, in grave condition following a coronary. So the warden went to visit him. "You've got to tell me something," he said to the poacher. "When I was hiding in the bushes waiting for you, how did you know I was there?" The old poacher turned his head and smiled.

"I didn't know you was there, son. Every mornin' for thirty years I went out on my porch and yelled the same damn thing."[14]

The lesson is that one way to solve the challenges associated with duration is to act continuously. Then you will never be too early or too late. Of course, acting continuously can be expensive and exhausting. Therefore, when you decide on the speed of your own actions, ask yourself what is sustainable. The poacher in the story found a rate that he could sustain over a long period of time, which enabled him to be successful.

Direction—the Way Things Are Headed

Speed refers to how fast something is happening; velocity adds the idea of direction. We often think that effective action depends on knowing which way things are headed, in effect knowing the velocity. And in many situations, the direction is clear. Most secrets will eventually come to light. Over time, fragmented industries will consolidate. Bubbles will eventually burst, and so on. But sometimes the direction of a change doesn't matter: all that matters is speed. This is particularly true when it comes to fashion. It matters less whether ties become wider or thinner, or hemlines move higher or lower, as long as there is something *new* to capture the customer's attention. In the 1980s, for example, Honda flooded the market with so many new models within an eighteen-month period that motorcycle design became a matter of fashion. Its rival Yamaha couldn't respond.[15] It's an interesting strategy to remember. In fact, extremely high rates of change are part of the reason some industries continue to prosper.

Objective or Subjective: Know the Difference

There is a world of difference between how quickly something happens and how quickly it *seems* to happen. The year will always have 365 days, for example, but with age it appears to speed by. I use the labels *O-rate* (objective rate) and *S-rate* (subjective rate) to remember to take this difference into account. Customer complaints are likely to be driven by the latter rather than the former. Yet, in the case of Apple, the difference between objective and subjective rate prompted an innovation. The company found that when users could watch a progress bar, they felt that the computer completed the task more quickly.[16] Similarly, during rush hour, highway signs sometimes display the time needed to reach a particular destination: 18 minutes until Route 280. Somehow, this is reassuring. Absent that estimate, frustration builds based on the subjective sense that we could be delayed indefinitely.

Meaning

How will various stakeholders *interpret* a given rate? Public relations firms advise companies to disclose bad news quickly. If they don't, people may think it means that they are hiding something even more awful. In the spring of 2008, Bear Stearns needed to unwind or sell certain positions. But if it acted too quickly, confidence in the bank would plummet. Individuals would worry that the bank didn't have adequate reserves, thus precipitating the very crisis that the fast action was intended to prevent. This situation comes up often enough that I have given it a name: a *rate-reducing dilemma* (RRD). Quick action is required, but doesn't occur because of the way speed will be interpreted. Because RRDs are almost always present in times of crisis, every risk assessment should take them into account.

Number

In any complex situation, there will always be several rates of speed in play at the same time, and the differences among them can create problems. Therefore, it is important to look for multiple rates and understand how they interact.

Think back to World War I, where the conflict was caused, in part, by the failure of diplomacy. Diplomats at the time could not cope with the volume and speed of electronic communication. Most of the gentleman who made up the diplomatic corps in 1914 "were of the old school... They still counted on the ultimate effectiveness of 'spoken words of a decent man' in face-to-face encounters."[17] Yet the Austrian ultimatum set a time limit that was unimaginable before the age of the telegraph and telephone, and required a fast response that was out of the question in the time given.[18] It was a matter of multiple rates at odds with each other.

What was true one hundred years ago is equally true today. The speed of modern communications often requires that we respond more quickly than we can think. The demise of stand-alone Internet banking in the early days of the dot-com boom provides an example. According to the *Economist*, until early spring 2000 "no self-respecting financial consultant would travel without [a] bar chart showing that the marginal cost of Internet banking transactions was a tiny fraction of the cost of branch banking."[19] The argument was that Internet banks would need fewer employees and incur only a fraction of the expense compared to bricks-and-mortar competitors. Internet banks should win hands down. But we know what happened. They failed. The reason was a difference between two rates: how quickly customers would agree to trust the Internet with sensitive financial information, and how quickly costs at Internet banks would increase. The former would take a long time. The Web was and is a dangerous place, subject to viruses, system outages, and hackers. But if building trust was a slow process, other processes were not. To gain market share, Internet banks had to advertise heavily and offer customers rates that could not be sustained. As a result, costs grew much faster than businesses.

The presence of multiple rates is a problem that bar graphs often fail to capture because they, like pie charts, are static. However long we stare at one, its parts do not move. Pie charts are like fast food: we consume them in one visual gulp. In a world in which speed and time matter, they may have little nutritional value.

Even beyond communications and technology, rate differences are common. One example involves aluminum baseball bats. Aluminum bats have many advantages: they are cheaper than wooden ones; they don't break; they allow batters to hit the ball farther; and when a batter misses the sweet spot, an aluminum bat doesn't hurt his hands as much as the old wooden one does. So the case for aluminum seems clear: more interesting games, more home runs—which fans like—and lower costs. And making the switch from wood to aluminum would not upset the competitive balance of the game. All teams would benefit equally.

So what's the problem? Perhaps you know the answer. The ball would rocket off the hitter's bat so quickly that the pitcher would not be able to catch it or move out of the way in time (the speed of the ball would exceed his reaction time). The result would be injuries, which is an especially troublesome problem for young players for whom the game is still supposed to be a game.

To anticipate these kinds of risks, you need to consider which rate differences will be present *when your product is actually used.*

RATE-RELATED RISKS

Failing to notice rates of change may lead to a variety of timing errors. Because what is printed on a page is static, we need to remind ourselves of movement. Cartoonists achieve this with a few strokes of the pen. As the next sections indicate, there are many reasons why we miss rate-related risks.

Normal Rates

Failing to take into account the normal speeds (N-rates) of "systems" (political, cultural, economic, financial, legal, and so on) can lead to any number of problems. For example, investors expect to receive performance reports for mutual funds at the end of each quarter. But these reports can't be emailed or shipped until they are approved by the firm's compliance office. The N-rate for compliance approvals is slow. Firms need to take that fact into account in order to meet industry deadliness.

In some cases, an industry or enterprise has multiple N-rates. In the oil sector, OPEC tends to be quick to cut output in order to shore up prices, and slow to ramp up production to prevent shortfalls.[20] Anyone interested in the price of oil needs to know about this asymmetry.

Question to ask: *Do I know the normal rate or rates of a particular system?*

Direction

Look for instances when a rate is increasing when it *should* be decreasing, or vice versa. We normally think that increasing demand will cause companies to hire, but that is not always the case. If productivity is increasing faster than the overall economy (a rate difference), it means that when there is an increase in demand, companies can meet it while still laying off workers.[21]

Question to ask: *Is the speed (or rate of change or progress) of a system moving in the direction I expect?*

Size—the Rate Envelope

The rate of change in your environment may be faster or slower than you can cope with. For example, the maximum speed of the slowest process can be too slow. (Recall the example describing the causes of World War I: the diplomatic response was too slow.) Conversely, the speed of the fastest process can be faster than we anticipate. When there is an advantage to being early, expect those who could benefit from speed to jump the gun. For example, anticipating an agreement in March 2000 that would increase oil production, "many OPEC members cheated and began to increase production early,"[22] which drove down oil prices faster than anticipated.

Questions to ask: *Looking at the cells of the Rate Envelope, do one or more cells have a value that will be problematic for a system or process that is important to me? Do I lack information about any of the cells?*

Duration

When a rate of progress is too slow, there are consequences. For example, when a company turnaround takes too long, managers find their jobs at risk; when an economy falls into a recession that does not end quickly, politicians pay the price during the next election.

Questions to ask: *How long will a given rate (of change, progress, and so on) continue? When will it change?*

Objective and Subjective Rates

Different stakeholders can judge the same rate differently. On the basis of their own subjective perspective, they may perceive a rate to be faster or slower than it is. As a result, they may act in ways you did not anticipate. What a company assumes is a rapid response to a complaint may seem like an eternity to the customer involved.

Questions to ask: *How will various stakeholders perceive this rate? Who will be satisfied and who will be disappointed, and why?*

Meaning

It is possible to misread the meaning of a rate. For example, you might decide that your proposal or bid was not seriously considered because it was promptly rejected. In fact, the other party acted quickly because it received and rejected a similar offer from another partner.

Questions to ask: *What does speed in a particular situation really mean? Am I misinterpreting it?*

Number

As we've seen throughout the chapter, coping with differing rates (of change, development, progress, and so on) can prove to be a challenge. In the war in Iraq, for example, the United States found that a police force could not be trained and mobilized quickly enough to deal with the power vacuum that the swift military defeat of Saddam Hussein created.

Questions to ask: *Are many things going on at the same time with different speeds? Which processes are moving faster or slower than others, and will the differences among them matter?*

RATE OPTIONS AND OPPORTUNITIES

The rate lens, like all the lenses described in this book, can be used every day to identify timing-related risks and opportunities in your environment.

Questioning

The rate lens can help you ask the right questions. For example, when inflation picks up, will it happen gradually, or will it speed up so quickly that it is as if someone pressed the price accelerator to the floor? Similarly, you can use the rate lens to help you plan your own activities. For example, how quickly should you proceed in launching a new product or adopting a technology? In industries where innovation matters most, of course, rapid speed to market is paramount. More and more, companies need to test new ideas with customers early and then iterate quickly, as opposed to keeping plans under wraps until a product or service is fully formed. But moving slowly can also be an opportunity. In some industries, such as luxury hotels and spas, one-to-one, personalized attention is worth more than rapid response. It is also possible to design a product that will enhance what is essentially a slow activity. Austrian glassware maker Claus J. Riedel was among the first to recognize that the bouquet, taste, balance, and finish of wines are affected by the shape of the glass from which they are drunk.[23] By altering the shape of the glass, Riedel made the slow sequence of actions and sensations involved in drinking wine even more enjoyable.

There are many opportunities to use rate-related questions in your work. For example:

- *Disclosure*: Should I let others know how quickly I am proceeding, or would it be better to disguise that fact or keep it a secret?
- *Interval*: Would it be better to continue at this pace for a longer or shorter time?
- *Meaning*: How do others interpret the pace or tempo of my work or actions? Can I influence what they think?
- *Limits—the Rate Envelope*: Which are the fastest and slowest components of the work I am doing, and what are their individual speed limits? Should I replace the slowest process with one that could be done more quickly, or choose another way to proceed?

Problem Solving

Using the rate lens can call your attention to differences in rates of speed, and these differences can solve problems. For example, one spring morning I watched a bulldozer attempt to scoop up a large cement slab. The piece was lying in soft dirt. Every time the scoop tried to get fully under the slab to lift it up, the bulldozer only succeeded in pushing it farther ahead. The operator finally solved the problem. He placed the scoop under the front lip of the concrete slab. Inching forward, he raised the slab up onto its edge, which bit into the soft earth, thus stopping the slab's forward movement. When the slab was almost vertical, the operator dropped the scoop. The slab hesitated, teetered, and then executed a perfect swan dive into the waiting scoop. What made this maneuver work was a rate difference: the operator was able to drop the scoop to the ground faster than the slab could fall.

I mention this example not because most of us work on construction sites but because rate-difference solutions are a part of everyday life. Yet because they go unnoticed, they do not become part of our conceptual toolbox. To be of use, they need to be identified and recognized so that we can carry them with us.

THE TEMPORAL IMAGINATION

One reason Rodin sculptures have a dynamic quality is that Rodin placed different parts of the body in positions they could not occupy at the same time, thereby creating a sense of movement as we try to reconcile the discrepancies. He created a subjective sense of movement (S-rate) in an object that was not moving at all (O-rate).

> What provides movement, Rodin said, is an image in which the arms, the legs, the torso, the head are each taken from a separate movement, therefore showing the body in a position that it has never been in, and imposing fictive links between the various parts, as though this confrontation of impossibilities could ... cause [a sense of transition] and ... duration to rise in the bronze and on the canvas.[24]

RATE: IN BRIEF

Characteristics of rates:

The normal rate (N-rate). Know the customary or expected rates of change for processes that matter to you.

Size—the Rate Envelope. Determine the fastest and slowest possible rate of change in situations you lead or manage, and understand the impact of their limits.

Duration. Consider how long a given rate will continue and whether it is sustainable.

Objective or subjective. Understand the difference between the real rate of change and how it is perceived.

Meaning. Be aware of how different stakeholders interpret the same rate.

Number. Look for multiple rates of speed or change and how they interact.

Risks associated with missing or misinterpreting rate include

- *N-rate risk.* We fail to take the normal speed of a system into account. (We know that a certain approval process is slow, yet we don't build in enough time and, as a result, miss a deadline.)

- *Direction risk.* We assume that different rates move in the same direction, when in fact they move in the opposite direction or have no influence on each other at all. (We expect an increase in demand to reduce unemployment, but if productivity is increasing much faster than the overall economy, companies can meet demand without hiring.)

- *The Rate Envelope.* The rate of change in your environment may be more extreme, faster or slower, than what you can cope with. (In the fast and furious technology and telecom sectors, even companies accustomed to a frenetic pace have a difficult time keeping up.)

- *Duration risk.* When a rate continues or drops off unexpectedly, we are caught off-guard. (An executive fails to anticipate consecutive quarters of stalled growth.)

- *Objective and subjective rates.* Failing to consider how stakeholders perceive the same rate can have negative consequences. (What a company assumes is a rapid response to a complaint may seem like an eternity to the customer involved.)

- *Number risk.* Coping with differing rates (of change, development, progress, and so on) can be a challenge when they overlap. (In the war in Iraq, the police force could not be trained and mobilized quickly enough to deal with the power vacuum that the swift military defeat of Saddam Hussein created.)

Identifying speed and rate of change also offers options and opportunities:

- *Questioning.* Remember to ask rate questions. (When inflation picks up, will it happen gradually, or will it shoot up almost overnight? What effect will it have on my business?)

- *Optimizing products or services.* Consider rate in design and process innovation. (Riedel designed glassware to complement the slow sequence of actions and sensations involved in drinking wine.)
- *Problem solving.* Managing rate can solve problems in any number of ways. (Recall the bulldozer example. The operator was able to drop the scoop to the ground faster than the slab could fall.)

five

Shape

Success is rarely a straight line.

—*Tom Perkins*[1]

I'd like to begin the discussion of shape by inviting you to take a short walk on the beach with the sculptor Henry Moore. I've timed it: it will take less than a minute.

> Sometimes for several years running I [Moore] have been to the same part of the sea-shore—but each year a new shape of pebble has caught my eye, which the year before, though it was there in hundreds, I never saw.[2]

> ... the sensitive observer of sculpture must ... learn to feel shape simply as shape, not as description or reminiscence. He must, for example, perceive an egg as a simple single solid shape, quite apart from its significance as food, or from the literary idea that it will become a bird. And so with solids such as a shell, a nut, a plum, a pear, a tadpole, a mushroom, a mountain peak, a kidney, a carrot, a tree-trunk, a bird, a bud, a lark, a lady-bird, a bulrush, a bone. From these he can go on to appreciate more complex forms or combinations of several forms.[3]

129

In the passage here, Moore was concerned with physical shapes. In this chapter, I will be concerned with temporal shapes—the various curves that describe how an event or process changes over time. Most of us spend our time thinking about substance: the needs of customers, the impact of new technology, how our product or service stacks up against a competitors, and so on. In this chapter, I would like you to acquire an artist's eye. I want you to learn to notice the temporal shape of an activity or process apart from its content, in the same way that Moore studied the shape of an egg apart from its use as a food or symbol.

Recognizing the temporal shape of a process is important in making decisions about timing, for a number of reasons. First, many timing decisions reference shape directly. Without thinking about it, we include shape in our rules of thumb: "buy low, sell high" is a common example of a heuristic that incorporates shape. Likewise, when to spend your advertising dollars depends on whether sales *peak* during certain times of the year or are relatively constant month to month. In both cases, a shape triggers a decision or action. Second, shape offers important clues about timing. Take the idea of a cycle. Suppose you were asked in 2010 to predict when U.S. combat operations would cease in Afghanistan. Your prediction would take into account the date of congressional and presidential elections, the time in the election cycle when politicians must defend their decisions. It would also be based on another cycle: the length of a tour of duty and the number of tours that the armed forces could ask of its soldiers without degrading its global effectiveness. Third, shapes warn us that timing matters. For example, when something rises too quickly, we know it will fall. When a bubble emerges, we expect it to burst. We just don't know *when*. The bubble shape reminds us to start paying attention and to consider timing.

The temporal world, like the spatial world, is filled with shapes. Some of these shapes warn us of risks; others point to opportunities. Because the best way to see temporal shapes is to plot them, I will use the words *shape* and *curve* interchangeably.

AN ABRIDGED CATALOGUE OF SHAPES

As with all of the timing elements, using shape to make decisions about timing begins with knowing what to look for. The best way to train our eyes to see shapes is by examining a few that we encounter frequently. We will focus on six main shapes.

1. **Point**—the absence of shape (a single point in time)
2. **Line**—the span that directly connects two or more points in time
    Straight. If you plot how a process changes over time and find that it doesn't change at all, the result will be straight line.
    Divided. Sometimes we divide what would otherwise be a continuous (time) line into intervals—for example, weeks into days.
3. **Curve**—a line that changes its slope or direction over time
    Accelerating and decelerating curves—curves that change their slope in a consistent direction, like those that describe how fast your car is going after you push the pedal to the floor or slam on the breaks
    Arc—a shape like a rainbow or the top part of a gently rolling hill
    S-curve—a curve that begins slowly, reaches a peak, and then levels off
4. **Cycle**—an interval of time during which events periodically repeat, visually characterized by curves that rise and fall, rise and fall
5. **Helix**—a corkscrew shape, like a coiled spring or the handrail of a spiral staircase
6. **Tandemizing shape**—a shape in which two curves move in opposite directions. Then one reverses so that the two are now moving in the same direction, that is, in tandem or in parallel with each other.

The Point

Although a point is the absence of shape, it can also be the starting point for various shapes. Figure 5.1 illustrates a shape that I call the *point and fan.*

At time 1, to the very left of the diagram, imagine that you are faced with several alternatives. You choose one. That choice leads to others, so at time 2, you choose again from the alternatives that are present, and so on with each successive time period. Over time, the diagram assumes the shape of a fan. The equation that describes this process is an exponential function that accelerates quickly. Because choice matters only if the alternatives you are choosing among are different, when you look three or four time periods downstream, it is hard to imagine what the world and the alternatives that you are choosing among will look like. This is especially true because others are doing the same, which can change the choices that you have available That is one of the

Figure 5.1 The Point and Fan

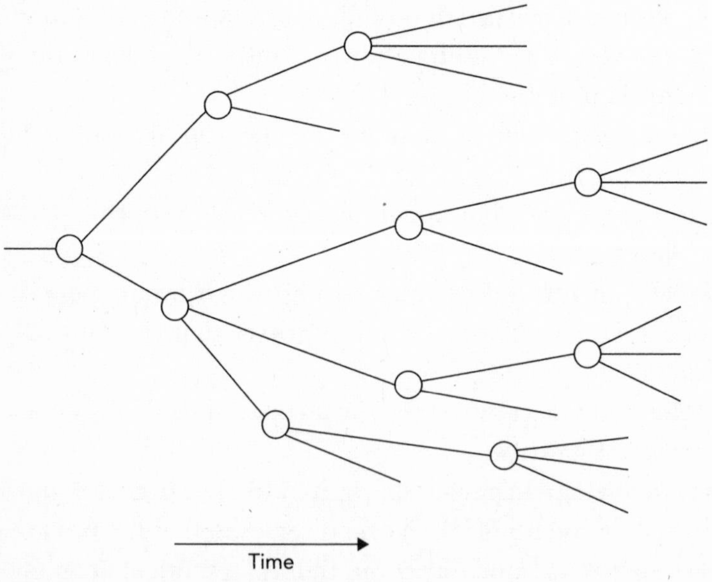

Time

reasons we don't think about the distant future. It is uncertain. That reality, however, can cause us to miss predictable risks.

For example, let's suppose that in fifteen years, baby boomers are fully invested in the stock market, in part to protect themselves from growing inflation. Then suppose the market plunges. Boomers, along with others, will exit in droves. They have to: they will be afraid they won't live long enough to see the market recover. Their exodus will cause the market to fall even further, thus creating a vicious cycle. I suspect that one reason this risk has not been priced into the market is that no time seems right to do so; that is, the problem lacks a timing solution.

This example has an important practical implication: do not assume that the distant future is necessarily less knowable than the more immediate future, as the point-and-fan diagram would suggest. Our deep belief in the power of choice to shape our future, which creates the widening fan, leaves the impression that the distant future is always more uncertain than the more immediate future. It may not be. We simply need to take a look and, while doing so, appreciate the irony that choice, the tool we use to control our future, creates the feeling that it is futile to know where we will end up.

Points come together to form an infinite number of shapes. Let's look at a few others.

Lines
I want to consider two kinds of lines: straight, uninterrupted lines and those that are divided.

Straight Lines
We like straight lines because they seem, well, straightforward, and hence predictable. What you see is what you get: no surprises, no deviations, no sharp turns. But is a perfectly straight line always a good thing?

We sometimes observe attempts to eliminate variation. For example, consider quality-control programs. Reducing variation can cut costs and improve quality, but it also has dangers. In the 1980s, for example, technology made it possible to track a person's attention and level of interest by measuring the size of his or her pupils. When a pupil dilates, it indicates interest; when it contracts, it signals disinterest. Market researchers measured the size of people's pupils as they watched television pilots, and advised network executives to eliminate the moments when interest flagged. But Jagdish Sheth, a professor of marketing at Emory University, pointed out that when they kept the emotional level high all the time, the pilot "failed miserably."[4]

We should not be surprised. When a heart monitor displays a flat line, life is over. Most human activities demand some degree of variability. When the musical performances of fine musicians are examined quantitatively, they are often found to be out of sync with the metronome beat. The musicians usually catch up in a measure or two, but if they are right on the beat all the time, their performance seems dull and uninteresting.

If variation is needed to give a performance vitality, its absence suggests something artificial or fake. In 2005, MIT professor Andrew Lo was looking for warning signs that a hedge fund was vulnerable to a crisis. What he discovered was that many "hedge funds were posting returns that were too smooth to be realistic." Digging deeper, he found that funds with hard-to-appraise, illiquid investments—like real estate or esoteric interest-rate swaps—showed returns that were particularly even. In these cases, he concluded, managers had no way to measure fluctuations and simply assumed that value was going up steadily. The problem, unfortunately, is that those are exactly the kinds of investments that can be subject to big losses in a crisis. Lo concluded that "measuring the smoothness of returns gives economists a good way to estimate the level of relatively illiquid investments in the hedge fund world ... without knowing the details of the investments."[5]

Lo discovered that straight lines can be as informative as their curvy counterparts if you take time to discover what they really mean. This principle applies to other shapes as well.

Divided Lines, Dynamic Sections
We commonly divide time into past, present, and future. When we place these divisions on a time line, the line looks like this:

```
    PAST              PRESENT              FUTURE
_____|_____|_____
```

By convention, at least in most English-speaking cultures, we place the events of the past on the left and those in the future on the right. This tripartite division of time is important because our most powerful timing rules, the ones we rely on to decide *when* to act, are *triples*. I illustrate these triples in Table 5.1. I've placed a YES in those cells when the window of opportunity is open and an action can be successful, a NO when it is closed, and acting is impossible or inadvisable.

As the table illustrates, decisions about timing depend on what is or is thought to be possible in the past, present, and future. If you want to understand the emotions associated with a timing

Table 5.1 Timing Triples

WHEN IS THE RIGHT TIME TO ACT?			
Past	Present	Future	Timing Rule or Implication
NO	NO	NO	Forget about it! No time is right.
YES	YES	YES	Timing doesn't matter. Any time will do.
YES	NO	NO	I'm sorry. It's too late.
NO	NO	YES	Not yet, but the right time will come.
NO	YES	NO	Act now! Opportunities are fleeting.
YES	NO	YES	You will get a second chance.
YES	YES	NO	Hurry. Act now, before it's too late.
NO	YES	YES	Finally. But don't worry: there's no rush.

decision, you need to consider all three time periods. For example, compare row 5 (NO–YES–NO) with row 7 (YES–YES–NO). The rows are highlighted. In both, the decision is the same: act now. But there is a difference. In row 5, this is your first and only chance. Doing what you want to do was impossible in the past, and it won't be possible in the future. Act now. In row 7, this is your last chance to take advantage of an opportunity that was always present. The decision is the same—seize the moment—but we feel differently about it depending on the timing triple that determines the decision.

Curves

I want to consider three kinds of curves: those that accelerate or decelerate, a special shape I call the dramatic arc, and the familiar S-curve.

Accelerating and Decelerating Curves

If you plot the shape of all the events and processes that matter to your organization, you will find very few straight lines. Most will be curves. One of the most important curves to watch for is one that starts slowly, but then rapidly accelerates or decelerates. An "exponential function" is a typical example. As inventor and futurist Ray Kurzweil says, such a function "starts out almost imperceptibly and then explodes with unexpected fury."[6]

There are many examples of exponential functions. Moore's law is perhaps the most famous: the number of transistors that can be placed on an integrative circuit doubles every two years, a trend that has continued since Moore first proposed it in 1965. But there are many others. In the years leading up to 2000, the increase of venture funding for Internet start-ups had an exponential shape: a slow start, followed by a dizzying climb. Another dramatic example is George Soros's explanation of the mortgage and credit crisis of 2008 in terms of the exponential growth of the CDS (credit default swaps) market. Here's what Soros said happened. I've put the last part of the quotation in italics because it is so extraordinary.

Hedge funds entered the market in force in the early 2000s. Specialized credit hedge funds effectively acted as unlicensed insurance companies, collecting premiums on the CDOs [collateralized debt obligations] and other securities that they insured. The value of the insurance was often questionable because contracts could be assigned without notifying the counterparties. They grew exponentially until it came to overshadow all other markets in nominal terms. *The estimated nominal value of CDS contracts outstanding is $42.6 trillion. To put matters in perspective, this is equal to almost the entire household wealth of the United States. The capitalization of the U.S. stock market is $18.5 trillion, and the U.S. treasuries market is only $4.5 trillion.*[7]

All of this raises the following question: Is anyone in your business watching for exponential functions and the mechanisms that produce them, such as accelerating curves and vicious cycles? If not, these shapes are likely to fall through the cracks, leaving you surprised by "sudden" risks and unprepared for fast-moving opportunities.

The Dramatic Arc

In most cases, a climax occurs not at the halfway point of an event but someplace toward the end.[8] No one reading a novel or watching a film wants the climax in the middle, leaving the rest of the story to drag on and on. Nor do we want the climax to happen at the very last moment. Bang. It's over. Instead, we want the climax to occur *toward* the end, but not *at* the very end. It's all in the timing. I call the shape that describes the asymmetrical placement of the climax the *dramatic arc*, illustrated in Figure 5.2. You will often find this shape whenever there is a goal-directed process. Tension rises to a peak as you near the goal and then falls as the goal is achieved.

The dramatic arc may seem far removed from a business or practical application, but that's not the case. It comes into play

Figure 5.2 The Dramatic Arc

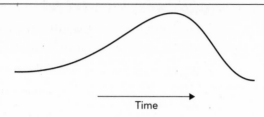

Time

anytime we manage a process that involves the build-up and release of tension, such as announcing an acquisition, or timing an exit. The *surge* strategy adopted by the Bush administration during the war in Iraq is an example of the dramatic arc. The timing of a surge places it after the midpoint of the war. The surge, similar to a sprint at the end of a race, not only signals an ending but also makes it inevitable by expending resources at a rate that cannot be sustained. It allows those who must defend an ending to say, "We have done everything we can."

If you need to terminate a project, an investment, or any other activity and you want the process to be well received, use the dramatic arc. (Unless, of course, the situation is dire. Then simply pull the plug.) The dramatic arc satisfies our esthetic sense: it feels right. And if you see one forming, know that an ending—or at least an attempt at an ending—is in progress.

S-Curves

Another very common shape is an S-curve. When you scan your environment and look into the future, you will likely see them.

Technologies, for example, often experience an early period of rapid growth, a leveling off, and then a steady climb to saturation. Reaching saturation, I should add, can take a long time. In the case of television, which had "the shortest span between early adopters and universal penetration of any medium,"[9] it took nearly fifty years for almost every household to have one. You can anticipate an S-curve by identifying the mechanisms that create it. Consider, for example, the rate at which fax machines were adopted. When fax machines were new, a small number of people bought an early version. Most people waited. There was no point in having one unless others had one as well. Then, at a certain point, it made sense to have one because each machine now had companions with whom it could communicate.

S-curves have a number of characteristics. In the beginning, nothing seems to be happening. Once the upturn begins, however, the question becomes *How quickly will it accelerate?* Researchers, such as the late sociologist Everett Rogers, who introduced the term "early adopter," have identified a number of factors to explain the acceleration of the curve. These include the comparative advantage of the product relative to others, its compatibility with existing products, whether customers can try it out before purchasing it, and whether its benefits are immediately clear. Although such a list is useful, it is only a starting point. Each factor has its own time course. For example, if there is a benefit to a product, *when* will customers notice it—immediately, or only after a period of time? *When* will the product be judged compatible or not compatible with other products—right away, after a trial period, or some other time? That is where the timing advantage is to be found—in a more detailed consideration of the factors that give the S-curve its shape. So the next time anyone includes an S-curve in her presentation, ask her to sketch the shape of the underlying curves that produce it.

Although the S-curve is useful in tracing the evolution of innovations that have run their course, it is equally useful for anticipating the life cycle and longevity of newer products.

Cycles
Every business environment is filled with cycles. These include financial (the quarterly reporting cycle), political (election cycles), technological (adoption cycles), and economic (the business

cycle). Every cycle has a number of characteristics, any one of which can be important for deciding questions of timing.

Period

A period characterizes the length of a complete cycle. For example, how long will it be from one recession to the next?

Some cycles are long, like certain weather patterns—the rise and fall of ocean temperature over decades, for example. Others are measured in hours and minutes, the twenty-four-hour news cycle being one example.

It's a useful exercise to list the cycles on which your business depends. Note their current length, and ask yourself whether they might become longer or shorter in the future. How quickly could that expansion or contraction take place, and how much advance warning would you have?

Regarding the length of the human life cycle, the poet Mary Oliver wrote, "A lifetime isn't long enough for the beauty of this world and the responsibilities of your life."[10]

Parts and Phases

Some parts of a cycle are of particular interest, as the Christmas shopping season is to retailers. In addition, some parts of a cycle may become longer or shorter than others over time. I've noticed that Christmas decorations seem to go up earlier every year, particularly if there is a downturn in the business cycle.

Think about which parts of a cycle are most important. For example, social scientists conducted a study in which they asked patients how much pain they experienced during a colonoscopy.[11] They found that the total amount of pain patients experienced was less important than the highest degree of pain they suffered at any point during the procedure, as well as the amount they experienced during the last three minutes. The researchers called this a "peak and end" pattern.

Sometimes a cyclical pattern will have two peaks. Researchers who study auto accidents find a two-peak pattern over a twenty-four-hour period. They see "an extremely sharp error peak at about 3 AM and an error peak about one-quarter that size at about 3 PM."[12] This is an example of a pattern that policymakers and legislators can take into account as they are considering traffic safety laws and guidelines.

It is important to consider all the phases of a cycle. For example, if you had to guess which high school sport had the greatest number of injuries, most of us would probably guess football or hockey. But according to a thirteen-year study in 1993, girls who ran cross-country in autumn suffered more injuries on a percentage basis than any other sport at the time. The reason is that they take the summer off. "In contrast, girls' track and field, a winter and spring sport that allows ample semester time for runners to get in shape, was ranked only ninth in [the] study, with less than half the injury rate of girls' cross-country."[13]

It is easy to miss a phase or overlook the need for an extra cycle. For example, some airports have perpendicular runways. Ordinarily, that configuration is fine, but when an incoming flight has to abort its landing, turn left or right, and circle around for another try, that flight pattern can put it dangerously close to an aircraft taking off from the runway perpendicular to its approach.

Once you have identified all the phases of a cycle, ask yourself what issues might emerge if a phase has to be omitted, postponed, or repeated.

Amplitude

Amplitude refers to the magnitude or height of a cycle, peak to trough. Is a cycle composed of a series of gentle hills and valleys, or is it made up of steep climbs followed by death-defying descents? Amplitude can be important. When the market for a product or commodity rises or falls precipitously, planning goes out the window. For instance, the headline in the *New York Times* in July 2009 read, "Volatile Swings in the Price of Oil Hobble Forecasting." In 2008, Southwest Airlines reported two consecutive quarters of losses—as oil prices spiked and collapsed all within a few months. "Prices were falling faster than we could de-hedge," said Laura Wright, the chief financial officer at Southwest Airlines, a company that bought long-term oil contracts in an attempt to insure itself against volatile prices.[14]

Symmetry

Is the curve of the cycle symmetrical? In other words, when a sharp downturn occurs, should you expect a sharp upturn?

According to Bill Dudley, head of U.S. economic research at Goldman Sachs, stock market cycles are asymmetrical. "The idea in the marketplace that you had to have a sharp recovery because you had a sharp decline is not borne out by the empirical evidence," he said.[15] Financial bubbles are also asymmetrical. The typical bubble has a "slow start, gradual acceleration in the boom phase, a moment of truth followed by a twilight period, and [a] catastrophic collapse."[16] If it would deflate gradually, the bubble would be less threatening.

As you scan your own environment for the shapes that matter, assume asymmetry. Ask yourself which is more likely, a curve that rises quickly and then trails off slowly, or a curve that builds slowly and then quickly declines? In probability theory and statistics, the measure of the asymmetry is called "skewness." If you haven't found a number of positively and negatively skewed curves in your environment, you are probably missing them. Assuming symmetry is a common bias of the conventional mind, like the desire to live in a state of perpetual equilibrium; it is simply unrealistic. When things don't work, we say that someone has thrown us a curve, and most curves, I would suggest, are asymmetrical. In baseball, a pitcher's slider breaks over home plate, not halfway to it.

Smoothness

Will a cycle be smooth and rounded, like an amusement park roller coaster, or full of sharp edges, like a serrated knife? The latter is a particularly important shape.

Figure 5.3 The Sawtooth Curve

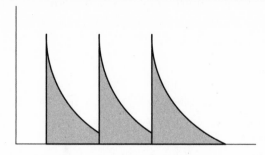

When HMOs were first introduced, for example, it was assumed that their large buying power would keep costs down. That didn't happen—in part because of what I call a *sawtooth curve*. Here is what I mean. When drugs, tests, or treatments are new, they are expensive. As more people use them, costs decline. But as soon as a better drug or treatment is invented, everyone wants it. The result is a series of spikes, illustrated in Figure 5.3. There is not enough time between the spikes for costs to decline significantly and stay there before the next spike begins.

In the case of the HMO, the experts failed to consider the likelihood of the sawtooth curve when they were analyzing pricing trends. Why? One reason is magnitude thinking. Price, we are told, is determined by the magnitude of supply and demand. Increase supply, and prices will decline; increase demand, and prices will rise. But, as we have seen, it is not that simple. In the case of the sawtooth curve, we don't need to know precisely how high the peaks are, or exactly how much time will elapse between them, to see the implications of this shape. We simply need to recognize that the peaks will be high and that the interval between them will be short. That is sufficient to temper the view that buying power alone will keep costs in line.

Number

How many cycles will there be in a given time period? Will one cycle of boom and bust follow another almost immediately? How many cycles is your business subject to, and what could happen if the number were increased? Multiple tours of duty for U.S. soldiers in Iraq, for example, caused fatigue and health issues.

Predictability

Some of the aforementioned characteristics are predictable, such as the length of a tour of duty in Iraq or the term of office for a state senator. Others, such as the length of the business cycle, are less predictable.

If the beginning or ending of a recurrent or cyclical phenomenon is predictable, expect company. In 2008, both Florida and Michigan jumped the gun and moved up the date of their primaries. If there is an advantage to being first, expect that people will respond by jumping in earlier than you anticipated.

Linkage Between Cycles

How does one cycle prepare us for the next? For example, how does a period of high inflation prepare us for the next time prices skyrocket?

The collapse of the World Trade Organization's "Doha Development Round" of trade negotiations in the summer of 2008 illustrates what happens when the link between cycles is not considered. The negotiations failed, in large part due to the success of the previous round of talks. The 1994 Uruguay round had stipulated that countries could convert farm quotas into normal tariffs. Concerned about a flood of imports, countries were permitted to impose short-term safeguard duties to guard against a surge. But what was created as a temporary solution became a crutch. In the Doha round, negotiators' inability to manage the issue and agree on a way to reform the safeguards was part of what sunk the talks.[17]

Another reason the talks collapsed was that countries from the developing world felt that the prior round of talks was biased toward the rich, so in the Doha round they wanted to redress the balance. Negotiators needed to consider how the end of one cycle (or round of talks) would influence the next. The same is true in business. Stop to consider how cycles are linked. One annual cycle of strong sales, for example, may set up an unrealistic expectation for success in the next cycle. Or, conversely, downsizing jobs in one cycle in response to a shrinking market may leave business units unprepared for the coming rebound.

Influence

Cycles also influence the shape of actions that are associated or coordinated with them. For example, what activities are sequenced or timed with the beginning or ending of the fiscal year?

A passage from the 1891 novel *Main-Traveled Roads* illustrates the power of a cycle to influence behavior. It describes a girl who waits for her boyfriend to visit her every Sunday, as seen through the eyes of the woman who employs her.

> "Girls in love ain't no use in the whole blessed week," she said. "Sundays they're a-lookin' down the road, expectin' he'll *come.* Sunday afternoons they can't think o' nothin' else, 'cause he's *here.* Monday mornin's they're sleepy and kind o' dreamy and slimpsy, and good f'r nothing on Tuesday and Wednesday. Thursday they git absent-minded, an' begin to look off towards Sunday agin, an' mope aroun' and let the dishwater git cold, right under their noses. Friday they break dishes, and go off in the best room an' snivel, an' look out o' the winder. Saturdays, they have queer spurts o' workin' like all p'ssessed, an' spurts o' frizzin' their hair. An' Sunday they begin it all over agin."[18]

When we think about cycles, we think about something that reoccurs, a process that goes up and down repeatedly, like the business cycle. But as the description in the passage suggests, cycles are more complex than simply periodic reoccurrence. Therefore, when you find a cycle, ask two questions: First, what external process or schedule governs, controls, or influences the cycle? Second, how would the cycle be influenced if that process or schedule changed? For example, what would happen if the fiscal year for your organization were shortened by six months or lengthened to eighteen months? What costs or benefits would result, and how could you capture them without actually modifying the fiscal year (which I assume is impossible)?

Vicious Cycles

Vicious cycles are situations in which one problem, or attempted solution, leads to another problem, which makes the first problem worse and starts the process all over again. For example, when a company needs to exit a very large position it holds in a market, that sale may cause prices to decline, thereby forcing the company to sell even more, which causes the market to drop further, and so on and on in a vicious cycle. The skyrocketing prices of homes during the U.S. housing bubble is another example of a vicious cycle. High prices and fast turnover fueled overbuilding, which created an oversupply of homes. That oversupply, among other factors, caused prices to plummet. Many owners suddenly found themselves owing more than their homes were worth. But as foreclosures rose, banks were reluctant to lend to buyers, thereby worsening the oversupply issue, leading to additional price declines and more foreclosures.[19]

Most serious crises have multiple vicious cycles at play. That's one reason they are crises. Organizations should keep track of the vicious cycles they may encounter—noting their cause, expected duration, and the strategies needed to terminate them. No strategic planning exercise should be considered complete without consulting this catalogue.

The Helix

A helix is a three-dimensional curve shaped like a wire that is wound uniformly around a cylinder or cone. That's the dictionary

Figure 5.4 The Helix

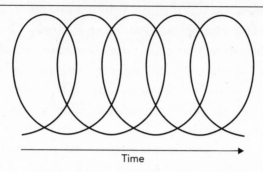

Time

definition, but ask anyone who knows what a helix is, and he will take his index finger and swirl it through the air in the shape of a corkscrew (see Figure 5.4).

The helix is an important shape when it comes to timing, for two reasons.

First, it helps us avoid a common error associated with feedback: the failure to take account of the passage of time. The image of a corkscrew reminds us that we receive feedback, not when we first ask for it, but at some time in the future. Managers, therefore, need to be conscious of what may have changed in the interim. Will those who initially requested the feedback still be with the company? When the feedback arrives, will those who receive it be in a position to understand and use it appropriately? Finally, will the information still be relevant? Surveys, in-depth interviews, and other types of feedback can be expensive. Before seeking feedback, be sure you can answer the questions here.

The second reason the helix shape is important has to do with planning. As I mentioned in the chapter on temporal punctuation, we like closure. In a busy world, managers want issues to be resolved "once and for all." Certain kinds of issues, however, never get resolved. They keep coming back, returning again and again at successive points in the future, thus tracing out the shape of a helix.

The key is to identify issues of this kind so that you are prepared when they return. A prime example is a dilemma. A dilemma is a choice that has three defining characteristics. First, the alternatives that define the choice are *incompatible*. They can't coexist. You must choose one. Second, each is *indispensable*. You can't summarily dismiss it because it represents something essential to you or your organization. Finally, each alternative is *inviolate*, meaning that it cannot be compromised or watered down. When all three characteristics are present, you face a dilemma. Whatever is not chosen is not eliminated, only repressed or sidestepped. It will therefore always resurface. So after you have chosen one alternative or course of action, ask yourself two time-related questions: (1) *When* will we see this issue again, and (2) What might be going on *at that time* that would make dealing with it particularly difficult?

Tandemizing Shapes

Thus far we have focused on single curves and shapes. To lead into the next chapter on polyphony, I will mention a pair of curves that I call *tandemizing shapes*. Tandemizing shapes are curves that have two phases. In the beginning, they move in opposite directions. Then one curve changes direction so that the two curves move in parallel, or in tandem. I illustrate two tandemzing curves in Figure 5.5, one positive and one negative, depending on which direction they turn.

Many risk management strategies assume the first phase: something (such as a stock) moves in one direction, while something

Figure 5.5 Tandemizing Shapes

else (a bond) moves in the opposite direction. In times of crisis, however, both can turn down at the same time—that is, move in tandem. Shapes that are negatively correlated can become positively correlated. And that shift may occur at precisely the wrong moment—that is, when their negative correlation is most needed to manage risk.

We like countercyclical strategies, offsetting rates, and shapes that cancel each other out because they smooth out or eliminate variability. But no one can eliminate change. Therefore, when a risk management strategy relies on components that are assumed to move in opposite directions, look for tandemizing shapes. If you cannot envision conditions when "tandemization" will occur, then you have less protection than you need.

SHAPE-RELATED RISKS AND OPPORTUNITIES

Most shape-related risks stem from a failure to consider shape and its impact. For example, an article in *Florida Today* noted that the Brazilian airliner Embraer was successful because it produced *just the right size plane at just the right time.*[20] Yet what the article failed to include in its description of good timing was any mention of shape. How steep was the demand curve for that aircraft, and when was the shape or slope of that curve obvious? When in the future will that aircraft no longer be the right size, and how rapidly will demand for it decline? In the Introduction, I said that our descriptions of the world are often time impoverished: they leave out many temporal characteristics. Our explanations, after the fact, also tend to miss elements such as shape.

Of course, the sculptor Henry Moore, mentioned earlier, wouldn't be surprised. He would appreciate the difficulty of the task. The shapes that he needed were all around him. He could find and examine a shape in its entirety at his leisure. That is not the case for the shapes that we need in our work. Those shapes unfold over time and require both memory and imagination to see them, neither of which we can always count on. The best protection against missing a shape is to have encountered many examples of it in the past. To that end, I suggest that you add to and update the catalogue of shapes that I have started here. Doing so will prepare you to look for those that are critical to your work.

When you know that a particular shape exists, you can use that knowledge to improve decisions, processes, and predictions. Consider a circadian rhythm, which refers to the body's rhythm of waking and sleeping in sync with the sun's twenty-four-hour cycle of rising and setting. As Abigail Zuger wrote in the *New York Times*, it is possible to picture a day when health care takes the circadian rhythms of disease into account. "Asthma testing would take place in the middle of the night for the most telling results... Cardiac patients would have life-threatening clots in their coronary arteries dissolved in the late afternoon, when the body's clotting system is at its weakest."[21]

Another way to use shape to manage risk and spot opportunities is to ask more precise questions. Consider the bubble. The questions people tend to ask are the same: Is there or is there not a bubble forming, and if there is, when will it burst? That's where the discussion usually ends. Instead, ask about shape (as well as rate, interval, and sequence). If the bubble does exist, will it pop, or will it deflate slowly, and if the latter, over what period of time? Also ask about mechanism. Is a vicious cycle involved? For example, if you are surrounded by houses that have been foreclosed, your own home will lose value, which will cause your neighbor's to lose value, which will cause your home to lose even more value, and so on. We say that we value transparency and perfect information, but if everyone sees the same shape at the same time and interprets it in the same way, expect herd behavior. In the case of a bubble, that can mean a panicked race for an exit before the bubble bursts. So remember to ask about the shape of the information curve: When will increasing numbers of individuals know certain facts and then act on them? Finally, ask yourself how much advance warning you are likely to have before a known bubble busts.

Seeking answers to these questions—even just raising them—will better prepare you for what might occur, particularly if you have researched past bubbles in your industry and looked for the answers to these questions in the historical record. Don't let fragments of information go to waste. We know, for example, that when an economic recovery begins and inflation returns, the Federal Reserve will be to slow to raise interest rates for fear of stopping the recovery in its tracks. Unless you plot two curves, one that shows the rising rate of inflation and the second that shows the predictable lagged response of the Fed, information about the lag will get lost.

Remember the mantra: *before precision, pattern.* If you find yourself sketching a curve that has an odd but important shape, you may want to name it, as I did with the tandemizing shape or sawtooth curve. This will help you remember it.

Finally, be aware of your own biases. We all seek the power and adrenaline rush of the decisive moment. When unfavorable conditions are present, we want them to end, period. Over time, we come to realize that we need to consider more time-extended shapes. For example, "more doctors and patients are starting to view cancer as a chronic illness—something to be treated, not cured."[22] This is an important historical shift with implications for how patients are treated. We want our lines short and, of course, straight. When we find a curve, we want it to be symmetrical and smooth with no gaps, discontinuities, or sharp edges. As a result, we are likely to be late in discovering shapes like the sawtooth curve and in understanding its implications. When something changes in a positive direction, we want it to continue, as was the case with housing prices: always moving up. When we can't answer a question—for example, when will a bubble burst—with *precision*, we move on and forget to ask other questions, such as those I mentioned earlier. The best protection in any business venture is to list the shapes that you assume will be present and then challenge them, keeping in mind your biases. For example, if you expect sales to ramp up smoothly, look for times when sales will jump and then fall back before advancing again. If you expect a project to end, expect some parts to continue on, even unofficially, like embers in a fire that takes a long time to die out.

There are many shapes that were not included in this chapter and others that were mentioned only in passing. Space was limited, and some shapes, like bubbles and cliffs (a precipitous drop or change in a prior condition) tend to dominate public discussion because of the fear and anxiety associated with them. I counted seventeen shapes that Henry Moore was interested in as he walked on the beach—eggs, shells, nuts, plums, and so on. I suspect that temporal shapes are just as numerous and diverse as spatial ones. We just need to look for them.

THE TEMPORAL IMAGINATION

I have focused on shapes that are easy to visualize, such as points, lines, and cycles. As I have indicated, there are many others. I use a shape from Laurence Sterne's novel *Tristram Shandy*, which he created to visually represent the narrative arc of his book, to remind myself to look for a variety of shapes, many of which do not have names (see Figure 5.6). One purpose of Sterne's novel,

Figure 5.6 Narrative Arc of the Novel *Tristram Shandy*

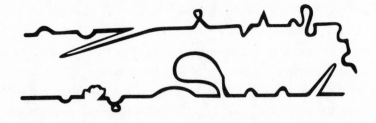

according to Howard Anderson, the editor of the Norton Critical Edition, was to reveal "the infinite ways in which conventional ideas of all sorts have handcuffed our minds and imaginations."[23] That is also an aim of this book.

SHAPE: IN BRIEF

There are many kinds of temporal shapes:

Points—the absence of temporal shape (a single point in time).

Lines—the span or segment that directly connects two or more points in time. If you plot a process over time and find that the process doesn't change at all, the result will be a straight line.

Curves—the shape of change. For example:
　Accelerating and decelerating curves—curves that change their slope, like the those that describe how fast your car is going after you push the pedal to the floor or slam on the breaks
　Arcs—a shape like a rainbow or the top part of a gently rolling hill
　S-curves—a curve that begins slowly, reaches a peak, and then levels off

Cycles—a process that periodically repeats, visually represented by curves that rise and fall.

The helix—a corkscrew shape like a coiled spring or the handrails of a spiral staircase.

Tandemizing shapes—shapes in which two curves start by moving in opposite directions, but then one reverses so that it is moving in tandem or in parallel with the other.

Risks and opportunities associated with shape:

- We like simple shapes. We want our lines to be short and straight; we want the curves we encounter to be symmetrical and nicely rounded, with no gaps or sharp edges. As a result, we are likely to be late in discovering shapes, such as the sawtooth curve, that don't have these characteristics.
- When something changes in a positive direction, we want it to continue, as was the case with housing prices: always moving up.

- To prepare your mind to consider shapes, create a catalogue of the shapes that are critical to your work.

- When you know that a particular shape exists, you can use that knowledge to improve decisions, processes, and predictions.

- Remember to ask more questions. Is there a bubble forming, and if there is, when will it burst? When we can't answer this question with *precision*, we move on and forget to ask other questions, such as, Will the bubble pop or simply deflate slowly, and, if the latter, over what period of time?

- Seeking answers to these questions—even just raising them—will better prepare you for what might occur.

- The best protection in any business venture is to list the shapes that you assume will be present and then challenge them, keeping in mind your biases. For example, if you expect sales to ramp up smoothly, look for times when they won't. If you expect a project to end, be prepared for parts of it to continue.

six

Polyphony

We can no longer depend on a story-line unfolding sequentially, an ever accumulated history marching straight forward ... for too much is happening against the grain of time, too much is continually traversing the story-line laterally.

—*John Berger*[1]

Polyphony in music is a form of composition in which multiple melodies are performed at the same time, each retaining its own individuality as it harmonizes with others. In the previous five chapters, we looked at a *single* time-extended pattern laid out horizontally, like a single melody, including its sequence, its rate of development or change, its overall shape, its starting and ending points, and so on. With the element of polyphony we add the vertical dimension. For most executives, there is always a lot going on at the same time, and to get the timing right, the task is to figure out how these *multiple* streams of actions and events interact with each another.

Because we are coming to the end of the set of lenses needed to conduct a timing analysis, I will also include in this chapter some simple examples of what a beginning timing analysis looks like in order to set the foundation for Chapters Seven and Eight. But first, we will examine two types of relationships that are present when actions and events go on at the same time. The first is *structural*: the extent to which one parallel event is aligned or overlaps with another. The second is one of *influence*: the extent to which one event or process masks, competes with, substitutes for, or amplifies another that is going on at the same time. Previously, I called our inability to find patterns when multiple actions overlap Copland's Constraint. The classical composer pointed out that when we listen to music, we can't easily follow more than four melodies at once. Here is Copland's description of polyphony and the difficulty it poses:

> Music that is polyphonically written makes greater demands on the attention of the listener, because it moves by reason of separate and independent melodic strands . . .

> . . . Polyphonic texture implies a listener who can hear separate strands of melody sung by separate voices, instead of hearing only the sound of all the voices as they happen from moment to moment. . .

> . . . Polyphonic texture brings with it the question of how many voices the human ear can grasp simultaneously. Opinions differ as to that . . . I think it can safely be maintained that with a fair amount of listening experience, two- or three-voiced music can be heard without too much mental strain. Real trouble begins when the polyphony consists of four, five, six, or eight separate and independent voices.[2]

One of the greatest challenges of timing is finding patterns when multiple streams of actions are going on at the same time. Although it is not a task that we are used to, it is, I would suggest, the task we now face in the twenty-first century. General Rupert Smith describes this new reality as it applies to modern warfare:

In the world of industrial war the premise is of the sequence peace-crisis-war-resolution, which will result in peace again . . . In contrast, the new paradigm of war amongst the people is based on the concept of a continuous criss-crossing between confrontation and conflict . . . Rather than war and peace, there is no predefined sequence, nor is peace necessarily either the starting or the end point: conflicts are resolved, but not necessarily confrontations.[3]

Unfortunately, we are ill-prepared for such a world. When we speak or write, we must place one word *after the next*. When we describe a particular situation, there are only a limited number of times we can use the word "meanwhile" before eyes begin to roll. When we reason, we demand that our conclusions *follow* logically from what came before it. *In short, we are serial creatures in a massively parallel world.* As a result, we are continually "blindsided" by events that seem to come, to use a baseball analogy, "out of left field." But a large part of the problem is that we have gotten the location of left field wrong. It is not left, but up. Many things are happening at the same time, and we can't keep track of them.

TRACKING POLYPHONY

In order to find all the parallel processes that have implications for timing, it is useful to break down any event or situation into what I call *tracks* and then examine each one. Let me give you an example. On the op-ed page of the *New York Times* in 1996, a woman told the story of her attempt to get divorced. The title of the piece was "34 Months and Still No Divorce."[4] What took so long?

Over the course of the legal proceeding, a number of things happened at or around the same time, including the following: "Three matrimonial judges were sent to other parts of the State Supreme Court system and replaced by three judges with no divorce-law experience.'' Her husband didn't show up for the trial, and it had to be rescheduled. The trial had to be rescheduled a second time because her husband's lawyers were preparing an appeal in another case. One lawyer had medical problems. Then the judge found himself in the midst of another trial, so he rescheduled the trial yet again. Finally, the woman was informed that the clerk's office at the State Supreme Court had misplaced all the files from her case.[5]

Presumably, this woman is now happily divorced, but the process took much longer than she anticipated. One approach for determining why this process was so lengthy is to think about all the parallel events and processes that were going on at the same time like multiple melodies being performed simultaneously by different instruments in a musical score.

Musical scores (you may want to look back at the Beethoven score I reproduced in the Introduction) have both a horizontal and vertical dimension. In this example, the horizontal dimension of the score describes the sequential nature of the legal system: hiring an attorney, filing for legal separation, meeting with the judge, and so on. In a divorce proceeding, certain steps have to be taken in a particular order. If the woman in this example had read the previous chapters, she would know that whenever events must happen in a particular order—that is, when a sequence has strict serial constraints—things can take much longer than expected. She would also know that whenever there is an acute need for closure—which is what a divorce is—any delay, particularly one that occurs at the end, can be particularly painful.

The situation the woman faced also had a vertical dimension: there were many things going on at the same time. In fact, the vertical dimension consisted of eleven different parallel tracks, one for each of the following actors or processes:

1. The husband
2. The wife

3. The wife's lawyer
4. Husband's lawyer 1
5. Husband's lawyer 2
6. Other cases for lawyer 1
7. Other cases for lawyer 2
8. Judge 1
9. Judge 2
10. Other cases for Judge 1
11. Other cases for Judge 2

If we want to add more detail, we could include additional lines for the other cases the lawyers and judges were involved in (items 10 and 11). I refer to the number of tracks in a score as its C value (C for Copland). In this example $C = 11$, which exceeds Copland's Constraint ($C = 4$) by quite a bit. That is not unusual; most situations are even "taller."

A high C value would not matter except for the fact that the actions of different parties need to be coordinated. If a hearing is scheduled and the wife doesn't show up or her husband's lawyer cannot attend, the process cannot go forward. I call this a *synchronous requirement*—certain things need to happen at the same time in order for an event to play out on time.

The woman's divorce was delayed in this example because of three factors: (1) a high C value: there is a lot going on in parallel; (2) serial constraints: there is a limit to the extent to which the different steps to finalizing a divorce can be omitted, condensed, collapsed, or inverted; and (3) synchronous requirements: certain actions or activities must take place at the same time. The steps and stages of the process are clearly punctuated. A hearing or meeting begins on a particular day and time. A high C value, when combined with strict serial constraints and synchronous requirements, dramatically increases the possibility of delay. That doesn't mean that a delay is inevitable, only that one is likely. Perhaps no one could have predicted that a lawyer would have medical problems or that a judge would be reassigned. But we *could* have predicted that any process characterized by a high C value, strict serial constraints, and synchronous requirements would be subject to delays. Moreover, the longer such a process was delayed, the greater the risk that chance events would intervene that would delay the desired outcome even more.

So the lesson to draw is that we need to pay attention to the tall stack of parallel processes that are present at every moment in time. We can if we look up. I use the following poem by Rita Dove to remind me to look vertically.

> Cancel the afternoon
> evenings morning all
> the days to come
> until the fires
> fall to ash
> the fog clears
> and we can see
> where we
> really
> stand.[6]

But before I suggest a number of strategies that will help you look for tall polyphonic structures, let me distinguish polyphony from multitasking. The agenda items in multitasking are already defined. The problem is simply that we can't do all of them at once. The challenge of polyphony is different. The tracks of a tall polyphonic structure are neither fully visible nor easily imagined. We have to search for them and the ways they influence one another. The challenge of polyphony is not juggling the known but looking for the unknown, just as we did when we were looking for "hidden" intervals or "hidden" rates.

USING THE POLYPHONY LENS

The polyphony lens tells you where to look and what to look for, specifically:

1. **Look vertically**. Identify what is going on *at the same time* that could affect your work or business.
2. **Look for structure**. Note how simultaneous events, activities, and processes are aligned relative to each other. Which lead, lag, overlap, and so on?
3. **Look for influence**. Explore how one event affects, causes, or influences others going on at the same time.

Look Vertically: What Is Going on at the Same Time?

Take a moment to think of a situation in your work or life where timing matters. There are few general rules about *how many* tracks will be needed to describe it. Every situation is different. But there are some general strategies that can aid in the process. They fall into two categories. The first set deals with the visible. The second set consists of looking for "forgotten" or "hidden" tracks. I'll begin with the first category.

Consider All the Visible Moving Parts or Dimensions

Begin by identifying each business or function (such as R&D, manufacturing, and marketing) that is related to the situation in question. Then look closer and outline the individual tracks that are associated with each of these moving parts. Remember to include all dimensions: economic (tracks for the business cycle), financial (tracks for the rise and fall of markets), administrative (tracks for changes in the workforce), technical (tracks for the invention and use of technology), political (tracks that chart shifts in political ideology), legal (tracks that monitor changes in rules and regulations), and sociocultural (for example, tracks that chart the rise and fall of social movements, changes in values).

In addition, do not forget contextual factors. Include tracks for stakeholders and for the actions and reactions of different agents and actors, for example. Think of context as a set of concentric circles beginning with the individual, followed by the group, the firm or organization, the industry, and the nation. The largest context is global, what is going on internationally. Give each "ring" its own track or set of tracks.

The idea is to locate all the moving parts in the context in which you find yourself. A useful rule is to give all "nouns" their own track. Whatever *might* have its own developmental sequence, its own rate of change, its own rhythm or punctuation, and so on gets its own track. Each of these has the potential to affect what is going on in your own situation.

Find All the Hidden or Missing Tracks

This step is a little more complex. We tend to miss processes that will affect our work and business because many of the ways we describe our world are "flat." To add height, we need to redescribe events. For example, consider the statement "A firm decides to manufacture and market a product." This sentence refers to a single time line: first A, then B; first manufacture, then market.

You can describe the same series of events as a polyphonic structure by considering them in parallel. Simply give each element its own track or time line—one each for the firm, the manufacturing process, the product, and the market. Each of these four elements will change and overlap over time. Firms are bought and sold. New technologies will change how the product is manufactured. Marketing strategies will evolve, as will the market for the product.

The move from serial to parallel brings questions of time and timing to the forefront. Is this the right time for this firm to be marketing this particular product? Will its marketing strategy change quickly enough? Those questions are not brought to the surface by a sentence that simply says, "A firm decides to manufacture and market a product." That is why redescription is useful. Because the world is complex, we simplify it; because it is moving, we stabilize it. We need to be conscious of the unconscious ways we do so (and work to overcome them), or we will miss the changes that affect our business.

Redescription is not an academic exercise. Look back at how General Rupert Smith described the changing nature of modern war. The word "crisscrossing" is the key. It is a hint that some kind of parallel structure will be needed to understand the whole. If we don't think in terms of polyphony, we will be puzzled and ultimately frustrated. Take an issue of temporal punctuation. When will a war be over? When will violence erupt again? In a serial world, such questions have answers. In the polyphonic world, those answers are much less clear-cut. Instead of a single answer, one question raises others: What do we need to do in parallel, and how will these various processes influence each other as we implement them over time?

Let's look at ways we can uncover and think about all the relevant tracks (events, situations, circumstances) that are either hidden or obscured by other tracks.

Forgotten Tracks   There are several types of tracks that we tend to forget. The first two "forgotten" tracks are a result of rates of change that are either too slow or too fast to notice or anticipate.

Termite tracks. Termite tracks describe processes in which the minimum speed of the slowest process is so slow that we don't notice that anything is going on. For example, one reason people have bad backs is that we have gotten taller while tables have gotten lower. According to A. C. Mandal, chief surgeon at Denmark's Finsen Institute, the average height of men and women has increased four inches over the past fifty years, while the average height of tables has been lowered by as much as eight inches. "This inevitably leads to more constrained sitting postures [and] is probably the main reason for the growing number of back sufferers."[7] Termite tracks represent processes that happen slowly but can eventually undermine the structural integrity of a system. A corporate culture, for example, can change very slowly and incrementally, as individuals leave the organization and are replaced. When that culture change reaches the tipping point, it can have an impact on business. Yet we may miss the warning signs because the change has occurred so slowly, as when autopilots in an aircraft change the direction of an aircraft so slowly that the actual pilots don't realize the change has taken place.[8]

High-speed systems. In Chapter Four (Rate), I mentioned the maximum speed of the fastest process. A high-speed process may be a natural occurrence, such as a raging forest fire, or it may be chain reaction, such as a bank run fueled by panic. I also talked about the high speed of symbol systems. When symbol systems become a significant part of our reality, be prepared for speed. Capital moves around the globe in nanoseconds as a result of networks that are based on symbols—computer code and algorithms. There is much that is present in the world that we don't see because of the speed at which it is taking place. So remember to add tracks for processes that can happen "in the blink of an eye," or, with computers, even faster.

Alternative Tracks   These tracks describe actions or events that represent alternatives to what is going on in other tracks. Recall the example of the woman getting a divorce. One reason it took so long was that the lawyers involved had other cases that demanded their attention. They couldn't do A, because they had to do B. So if you want to know how long your kitchen renovation will take, ask the contractors how many other jobs they will be working on at the same time or, for that matter, how many they *could* be working on if the right opportunity presented itself. The answer you receive will tell you a lot about when your kitchen is likely to be completed. Suppose that a firm has a line of business in a market that is deteriorating. When should the firm close down the business and exit the market? Without identifying alternatives—for example, other more profitable business opportunities—many firms will continue to rationalize sunk costs and hope for a turnaround. The best way to make a timely exit is to have an alternative handy when you need one. And the best way to do that is to give each possible alternative to your current course of action its own track. That way, pardon the pun, you can keep track of it.

Alternative tracks should be included in a discussion of supply and demand. The standard view is that when the price of a product falls, customers will buy more of it; when prices rise, they will buy less. But that is not always the case. Sometimes when prices fall, customers feel richer and, as a result, *buy something else* that they previously couldn't afford rather than more of the same product. That is what economists call a *Giffen good* after Robert Giffen, a Victorian-era British statistician who first identified this phenomenon.[9] So ask yourself: How might the needs of my customers change in ways that would cause them to seek a very different product or experience when the price of my product changes?

Interpretation Tracks Choosing the right time to act depends on how a situation is interpreted. When a country starts moving its bioweapons from one location to another, does that mean that it is preparing to use them? If so, is immediate action required? The best way to remember that timing depends on how events are interpreted is to give each interpretation its own track.

In 1993, police at the University of Pennsylvania acted to prevent black students from seizing copies of the student newspaper during a protest against a conservative columnist. A subsequent report of the incident said that the "officers should have recognized that the students' attempt to remove all the papers, although it violated university policy, was 'a form of protest and not an indication of criminal behavior.'"[10] If the students were engaged in criminal behavior, then the police acted in a timely manner. But if students were engaged in lawful protest, then the police probably acted too quickly. If the police were guilty of a timing error, it had to do with their interpretation of events.

If this story had only one possible interpretation, then the events it comprises could be placed, one after the other, on a single track or time line. But if different interpretations are possible, you need multiple tracks—one for each different "reading" of what might be going on. Ask yourself three questions: (1) *When* will I know which track or interpretation is correct? (2) What might be going on *at that time* that would influence my judgment? And (3) Given what I think is the right interpretation, *when* should I act?

Reaction Tracks   When a change—a new organizational policy, for example—is proposed or introduced, expect a reaction: perhaps support, perhaps opposition. As Newton would say, for every action, there will be an equal reaction. There are four timing questions to ask about reactions. They involve issues of temporal punctuation, shape, and rate:

1. When will the reaction or opponent process start?
2. How quickly will it develop?
3. When will it reach significant size?
4. When will it be over?

In short, what is the overall shape of the curve that describes how the reaction begins, develops, and finally runs its course?

The best way to keep track of a possible reaction is to give the reaction its own track. That way you can consider its shape and timing from the very beginning. If you put actions and reactions on the *same* track, the tendency will be to think of a possible reaction as a future event, which can put it out of sight and hence out of mind.

Goal Tracks   Individuals and organizations often have multiple goals or objectives: ensuring profit; enhancing their reputation; creating wealth for the next generation, in the case of a family business; and so on. Sometimes these goals are aligned, sometimes not. And over time some goals may change; one goal may replace another. Recall the dollar auction I talked about in Chapter Four (Temporal Punctuation). For many individuals, the motive to maximize gain was ultimately replaced by the motive to avoid loss, because, as you recall, the runner-up had to pay what he last bid. If you don't include separate tracks for different goals and objectives, you may be too slow to realize that they should change.

Qualitative Tracks   Include tracks that describe events, processes, or activities that are important, but difficult to quantify. The breakup of the Soviet Union serves as a cautionary tale about what happens when we fail to take into account what is not easily counted, namely, "the passions—the appeal of ethnic loyalty and nationalism, the demands for freedom of religious practice and cultural expression, and the feeling that the regime had simply lost its moral legitimacy."[11] Because many experts on the Soviet Union didn't consider these factors, instead relying on what they could more precisely model—that is, economic and military factors—they missed when and how quickly the breakup would occur. Regardless of the business you are in, remember to consider qualitative tracks. What cannot be quantified will often be dismissed as soft or subjective, especially in organizations that prize precision and insist that all decisions be based on "the numbers." But, as in the case of the breakup of the Soviet

Union, that attitude can lead to timing mistakes and missed opportunities.

■ ■ ■

Once you have identified the visible and hidden events and situations (tracks) relative to your environment, you can start to examine them in a deeper way in terms of how they affect and intersect each other.

Include a Sufficient Number of Tracks

Now that we have looked at ways to find tracks that are hidden or that we are likely to miss, it's appropriate to ask, *How many are enough?* This is like asking about a skyscraper, How tall is tall enough? The answer depends on the purpose of the building. Was the skyscraper built as a symbol: the centerpiece of a city skyline? Was it built to prove a point: to break the record for the tallest building? Was it constructed to stimulate commerce: to create a new space to attract businesses? The height of a building depends on its purpose. The same is true when we use the polyphony lens to make timing decisions. I can't say how many tracks you will want to include and analyze. But my experience tells me that you will need a C value greater than 20 to make a well-informed decision.

As part of a corporate strategy session, I worked with the head of IT in an insurance company to consider certain business scenarios. We were writing tracks on his whiteboard. Once we had about twenty tracks, he stood back and discovered that the decision about when to upgrade the company's computer system would affect the entire strategic direction of the firm. The polyphony lens helped him see beyond his own silo. I had a similar experience working with a financial firm. The members of the firm were concerned about matching their competitor's pricing. We began to describe the industry the firm was in, adding more and more tracks to capture its complexity. At around twenty, we discovered that changes in the industry would likely make the issue of price competition moot. Price would no longer be the primary factor driving profitability.

So how many tracks do you need? One maxim is what I call the *second dozen rule*. It has been my experience that the first dozen tracks simply display in visual form what you already know. It's the second dozen that allow you to see your situation in a new light.

Look for Structure: How Are Events, Activities, and Processes Aligned Relative to Each Other?

The polyphony lens directs our attention to how concurrent processes and events are aligned with each other: which occur at the same time and which will be separated in time. Either condition (overlap or nonoverlap) can be a source of business risks or opportunities.

Synchronous Risk—the Risk of Overlap

A dozen years ago, NBC discovered, much to its embarrassment, that viewers didn't watch the 2000 Australian Olympics in the numbers that it—and its advertisers—was counting on. Part of the problem stemmed from the date of the games, which started later than normal because Australia, the host country, was in the southern hemisphere and the seasons are reversed. According to the *Wall Street Journal*, the executives at NBC and elsewhere blamed poor ratings on competition, including the pennant race in baseball as well as NFL football games. They also acknowledged that the time difference between Australia and the United States was a factor.[12] Some even went so far as to wonder if Americans had lost interest altogether in the Olympic Games.

Eight years later, however, the Olympics in Beijing proved that the event could still draw a huge viewing audience. In fact, media outlets reported unprecedented interest in the games and the largest television audience in Olympic history. In 2012, the London Olympics were a huge success. "The Games averaged more than 30 million viewers a night, and well more than 200 million individual viewers in all."[13] So where did NBC go wrong in 2000? At least part of the answer is that NBC didn't understand the implications of all the overlapping events and circumstances that would be present, specifically:

- *Weather.* The Olympics were scheduled in the fall, as opposed to earlier in the summer, in an attempt to avoid the Australian winter.
- *The political calendar.* There was a presidential election going on in the fall that competed for media attention and viewers.
- *The ebb and flow of patriotism.* The end of the Cold War, years before, eliminated a clear rivalry, making the games less symbolically important. The Olympics was now more a contest between athletes, and less a contest between nations or ideologies (an example of termite tracks).
- *Technology.* The rise of the Internet, which makes information available on a real-time basis, made the time delay in broadcasting the events a difficult challenge.
- *Competition.* The Olympics competed with the baseball and football seasons (an alternative track to what was going on).

Using the polyphony lens, you can better see what overlapping conditions are at play and how to respond to them. If NBC had anticipated the issues created by so many concurrent events—and it could have—it might have found ways to benefit from the time delay. For example, it could have used detailed close-ups and slow-motion replays to show exactly how an athlete won the gold. Or it could have inserted real-time "Olympic update" advertising during pennant games, to remind viewers of the Olympics. The key point is that using the polyphony lens could have revealed in advance the challenges NBC faced.

Because there are always many overlapping events and conditions, synchronous risk can be found just about everywhere. For example, on August 1, 2007, a bridge over the Mississippi River in Minneapolis collapsed, killing 14 and injuring 145. What investigators subsequently discovered was that more than half the weight on the main river span was concentrated on a narrow, 115-foot stretch of roadway that straddled the point where the collapse began. As part of a resurfacing project, fine and coarse aggregate used in paving materials had been placed directly above where the National Transportation Safety Board later found the design flaw that sent concrete and steel crashing into the Mississippi River.[14]

To understand what happened, let's look back in time. A bridge is built. Traffic begins to flow, heavier at rush hour, lighter at other times. After many years, the bridge needs repairs. In order to prevent the collapse, one had to anticipate how the repair of the bridge would interact with increasing rush hour traffic. Over time, vehicles became heavier. The population increased, and with it, rush-hour traffic. (These slow increases are examples of termite tracks.) As a result, the total weight on the bridge increased. That, combined with the weight of repair materials and equipment, contributed to the collapse.

Subsequent investigation also found a design flaw in one component of the bridge—it was too thin. That was certainly a factor. But the overall lesson is clear. To anticipate synchronous risk—the danger of overlapping events—consider downstream conditions that might co-occur from the beginning. One reason we don't do that, ironically, is that the usual way we think about cause and effect keeps our mind focused on what is essentially a single time line. We focus on what *follows* what, rather than on what is going on at the same time—which is where synchronous risks are to be found. As Ben Bernanke pointed out, the 1929 stock market crash didn't *cause* the Great Depression; rather, the Great Depression was caused by "a series of unrelated international financial events" that were going on at the same time.[15]

One obvious solution to the problem of synchronous risk is to create an asynchronous solution. This is what hedge funds do when they limit disbursement to staggered redemptions. In effect, these staggered redemptions prevent everyone from withdrawing his or her money at the same time in the event of a panic situation, allowing time for cooler heads to prevail and market conditions to change in a way that would convince people to keep their money invested.

Let me give you another example. The economist Richard Thaler proposed an asynchronous solution to the problem of inadequate saving by American workers (one still waiting to be implemented as far as I know). The plan would incentivize individuals to allocate a portion of their future salary increases toward retirement savings. They would commit to the allocation well in advance of their next salary increase, but the stepped-up contribution would not take effect until the increase hit their paycheck. By timing the contribution to coincide with the pay increase, workers are assured that their current take-home pay would not fall.[16] The timing of additional income and additional savings would be synchronized. Perfect harmony.

Overlapping events and circumstances can therefore have positive results, what we might call synchronous rewards. For example, the director Peter Brook says that overlap protects him against failure: "I never experienced the end of work . . . I always made sure that I had another production set up before the current one was ended, to cover the danger of failure."[17]

Planning to do several things at once is also efficient. Trains running to Grand Central Station, for example, update their schedule at the same time that they make adjustments for daylight saving time. Dan Brucker, a spokesman for the Metro-North Commuter Railroad Company, said the overlapping adjustments are simpler, enabling riders to acclimate to the changes in schedule.[18] Careful consideration of overlapping events creates opportunities to generate positive outcomes and better manage risk.

Synchronous Requirements—When Conditions Must Be in Sync

Synchronous requirements refer to conditions that must be simultaneously present for a plan or activity to succeed. For example, a technology can be too early if the conditions needed for its success, including market readiness and infrastructure requirements, are not present and synchronized. One example that comes to mind is the pneumatic tire (a tire filled with air). Although Robert Thompson patented it in 1845, he never successfully commercialized the product. It was not until 1880 that the pneumatic tire was widely marketed by Robert Dunlap. By that time, bicycles had come on the scene, and pneumatic tires were ideal for providing a smooth ride.[19] Thompson's timing was off because certain conditions were not present when he introduced his innovation.

Many situations have synchronous requirements. The best example in recent memory is the flight commanded by Capt. Sullenberger, the pilot who successfully landed in the Hudson River after a bird strike. He described his task as follows: "I needed to touch down with the nose slightly up ... with the wings exactly level ... at a descent rate that was survivable ... just above our minimum flying speed but not below it. And I needed to make all the things happen simultaneously."[20]

What Sullenberger did was extraordinary. It required training, experience, and nerves of steel. But all of us perform actions that require synchrony whenever we make a decision, because for something to count as a decision, three conditions must be simultaneously present: first, we must perceive that we have a choice; second, the choice must be among alternatives that are recognizably different and that lead to different outcomes. Otherwise, we might as well flip a coin. Finally, we must experience a sense of efficacy. If we believe that forces beyond our control have already decided the outcome, then choice is only a formality. It is only when these three conditions are simultaneously present that an action becomes a decision. That is why it is sometimes unclear whether we have actually made a decision, rather than acted out of habit or in line with custom. We like to talk about decisions to dramatize the moment of making them. But, on closer examination, a true decision is not a single action, but a confluence of conditions. That is one reason the polyphonic lens is important. It is easy to forget about synchronous requirements.

Synchronous requirements are important, but in some cases there is an advantage in being *out of sync*. In a sense, that is what innovation is all about: being first. Offering customers something new requires being out ahead of existing products or services. Being out of sync can also be the source of scientific discovery. According to Einstein, the pace of his development as a child was out of sync with the norm—and that might have contributed to his discovery of relativity. He put it like this: "The normal adult never bothers his head about space-time problems. Everything there is to be thought about, in his opinion, has already been done in early childhood. I, on the contrary, developed so slowly that I only began to wonder about space and time when I was already grown up. In consequence, I probed deeper into the problem than an ordinary child would have done."[21]

A CLOSER LOOK AT
SYNCHRONOUS REQUIREMENTS

The polyphony lens is useful in planning everything from business opportunities to travel plans. For example, according to the *New York Times*, a Los Angeles–based telecom engineer named Matt Holdrege wanted to change flights following a last-minute flight delay at his departure gate in Paris. The delay, blamed on mechanical difficulties, had the potential to stretch on and on. So when the flight crew rolled up the stairs to allow the mechanic on board, Holdrege used his cell phone to book a new nonstop flight to Los Angeles on British Airways. Then, just as the flight attendants seemed ready to let him leave, the mechanical problem was fixed. He decided to remain on board, and the plane eventually took off.

Unfortunately for Holdrege and the other passengers, the story does not end there. The plane had idled in Paris for so long that the crew

Figure 6.1 Holdrege's Flight

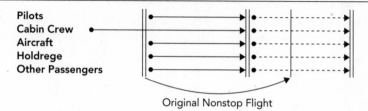

Original Nonstop Flight

couldn't fly to Los Angeles without exceeding the legal limit on hours worked. As a result, the plane had to land in Washington and wait for a replacement crew, further lengthening the already long delay.[a]

There was nothing preventing Holdrege from inquiring about the likelihood of additional delays, but he didn't. The question is, why? On the surface, the answer is simple. He didn't work for the airlines, so he had no reason to know how long flight crews could fly without taking a break. That's the conventional wisdom, and it is fine, as far as it goes.

But when we probe deeper, the story changes. A simple oversight becomes a symptom of more fundamental difficulty. To show you what I mean, let's look at the temporal architecture, sketched in Figure 6.1, of the flight Holdrege was on.

Each element of Holdrege's flight has its own line or track. There are five principal tracks, drawn as arrows to indicate the direction of movement: one for the pilots, one for the cabin crew, one for the aircraft, one for Holdrege, and one for the other passengers. The line for the cabin crew begins before the plane takes off, and terminates before the intended conclusion of the flight, thus forcing the interruption of the other lines.

Although they are not shown, two clocks are present. One displays the departure time for the flight; the other keeps track of how long the cabin crew can work.

A musical analogy can help us experience Holdrege's situation. In your imagination (or on a real piano), place the five fingers of your left hand over any five keys. Then bring your hand down vigorously (the takeoff). Listen to the sound of the chord (the muffled roar of a plane in flight). Then lift your fingers for the landing. Now do the same thing, but this time, let's assume that your middle finger grows tired in midflight and has to be replaced by a finger from your other hand. You can immediately see the problem. What if that finger was busy playing another chord? And even if it wasn't, the replacement would have to be done smoothly or the chord representing the plane in flight would be disrupted.

The chord is an important image. It reminds us to *think vertically* and to look for what is already visible in the present. Even in the simplest situations, the number of paths and trajectories we have to keep track of is greater than we might have thought. In this example, it's five. That is certainly more than our mind, limited by Copland's Constraint, would prefer. But there was another barrier that Holdrege needed to overcome—namely, the power of habit. He was used to seeing cabin attendants go about their tasks. He didn't think about the fact that all roles and visible actions have a temporal infrastructure that accompanies and supports them. He would recognize the description I have given of the temporal architecture of his flight. Still, thinking vertically and taking account of serial constraints would not be a part of his usual way of making decisions. That would require using the polyphony lens.

a. M. L. Wald, "When Can You Deplane Early?" *New York Times*, September 5, 2004, Practical Traveler sec., 2.

Look for Influence: How Does One Parallel Process Affect, Cause, or Influence Others?

After you have considered issues of alignment and overlap, the next step is to think through how the different events or processes might influence one another. Although not comprehensive, the following sections are a useful starting point for thinking about influence.

Causation or Creation

One action can cause or create another. For example, the solvency of some institutions, including banks, depends on the confidence of others. So when reality looks bleak, the leaders of financial institutions often express confidence in the future. To do otherwise would create the very conditions they seek to avoid—a panic and a further loss of confidence. However, if conditions worsen, the same leaders will be blamed for not disclosing how dire the situation was in the first place. The result is that when a crisis does emerge, it will often seem to appear "overnight" (the maximum speed of the fastest process is very fast), when, of course, the conditions that created it were long in the making. What is said or not said on one track (by one group) defines and creates the reality on another track (for another group).

Competition

It is not uncommon for individuals within a company to compete to secure resources—whether funding, technology, or manpower—for projects. Yet, when competition is extreme, it can divert attention from external opportunities. When there is turmoil inside a company, expect managers to miss or mistime market opportunities, particularly when those opportunities are unexpected or fleeting. Knowing when to act requires paying attention to one's environment, and that includes the dynamics of internal competition.

Cooperation

Different firms influence each other through cooperation in any number of ways, such as when they cooperate to establish industry standards or collaborate to fund the same lobbying effort. Internally, different functions within an organization, such as R&D and marketing, may pursue their own interests, but they must also cooperate to some degree if the overall goals of the organization are to be met.

Masking

One ongoing process can mask another. For example, Anthony Harris, director of the Criminal Justice Program at the University of Massachusetts, noted in 1997 that whereas the rate of aggravated assaults "skyrocketed by several hundred percent over the past four decades, the murder rate has remained flat, never increasing or decreasing by more than 50 percent."[22] The reason given was that "the murder rate is being artificially suppressed because thousands of potential homicide victims each year are now receiving swift medical attention and surviving. Americans, in other words, aren't any less murderous—it's just getting harder for us to kill one another." Recent shootings with assault weapons may have tempered that view, but improved emergency care and response time save patients from becoming murder statistics. In short, the number of murder attempts may have been on the rise (track 1), but better treatment (track 2) allowed more victims to survive. The latter trend masked the former. In order to discover this fact, a single category of action, like a murder, which we assume occurs at one point in time (cat-point thinking) should be viewed as the consequence of a sequence of actions that develop on different tracks.

Amplification

When different actions or events occur at the same time, one can amplify or intensify another. For example, if everyone cuts back on spending at the same time during a recession, that collective action can make the recession worse. There are also predictable times when we can expect amplification. During elections, for example, politicians will express concern about issues, such as obscenity in the media, so as to inflame the passions of a certain segment of the electorate. When the election is over, those issues will fade away.

Cancellation

Two parallel processes may cancel each other out. Military analyst Daniel Ellsberg recalled a conversation he had with Secretary of Defense Robert McNamara during the Vietnam War.[23] The question at the time was whether Washington's efforts at pacification were working. Ellsberg said that things were the same as a year ago. McNamara, for his part, pointed out that they had added a hundred thousand troops in that time and nothing had changed—meaning that the situation had in actuality gotten worse.

Imitation and Entrainment

There are many examples in which one process imitates another. One reason George Mitchell succeeded in negotiating a peace agreement in Northern Ireland in 1998, for example, may have been the precedent set by the peaceful transition away from apartheid in South Africa in the early 1990s.[24]

By entrainment, I mean a situation in which one process mirrors the rhythm of another. For example, a few years ago, the French decided to address their unemployment rate. Their solution: reduce the workweek to thirty-five hours. The strategy was simple. If companies wanted to maintain the same level of productivity with shorter hours—which they did—then they would have to hire more workers. After all, productivity equals the number of workers multiplied by the number of hours they work. Therefore, if productivity is to remain the same and if the number of hours each worker works goes down, then the company must hire more workers to make up the difference. *C'est logique!* (It's logical.)

But it didn't happen. When work was slow, companies gave workers time off, and when demand picked up, they asked employees to work more hours without overtime. Over the course of the year, the hours they worked averaged out to thirty-five per week, but the number varied from week to week and month to month. What the companies did was to synchronize two rhythms: the changing need for workers during the year with their ability to regulate the supply over time. The French, I should point out, finally abandoned their thirty-five-hour workweek experiment—without regret, as Edith Piaf would say.

Control

Some patterns control or govern others. Think about how much of our work and nonwork lives are controlled by the clock and calendar, for example. Control over time is one of the most powerful forms of control we have. The Nazis even had a word for it, *Gleichschaltung*, "the attempt to bring all of society into line, to synchronize it according to the imperatives of a totalitarian regime, to bring it into a unified time and beat."[26] In addition, every bench scientist I know will complain at some point about financial and bureaucratic controls that limit his or her creativity and make discovery difficult.

Substitution

One track can substitute for another. For example, a broadly diversified company will try to focus Wall Street's attention on its one business that is succeeding when the others are losing money.

Exchange or Market

Multiple tracks can come together to form a market or network, as when individuals, groups, or firms from different tracks buy from and sell to one another as part of a supply chain.

Engagement

Companies engage with each other to varying degrees. In some cases, a company may be only vaguely aware of what another is doing. In other cases, it may decide to actively monitor the other's activities. In still other instances, it may decide to actively compete with or influence what another firm is doing.

Independence

Not everything is connected. Some activities and streams of action do not influence each other at all. They simply coexist. My favorite example comes from a prose poem by the influential Russian painter Wassily Kandinsky:

> Once upon a time, a man in Weisskirchen said: "I shall never, never do that." At exactly the same time a woman in Mühlhausen said: "Beef with horseradish."[27]

Perhaps in some quantum-mechanical way, those two actions are related. But for practical purposes, I think it is safe to assume that they are quite independent of each other.

■ ■ ■

We have been using the polyphony lens to look at the external environment. Now, take a moment to write down three or four actions or events that are part of your life and work. Ask yourself two questions: (1) What is going on at the same time? and (2) Which things are happening separately? In addition, how do these different actions or processes influence each other?

Let's suppose that firms A, B, and C are competing for the same customers. The competition is intense. But while that fight is going on, another set of actors (firms, lobbyists) are actively trying to influence proposed regulations that will affect the entire industry. Firms A, B, and C may be so focused on competing with each other that they fail to follow these developments and so are unprepared for the change that is coming.

The goal of the polyphony lens is to examine relationships (in terms of both structure and influence) among the many processes and events that are going on at the same time. We do this informally all the time. This chapter is simply an invitation to undertake this process much more systematically and completely.

POLYPHONY-RELATED RISKS

Every day, we hear about the ups and downs of the Dow, but little about the billions of transactions that take place on other largely opaque exchanges and markets. In fact, there is a lot going on that is invisible to the average investor. For example, suppose someone told you that you could buy a security in units of $25 that returned a monthly interest payment for as long as thirty years at a guaranteed rate between 3 and 8 percent, and at the end of thirty years you could get your money back. It sounds too good to be true … and it was. Yet Wells Fargo, the bank who offered it, says that it fully disclosed the risks involved to investors. The problem was that circumstances changed in ways no one anticipated. Newly passed legislation intended to reform Wall Street and protect consumers made it possible to terminate the securities on which this offering was based. The decision to do so was based on interest rates, and because few institutions were involved (the market was small), what one company decided to do affected everyone. In order to know what the real risks were, an investor would have to monitor changes in legislation, interest rates, and market size, and how all those changes taken together might be viewed by all the companies involved. No one was doing that.

Floyd Norris, who wrote about this situation in the *New York Times,* attributed the problem in part to the fact that Wells Fargo had a "contrary interest from its customers for the life of the security" and that it did not "clearly explain what could go wrong."[28] But the problem is not just mismatched incentives or a failure of explanation. One cannot explain what has not been adequately described. What is needed is a category called Polyphonic Risks, which describes the risks that arise when multiple actors each pursue their own self-interested course of action *at the same time.* Only that kind of polyphonic analysis will allow investors to assess the real risk of their investments.

Although we can't monitor every situation, event, competitor, or process, we can train ourselves to broaden our peripheral vision to include the effects of multiple streams of action as they interact and influence each other over time. When someone suggests that you, as an individual or institution, sponsor a project of some kind or make an investment, the question to ask is how many events, actions, or activities will be going on at the same time and how their interrelationship might affect the outcome you desire.

Even in physical structures, such as bridges, synchronicity has an impact. According to engineer and author Henry Petroski, people do not usually walk in lockstep, but if the bridge on which they are walking begins to sway, they tend to synchronize their steps in an attempt to keep their balance. The result is a positive feedback loop, which makes the bridge sway even more. [29]

New York Times columnist Thomas Friedman believes that going forward we will encounter more instances of synchronous risk on a global scale, and he points to conflicts in the Arab world and Europe in 2012 as evidence. In the Middle East, he said, "this hyperconnectivity simultaneously left youths better able to see how far behind they were—with all the anxiety that induced—and enabled them to communicate and collaborate to do something about it." In the European Union, hyperconnectedness revealed "just how uncompetitive some of their economies were, but also how interdependent they have become. It was a deadly combination."[30] In both cases, the synchronous risk was a result of globalization and information technology moving the world from being connected to hyperconnected.

The question to ask in business is whether the same conditions of connectivity and interdependence will cause a spike in inflation if the world economies begin to recover at the same time. And with respect to timing, how much advance warning will we have relative to the lead time we need to manage this risk?

When we don't consider polyphony, we can draw the wrong conclusions. For example, the cash rebate website Extrabux did an analysis in 2012 to determine the best time for students to buy and sell their textbooks online. It found that August 20–26 and January 7–13, the beginning and end of the fall semester, were the best windows of opportunity. That's common sense. But what was interesting is what Extrabux discovered about the relationship between supply and demand. It found that prices online sometimes decrease as demand for the products increases.[31] Most of us believe that it should work the other way around: when demand is high, prices should rise, not fall.

We need to take a closer look to see why this phenomenon occurs and how it relates to polyphony. To do that we need to consider the actions of both buyers and sellers as they interact with each other over time. As the beginning of the semester approaches, students realize that there will be no market for their used books once classes are fully under way and that the professor might not assign the same book the following year. Sellers of a product nearing its expiration date will become increasingly desperate, especially if they need the money to buy their own books for the new semester. That's why, although there are more buyers, prices will be lower. Sellers must sell a product that has a short shelf life, and buyers arrive in large numbers to take advantage of the situation. It's all in the timing. In order to predict this effect, we need to imagine a polyphonic structure that describes multiple actors each pursuing a similar or different course of action at the same time.

POLYPHONY OPTIONS AND OPPORTUNITIES

In the same way that multiple overlapping events and actions pose risks, they can also create opportunities to innovate. Using the polyphony lens to improve timing can take a number of forms.

Adjust the Height

Any one of us can choose to do more (or fewer) things at the same time. Multitasking has personal costs as well as benefits. But at the organizational level, there are larger issues at stake. Acquisitions and divestments, which increase or decrease the number of activities a company needs to manage simultaneously, are height adjustments, as are decisions about outsourcing or global staffing, which change the number, kind, and timing of actions that must be managed simultaneously. Depending on the goals of a company, and its structure, choices need to be made between breadth and depth, expansion and focus. Subtracting height—engaging in fewer activities, which means fewer tracks—is as valid an option as adding more tracks to manage.

Modify the Structure

Considering different patterns of alignment and overlap (in roles and structure) may open the door to new opportunities. Entire industries have been created or contracted as a result of the Internet, for example, which eliminates the need for some of the traditional retailing features of business and brings customers closer to product creation.

Anytime one can work in parallel, rather than simply in sequence, there is an opportunity to save time and perhaps money. An example from the construction industry is what is called a design-build process. A design-build contractor is responsible for both the design and construction of the project, with the two phases overlapping. The overlap often reduces the time it takes to complete the project and saves money.

In medicine, bringing processes back in sync has led to innovative therapies. For example, even after a limb has been amputated, some individuals continue to be plagued by residual pain. Dr. Vilayanus S. Ramachandran, a professor of neuroscience at the University of California at San Diego, devised a simple method for eliminating the phantom pain.[32] He created a box with an angled mirror. When the patient places his hand in the box, he sees two arms, one the mirror image of the other. The patient is instructed to move his arm as if he were conducting an orchestra. His eyes see two arms moving, but he receives feedback only from the one. The brain becomes confused and simply shuts down the circuits that were involved, which removes the feeling of pain.

Boeing identified a business opportunity after falling out of sync with suppliers. In 1997, aircraft production had to be shut down for a month because parts weren't available following a flood of orders. This led to a year-end loss and \$2.6 billion in charges against earnings over two years.[33] Following that painful experience, Boeing decided to manage the problem by giving customers options. Customers could place a firm order, entitling them to a set delivery date, but giving them the ability to cancel or postpone within a year or so of delivery. Alternately, customers could choose what Boeing called a "purchase right," which guaranteed a price but no fixed delivery date.[34] A team at Boeing keeps a close watch on these different categories of customers and their shifting needs so that it can "award delivery slots to important or inpatient clients in the event that certain customers get in trouble and don't want the planes they had sought." In effect, Boeing implemented a polyphonic multilevel design by monitoring what was happening to different categories of customers over time as the environment changed.

Use Influence

Some polyphonic options involve how one process influences another. Think about the amount of capital that banks must keep in reserve. Too much will hamper the legitimate activities of the bank: it won't be able to lend, which will harm the economy; but too little will leave the bank vulnerable in a time of crisis. Charles Goodhart, a professor at the London School of Economics, proposed a solution to this problem that involved polyphony.[35] He suggested that regulators should track the pace of loan growth and the rate of increase in asset prices. When these move sharply above trend, banks need to find more capital. In effect, Goodhart argued that the way to manage and regulate a dynamic system was to monitor critical variables as they change in relationship with each other over time. One variable would influence another.

You can utilize information about how one process can influence another in any number of ways. For example, a study led by Dr. William Keatinge of Queen Mary and Westfield College in

London compared health and climate records in Europe and discovered a relationship between changes in temperature and the incidence of coronary thrombosis and strokes. Coronary thrombosis cases peaked two days after drop in temperature; strokes peaked five days after a drop. According to the *Economist*, the data were used to create "a computer model that combined meteorological, demographic and medical data to predict demand for medical services. A four-week trial ... resulted in operating savings of £400,000."[36]

■ ■ ■

As you think about polyphonic risks and opportunities, remember that the trick is to suspend your usual classification system, which can be overly narrow. The issue before you may appear to be predominately one of finance, manufacturing, marketing, sales, global strategy, or, for that matter, climate change. But framing an issue exclusively in terms of any one of these categories can lead you to ignore its wider context. What matters, when it comes to timing, is finding and examining multiple, ongoing streams of action and events. That is what the polyphony lens is designed to do. The goal is to expand your peripheral vision, which is where unnoticed risks and opportunities are to be found.

THE TEMPORAL IMAGINATION

One of the most frustrating conditions is waiting. You have arrived at a destination, but another person, or something you want, need, or depend on, has not. You have to wait, and if you are in a hurry, the time you spend waiting can be painful. That was the case at the airport in Houston. Passengers quickly arrived at the baggage claim, but their luggage did not. A classic polyphony problem: you exit the plane and proceed to the baggage claim. Your baggage is unloaded and transported to the baggage claim.

Which will get there first, you or your luggage, and by how much? In Houston, passengers got there first, and they complained about how long it took for their luggage to arrive, which was seven minutes on average.

The obvious solution was to get the luggage to the baggage area faster. I can imagine a small army of time-and-motion experts armed with clipboards and stopwatches, à la nineteenth-century efficiency expert Fredrick Taylor, monitoring and measuring every movement that was involved, perhaps even studying how baggage was loaded into the plane in the first place. But that was not the solution the airport implemented. Asynchronous risks, the risk that something will happen before or after something else, demand synchronous solutions. So what the airport did was to move "the arrival gates away from the main terminal and [route] bags to the outermost carousel. Passengers now had to walk six times longer to get their bags. Complains dropped to near zero."[37] It's not how long it takes to get your bags but synchronous arrival, seeing your bag come down the conveyer belt just as you arrive at the carousel, that makes for a happy passenger. The Houston solution took imagination and an understanding of polyphony, and it probably cost next to nothing.

POLYPHONY: IN BRIEF

The concept of polyphony draws our attention to the fact that many actions, events, and processes occur simultaneously, each with its own trajectory or path that it follows over time. The polyphony lens tells you where to look and what to look for:

Look vertically. Identify what is going on *at the same time* that could affect your work or business.

Look for structure. Note how simultaneous events, activities, and processes are aligned relative to each other. Which lead, lag, or overlap?

Look for influence. Explore how one event affects, causes, or influences others going on at the same time.

The following are risks and opportunities associated with polyphony:

- When four or more events overlap (Copland's Constraint), it is easy to miss the consequences of their interaction.

- Some events have synchronous requirements, meaning that certain conditions must be present together for a plan or activity to succeed. When these are not satisfied, the outcomes that depend on them will not happen.

- Asynchronous risks are the risks that an event may occur before or after another, when it would be better if they occurred at the same time. Making sure that some things occur together can be as important as keeping other things separate.

- When events overlap, one can mask or overshadow another, leading to mistakes or misinterpretation. If one division of a company is a market leader, for example, underperforming divisions within the same company can remain below the radar.

- Think about complex situations in terms of parallel processes or "tracks." How do events on one track affect events on another?

- Review important processes going on at the same time, and decide what you can stop doing so that you can focus on what matters most.

- Sometimes a new product can be created by inventing a process or product that can accompany and improve another ongoing activity—for example, Riedel glassware (discussed in Chapter Four).

seven

Using the Lenses

The Timing of Dissent

A "No" uttered from the deepest conviction is better than a "Yes" merely uttered to please, or worse, to avoid trouble.

—*Mahatma Gandhi*[1]

The first step in conducting a timing analysis is to learn to see the world through each of the six lenses described in the previous chapters. Doing so can bring into clear focus what is wrong in a situation and how it can be corrected.

Let me give you an example. It's the story of a small pharmaceutical company. A meeting has been called to decide whether to go ahead with marketing the company's new weight-reducing drug, Biritonin. As a participant in the meeting, you are painfully aware that a bad decision is about to be made. You know it is likely to end in disaster, but no moment seems right to object without putting your job on the line.

Here is a transcript of the meeting.[2] Those present include

Jonathon—president of the company
Bob—director of marketing
Sue—attorney
Fred—liaison with the government, also an attorney
Richard—head of R&D

1. Jonathon: All right. Now that Bob's here, let's start. We have only one item to discuss today, and I think we can wrap that up rather briefly: whether or not to proceed with the marketing of Biritonin, our new weight-reducing drug. Now, before we begin, there are some things I'd like to say rather informally. One of the reasons I'm excited about Biritonin is that it can allow us to continue the growth we've experienced recently. It can also allow us to increase our dividends to our shareholders. I know that some outside test reports have come in that are not completely positive, and I want these brought up-to-date. All right. I'll turn it over to you, Bob. Why don't you give us a quick rundown on the marketing?

2. Bob: Since you've all received my memo with the basic market strategy, let me just touch base on a few things. We project paying back our investment in fourteen months. After three years, we expect a $2.3 million cumulative profit, which represents a return on investment of 29 percent. Now, simply put, this means we could make a lot of money... and at the same time, we could make a lot of unhappy fat people a little thinner, a little happier.

3. Sue: What about the competition? Do we have anything to worry about?

4. Bob: Well, I think we've got the most effective product in Biritonin. I estimate a 20 percent share of market in two years.

5. Jonathon: Fred, what about the government? Have you got all the necessary clearances?

6. Fred: We're OK. Of course the FDA may reexamine after a year on the market, but for now we're free

and clear. The problem is those outside tests...
the unfavorable results ... well ... those FDA guys
love to be troublemakers.

7. Sue: Sure, it gives them good press—the government
protecting the poor taxpayer.

8. Jonathon: Richard, as the house pessimist, how do you read
those reports?

9. Richard: Obviously, my department wouldn't have recom-
mended Biritonin unless we felt it basically safe.
But still, some of these reports that came back
from that sample group of doctors aren't too
good.

10. Jonathon: What percentage, Richard?

11. Richard: What?

12. Jonathon: What percentage of the reports is negative?

13. Richard: Oh, very small, less than 5 percent.

14. Sue: How serious are the symptoms?

15. Richard: Oh, well, one doctor reported vomiting with one
on his patients. Another suspected blood clots.
One patient had dizzy spells.

16. Fred: Not very dramatic stuff.

17. Bob: Well, they sound like the kind of symptoms that
could be brought on by anything.

18. Richard: That kind of data is not very conclusive. Besides,
we pick our physician sampling at random. Why,
some of those doctors could be quacks or professional cranks. But we know we've got the best
people in our lab. They're the ones we ought to
trust.

19. Jonathon: Sue, do you see any liability problems?

20. Sue: Well, a lawyer always sees liability issues. The best
answer would be to test further.

21. Bob: Oh, my God! If lawyers had their way, the whole
drug industry would still be making just aspirin.

You've got to take some risks in this business. Besides, we're not selling Biritonin over the counter. It's a strictly prescription-only product.

22. Richard: Any doctor who doesn't feel sure about it doesn't have to prescribe it.

23. Sue: Not only that... We've built one of the finest reputations in the field by dealing squarely with the public. We're not about to endanger that with a faulty product.

24. Jonathon: OK. All right. Let's try to stay together on this. I'm sure Sue wasn't trying to upset the apple cart. Bob, what about this memo from Dr. Heller [the company's chief research scientist, who isn't attending the meeting]? He wanted to address the meeting. Did you talk to him about it?

25. Bob: That's why I was late. He caught me just as I was coming in. Conservative, as always... basically conservative. It was the usual stuff about wanting to test more, and so on. But being rushed as we were, I basically tried to relay the information. Otherwise we'd just be sitting here for thirty minutes listening to him.

26. Jonathon: Fred, he's in your group. What do you think?

27. Fred: The rest of the group is very confident. They've been very conscientious.

28. Sue: We don't have anything to worry about.

29. Jonathon: Anyone else? *(Pause)* All right, I guess it's unanimous. We go with it.

The meeting is fiction, the dialogue modified from an old black-and-white 16 mm film on group process. No drug company made this decision, but the dynamics that are present are all too real, as anyone in business can testify. The question is, what went wrong, and how could it have been prevented?

Let's take a moment to consider the risks the company is running. Given the number of people who are obese and a projected 20 percent market share, the number of people taking this drug is, forgive the pun, quite large. Side effects, some potentially lethal, were estimated to be "less than 5 percent," but 5 percent of a very large number is a very large number. With potentially hundreds of deaths, the company would be facing a PR disaster. The sales of its other drugs would be put in jeopardy as public trust in the company plummeted. The transcript provides no evidence of competitive pressure or financial exigency that would argue, or at least rationalize, moving full speed ahead. So the decision to market the drug without first hearing from Dr. Heller, the company's chief research scientist, is irresponsible. But, as the meeting unfolds, it seems extremely difficult to block the outcome. The lawyer tries and fails.

We have all been in meetings like this. Is there anything you could say that would postpone the marketing of the drug as well as get a nod of approval from everyone in the room, including Jonathon? For most people, that task seems like mission impossible. But as we will see in this chapter, it is not. The key is to examine the dynamics of the meeting through all six timing lenses. Each lens will help clarify why dissent is difficult. Once we identify the difficulty, we will be able to find ways to overcome it. I'll number each of these suggestions so that we can assemble them into an effective strategy by the end of the chapter. Let's begin by noting the risks the company is running by marketing the drug.

Soon after comment 15, when the negative side effects are first mentioned, it might occur to you to say something like the following:

(1) Now, correct me if I'm wrong, but didn't you say, Bob, that we expect a 20 percent market share in only a few years? That's terrific. That's an awful lot of people and an awful lot of

profit. [Pause] But it occurs to me that if even a small percentage of people experience serious side effects, we could face a serious problem. After all, a small percentage of a very large number is a very large number. We could have hundreds of people ill because of this drug, and if that happened, our entire company—all of our other products—would be affected. Our reputation would be on the line.

Unfortunately, this comment is dangerous because it threatens the authority of the president. There are many ways to think about power, but from a timing perspective, power means the ability control a number of temporal elements, specifically sequence, punctuation, rate, interval, duration, and shape.

- Jonathon can open and close the meeting at any time. He controls its length (duration), its beginning and ending (punctuation), and its pace (rate or tempo).
- The meeting has a back-and-forth shape as different participants speak and respond to each other. He decide who speaks and for how long (intervals).
- Jonathon can speak at length, any time, on any topic.
- He can expand or compress intervals and hence windows of opportunity. He can cut people off or demand a more detailed answer.
- Most important, Jonathon controls the sequence of the meeting. In fact, he has inverted the normal order of a decision meeting. To see how doing so limits dissent, let's look at the meeting through the sequence lens.

THE SEQUENCE LENS

Jonathon opened the meeting by saying, "We have only one item to discuss today, and I think we can wrap that up rather briefly." In effect, the decision to market the drug has been made. Everyone

Figure 7.1 Sequence Inversion

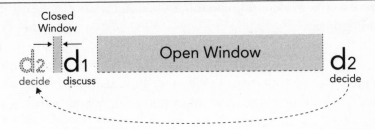

in the room knows it. I've diagrammed this state of affairs in Figure 7.1.

The normal sequence of events in a meeting such as this is to first discuss the matter under consideration and then, at the end, make a decision. The window is open for debate and discussion *before* the decision has been made, but not after. Once an issue has been decided, dissent is literally "out of order" (the closed window). Jonathon has inverted the normal sequence. As a result, any dissent is difficult and risky.

Sequence inversion problems, however, have solutions. I'll mention three.

Reinvert

Reinvert the sequence and open the window for debate by claiming that a decision has *not* been made. You could say, for example,

(2) I don't think we need to make the decision today, so I would like to reopen the question.

Such a statement, however, is a direct challenge to the president's authority. No one will make such a statement. Two other solutions stand a better chance.

Rescale

If the sequence "debate then decision" could somehow be ignored, then the problem of sequence inversion would not exist.

One way to do this is to look back from the distant future. Five years from now, who will remember the exact timing of events? So you might say,

(3) Well, the most important thing is not whether we make the decision today or next week. When we look back at this decision five years from now, the most important thing will be whether we got it right, not on what day or week we decided the issue.

Increasing distance, whether in time or space, diminishes our ability to distinguish objects and the time in between them. What we see as distinct close up merges and blurs at a distance.

Claim Irrelevance

The purpose of an action determines its timeliness. In this example, the meeting has two purposes. The first is to ratify a decision that has already been made. The second is to "be brought up-to-date." If the purpose of the meeting is the latter, then the issue of sequence inversion is irrelevant because no decision is required.

(4) But didn't you say, Jonathon, that the purpose of this meeting was to be brought up-to-date? We've been acting as if we have to make a decision now.

Nonetheless, redefining the purpose of the meeting is not without risk. Only those in authority can change the purpose of a meeting. A subordinate cannot, without being insubordinate.

THE PUNCTUATION LENS

The punctuation lens directs our attention to commas, pauses, periods, and other marks that segment the continuous flow of time. The following are a number of ways in which marks of punctuation and their placement can be used to help create the conditions for effective dissent.

Insert Punctuation

One reason individuals remain silent is not simply that they are afraid to speak or feel that they have nothing to say, but that the unfolding course of the meeting, and the flow of time itself, lack *intrinsic punctuation.* One moment follows the next, which blends with and follows the one before. And before you know it, the meeting is over. Punctuation has to be consciously inserted. For example, you could explicitly ask for a pause. You might say,

(5) Could we pause a moment and try to think this through?

Usually, only someone in authority can ask for a pause, which is why I framed the request as a question. Another option depends on timing. The longer the meeting goes on, the more complex the issues become, and the more it seems appropriate to say, "Could we pause for a moment to see where we are?" The answer can take the form of a summary, which becomes an opportunity to make the case for postponement.

Repunctuate

As you recall from the chapter on punctuation, an event, such as marketing a drug, can be grouped with the past or with the future. It can be seen as the last step in the long process of drug development, which one wants to bring to an end, or as the first step in a new marketing campaign, in which case caution prevails because first impressions matter. So if you want to slow a process down, you might say,

(6) We should get the first few steps right in order to create the right first impression in the consumer's mind. If we don't, it could take a long time to repair the damage.

Set a Deadline

Conducting additional research to determine the type, probability, and severity of side effects in different populations raises the specter of a process without end. From a business perspective, this is a fatal condition: the drug might never be marketed because no scientific study controls for every contingency and is ever 100 percent certain. In the context of this meeting, there are two possible solutions. One involves punctuation. The other references an interval, which, by comparison, makes a short delay worth it. For example, you could say,

(7) While it makes sense to look into these side effects, we don't want to be held up forever. Let's get an estimate of how long it will take to get some reasonable closure on this issue, and then set a deadline. Then we should weigh the risk associated with that kind of delay against the time it would take us to recover if the drug turns out to have more serious side effects than we anticipated.

Use Punctuation to Create Boundaries

When there is a clear and strong punctuation mark, like the decision to market the drug, you can emphasize how things change from before and after that boundary is crossed. Thus someone who wants to postpone the marketing of the drug might say,

(8) Once the drug is out there, a lot of things will be out of our control; we will have additional public scrutiny. If the side effects turn out to be more serious than we think, will the public continue to trust us? Lack of trust could threaten our entire product line. It is prudent to pause. Marketing the drug is a big step.

Affirm Common Values

The path between making an objection and, as a result, being marginalized or rejected as a member of a group can be a slippery slope. One statement leads to another, and before you know it, your comments are viewed as not helpful. The path from giving constructive criticism to being seen as a troublemaker has no clearly marked boundaries. One approach to the lack of punctuation is to affirm common values. Doing so makes it more difficult for others to reject you as a valued member of the group, even if your views challenge their own. So you could say,

(9) Well, it's clear to me that we all want this product to succeed. If we dot the i's and cross the t's, we can smile all the way to the bank.

THE INTERVAL AND DURATION LENS

One reason dissent is so difficult is that Jonathon has implied that the decision has already been made. From his point of view, postponing the drug is not desirable: it is not the outcome he wants. However, there are two intervals associated with the ED2 + R sequence, introduced in Chapter Three, that will allow Jonathon to save face and declare the meeting a success. The first interval precedes the ED2 + R sequence. It is the time between when a warning is issued and when the conditions warned about occur or exist. If the information about side effects were seen as part of an early warning system that worked, that would allow the meeting to be considered at least a partial success. For that "framing" to work, however, a warning must not be too early (the "time until" the expected crisis must be relatively short). Otherwise, the warning would be seen as premature or perhaps be dismissed as a false alarm. Here's one way to solve the problem. You could say,

(10) Now if Bob is right . . . we will achieve a very large market share very quickly. But the greater the market share, the greater our risk if there really is a problem with side effects. The irony is that the more we are successful, the more we have a problem.

And that problem . . . could affect our next fiscal year in a very significant way. It seems to me that if we are this close to that much risk, it's prudent to invest no more than a few weeks as an insurance policy to make sure that these side effects are not the tip of the iceberg. What we really have here in this data is an early warning system that worked. Maybe it is a false alarm, but I am certainly glad to find out now rather than later when it is too late.

Another way to think about the situation in terms of intervals is to use the R term of the ED2 + R sequence. Early warning gives you more time (a longer interval) to <u>r</u>esolve any problem that exists. It also helps you avoid the synchronous risk of having to deal with troubling side effects just when other issues might surface to demand your attention. So you might say,

(11) I don't think these side effects will turn out to be anything, but if we look into them now, we can get a head start on addressing them. By starting early, we won't have the added difficulty of trying to deal with a potential public relations disaster at the same time that we are dealing with other issues.

Highlight a Point of Order
The intervals of the ED2 + R sequence are also important for another reason. All meetings come with a defining set of norms and values. When a critical norm is threatened, whoever detects the threat first should immediately inform others. The time between <u>d</u>etection and <u>d</u>isclosure should be as short as possible. That is what a "point of order" is for. It identifies a threat that can be fatal to an orderly process. For that reason, as Robert's Rules of Order make clear, a point of order is always in order.[3] It can be raised at any time. Thus a window opens to object whenever what is being done threatens a core value of the group.

(12) You know, as I listen to this discussion, there is a critical principle that I think we have always believed in, and that is, we

don't rush to judgment. But at the same time, we don't sit around twiddling our thumbs. Either extreme would be a fatal.

Be Aware of the Passage of Time

We know from Jonathon's opening comment that the meeting is largely ceremonial; he expects it to be brief. Dissent risks prolonging it. There are two possible approaches to the problem of length.

Compression

Choose a strategy for expressing dissent that is known to be short, one that fits a small window. Here's an example:

(13) Well, let me for a brief moment play the devil's advocate. This is an important decision, and it is important that we look at all sides of the issue. If Bob is right and the drug has a potentially very large market, then the number of potentially serious side effects is also very large . . .

Playing the devil's advocate does not take long. It is a time-limited ritual and has the advantage of any well-established habit. It is a well-traveled path. There will be no surprises or long delays. Playing the devil's advocate is therefore fast. It is also widely accepted. It is understood as a helpful tactic used to advance the group's goals and objectives, not undermine them.

Elimination

Signal that you know that there are severe time constraints.

(14) Let me just skip to what I think is the central point here.

Focus on Time Until

In Chapter Three, I discussed the difference between "time since" and "time until." The time since the drug has been under development is long, but the time until a problem might develop is short. One could therefore say the following:

(15) It seems to me that if we are *that close* to so much risk, it's prudent to invest a few weeks as an insurance policy to make sure that these side effects are not the tip of the iceberg.

Use the "Last Chance" Rule

A common timing rule is this: take advantage of your last chance. But this rule, which might have triggered action, cannot be applied here because no one except Jonathon knows *how long the meeting will last.* The last-chance rule also runs into another problem. Everyone knows that an objection should not be raised at the last moment. "Why didn't you speak up earlier?" someone will say. One could modify statement 14 by saying,

(16) If it not too late to volunteer for some extra work, just let me say that I'm happy to follow up on those few reports, because if there is any substance to them whatsoever, that would clearly affect our marketing strategy in a profound way. Probably a waste of time, but I am happy to do it.

It is never too late to take on an additional work.

When we look at this meeting through the interval lens, we see what is missing—namely, a way to know how close the meeting is to reaching a final decision. If you knew when that moment would occur, you would know how long you could wait for someone else to make the case against marketing the drug before you would be forced to do so. But the clock that governs the pace and length of the meeting is not to be found on the wall or on anyone's smartphone. The only clock that matters is inside Jonathon's head. Only he can see it, and only he can tell you what time it is. In fact, he already has. According to Jonathon's *subjective clock*, the time for a decision has already passed.

THE RATE LENS

The rate lens and the interval lens give us two views of the same phenomenon. What moves quickly, takes less time; what moves slowly, takes more. So what one sees through the interval lens, one can also see through the rate lens. But like two tools that perform the same job, one tool may feel more natural or, for some inexplicable reason, may be the source of more creative ideas and solutions than the other. We all have our personal preferences. Sometimes using different language to describe the same phenomenon provides the "aha" that was missing. So here are some brief observations about the meeting as seen through the rate lens.

From Jonathon's introductory comments, we know that he expects the meeting to be short. As a general rule, short meetings are also fast paced. That is their *normal* speed: no pauses; no long periods of silence; no time-outs to regroup, recharge, or reflect. It is always useful to know the normal speed of any situation you must manage. That way you can come prepared to lead a rapid-fire exchange of views or a long, drawn-out, mind-numbing marathon filled with detailed charts and graphs.

When I think about how quickly something might happen or how long something might take, I always find myself coming back to one cell in the Rate Envelope (see Table 4.1), the one that asks about the *minimum speed of the slowest process*. Decision making will be slow if an issue is complex and requires careful consideration. But it can't be allowed to drag on so long that it seems as if a decision will never be made. Anyone who plays Hamlet in the boardroom won't last long. It will be his final act. So if we think about the normal speed of a short meeting and the normal speed of a thoughtful decision process, we know there is a conflict. If the issue is complex, either we must agree that a decision has already been considered and made or agree to extend the time to make it.

In the rate and interval chapters, I mentioned that different stakeholders might interpret the same rate or interval differently.

For the lawyer, postponing marketing the drug might avoid a problem. But for the director of marketing, it could mean finding that another company has beaten him to the punch by announcing a new "breakthrough" drug for obesity. In deciding how and when to argue for a delay, it is always wise to know how others will interpret a longer, slower process.

THE SHAPE LENS

There are five shapes that describe the dynamics of the meeting: cycles, lines, the helix, the point and fan, and the dramatic arc. Thinking about these shapes will give you another way to understand why an objection to marketing the drug is difficult, and how those difficulties can be overcome. For example, because the meeting is intended to end with a decision, the underlying metaphor is that of a scale on which different arguments, pro and con, will be placed. That is why the devil's advocate ritual is accepted: it helps place items on the scale, which we can think of as a divided line or seesaw. An action is timely if it fits with the shape of what is being referenced at the moment.

Cycle Strategies and Tactics
Jonathon will want to hear from everyone at least once as his or her expertise becomes relevant. The meeting, therefore, requires at least one full cycle before a decision can be reached. The number of cycles, however, will be small. We would not expect the discussion to go round and round endlessly. There are a number of ways you can use the cyclical shape of the meeting to argue that marketing the drug should be postponed. By keeping track of who has and has not spoken, you can decide how best to time your objection—before or after a known point of view. For example, because you can predict what the lawyer will say and how marketing is likely to respond, you can state the lawyer's position and refute it before she expresses it, or wait to respond

until after she has spoken. Knowing that there is a cycle also gives you information about how close the meeting is to ending—that is, how much time remains for you to make your point. After everyone has spoken once or twice, you know that the window for dissent is rapidly drawing to a close. Hence, be prepared to act.

Straight Lines and the Helix

The best way to keep a meeting short and on track is to proceed in a straight line. One topic should lead to the next; there should be no detours, no pauses, no interruptions, and no coming back to the same issue over and over again. When our world becomes complex, we hunger for simplicity, for the appeal of a straightforward linear process, even if one has to pause between steps. However, this meeting curves. The discussion, as it moves forward, circles back through all the necessary points needed to make a decision (marketing, government clearance, side effects, and so on). The underlying shape of the meeting is therefore not a straight line but a helix. The twists and turns of that shape, experienced as the meeting progresses, support an argument to pause and investigate side effects now, because those in the meeting are viscerally experiencing how unpleasant it is to go back and revisit an issue that could have been resolved earlier.

The Point and Fan

As the group looks into the future, it knows that if side effects become a problem, it will face a choice about whether to withdraw the drug from the market. It will have to manage the negative publicity that comes with serious side effects. It will have to make sure that its other products are not harmed. There will be a lot to consider. The choices the company will face will multiply and come to resemble a point-and-fan diagram as one choice leads to another. The more the future looks like a point-and-fan diagram, rather than a single straight-line path from product launch to profit, the more uncertain the future seems, which leads to the following timing rule: in the face of great uncertainty, proceed slowly and with caution.

The Dramatic Arc

The dramatic arc is important in understanding the sense of urgency that Jonathon and Bob feel in getting the drug to market. For most drugs, the development process is long. Rewards come only at the end. Thus, by the time the meeting is called, everyone needs the release and reward that marketing the drug provides. Ideally, the rise and fall of tension surrounding the development and marketing of a drug should follow the shape of the dramatic arc. Tension builds during development and is released during marketing. A pause to investigate side effects puts a dent in this shape and postpones the anticipated moment of release. When you know what a group will find frustrating, you are better prepared to help them work through it.

THE POLYPHONY LENS

The polyphony lens directs our attention to the possibility of parallel processes. You could suggest that two activities go on at the same time:

(17) Let me volunteer to follow up a bit with Heller. I don't think there is anything to it, and we should certainly proceed with the marketing. I'll let you know right away if I find anything. I think it's unlikely, but it is a good idea to retain Heller's goodwill. He's one of the best scientists we have.

Comment 17 extends the decision-making process beyond the boundaries of the meeting. The meeting ends, but another process continues. This is the continuity component of the SJPCW sequence that I discussed in Chapter Two, on punctuation. A follow-up means that a second process will go on in parallel with the decision to market the drug.

Delay in marketing the drug as side effects are investigated is not the most desirable outcome. But the cost of a delay is more than balanced by its potential benefit, catching a mistake before it is too late. You can also partially offset the cost of a delay by being willing to assume the burden for having caused it.

PUTTING IT ALL TOGETHER

Some reasons why dissent is difficult are constants in the sense that they are always present. (For example, Jonathon's comment at the beginning of the meeting that suggests that the decision has already been made.) Other reasons are present at certain points and absent at others. For example, only one person can speak at a time, and it is difficult to interrupt. So if someone else is speaking, you can't, and vice versa. Other forces increase or decrease in strength over the course of the meeting. Jonathon indicated that the meeting was to be brief, so the longer it goes on, the more it violates his expectation, and hence the more difficult it is to say anything that would prolong it.

There is always a reason to remain silent, which leads to what I call *the tragedy of the temporal commons.* When you examine the transcript line by line, you will find compelling reasons to remain silent at every point in the meeting. But complete silence courts disaster. So what is sensible for each moment is not sensible for the collective (for all the moments). So, what to do?

In managing any complex situation, no single action is likely to be sufficient. The same is true of this meeting. No single statement is likely to be effective. You will need to assemble the components that were revealed through the six lenses into a sequence strategy. Here is an example.

(9) Well, it's clear to me that we all want this product to succeed. If we dot the i's and cross the t's, we can smile all the way to the bank. (1) Now, correct me if I'm wrong, but didn't you say,

Bob, that we expect a 20 percent market share in only a few years? That's terrific. That's an awful lot of people and an awful lot of profit. [Pause] But it occurs to me that if even a small percentage of people have serious side effects, we could face a serious problem. After all, a small percentage of a very large number is a very large number. We could have hundreds of people ill because of this drug, and if that happened, the entire company—all of our other products—would be affected. Our reputation would be on the line. (4) But didn't you say, Jonathon, that the purpose of this meeting was to be brought up-to-date? We've been acting as if we have to make a decision now . . . (3) The most important thing is not whether we make the decision today or next week. When we look back at this decision five years from now, the most important thing will be whether we got it right, not on what day or week we decided the issue. (10) Now if Bob is right . . . we will achieve a very large market share very quickly. But the greater the market share, the greater our risk if there really is a problem with side effects. The irony is that the more we are successful, the more we have a problem. And that problem . . . could affect our next fiscal year in a very significant way. It seems to me that if we are this close to that much risk, it's prudent to invest no more than a few weeks as an insurance policy to make sure that these side effects are not the tip of the iceberg. What we really have here in this data is an early warning system that worked. Maybe it is a false alarm, but I am certainly glad to find out now rather than later when it is too late. (7) [And] while it makes sense to look into these side effects, we don't want to be held up forever. Let's get an estimate of how long it will take to get some reasonable closure on this issue, and then set a deadline. Then we should weigh the risk associated with that kind of delay against the time it would take us to recover if the drug turns out to have more serious side effects than we anticipated. (8) Once the drug is out there, a lot of things will be out of our control; we will have additional public scrutiny.

If the side effects turn out to be more serious than we think, will the public continue to trust us? Lack of trust could threaten our entire product line. It is prudent to pause. Marketing the drug is a big step.

■ ■ ■

In Chapter One (Sequence), I mentioned Julio Cortázar's novel *Hopscotch,* in which he gives readers a choice of the order in which to read the chapters of his book. So here are some suggestions for other sequence strategies. Each responds in different ways to what is going on in the meeting, including what is not contained in the transcript, other facts about the company and the individuals involved, their the nonverbal cues, and so on.

Sequence: 5, 1, 4, 10, 8
Sequence: 1, 7, 11, 17
Sequence: 14, 1, 10, 11, 8

I'll let you decide whether any of these sequence solutions would work given the dynamics and organizational culture present in this particular meeting. What is clear is how much closer we are to an effective strategy compared to where we were after reading the transcript at the beginning of the chapter. Using the lenses has given us a window into the largely invisible temporal structure of the meeting and allowed us to fashion a beginning response to the problem of dissent.

LESSONS LEARNED

The example in this chapter provides a number of lessons, not the least of which is that timing issues are not always obvious. The temporal structure of the meeting had to be uncovered. We needed the lenses to find out exactly why dissent was difficult and how those difficulties could be overcome. It is hard to deal with an enemy that is invisible. What's more, we needed all six lenses to see all the elements of temporal architecture that defined the structure of the meeting. When you find yourself making a decision based on only one or two elements—a looming deadline (a punctuation mark), for example, or how quickly something is changing (rate)—remember to consider others. They may warn you of risks or opportunities that you didn't know existed.

Although there are other ways to understand what went wrong in this meeting—poor decision making, inadequate leadership, groupthink, a flawed group process, an organizational culture that silences dissent, and so on—a timing analysis offers a unique perspective. It brings to the surface what other frameworks and models miss, or mention only in passing.

More than two thousand years ago, Aristotle watched ships disappear mast-first over the horizon, and realized—perhaps for the first time in history—that the earth was curved and not flat. If we had been the ones to notice that fact, how many of us would have dismissed it as an optical illusion, the bending of the light reaching our eyes rather than the bending of the land under our feet? Aristotle needed the principles of geometry to convert seeing into insight. That is what the timing lenses do— they reveal patterns that convert seeing into insight.

The analysis I have provided is intended to help those in subordinate positions find a way to prevent the immediate marketing of the drug. But it also holds lessons for anyone in power who wants to benefit from what his or her subordinates know and think. The question to ask is, Have you structured your activities in a way that creates a window of opportunity for others to safely express dissenting views? You can't rely merely on the goodwill or the courage of your subordinates to tell you what you need to know. You need to create moments when truth telling is possible, and that means, among other things, paying attention to timing.

You need to create the right conditions and the right moment. As in this example, when you know what closes a window, you can find ways to open it.

The next chapter offers a more structured approach to conducting a timing analysis. It breaks the process down into seven steps. As you go through them, your understanding of timing will deepen and grow more sophisticated. You will be much more likely to get the timing right.

eight

A Timing Analysis

Seven Steps

... not to give a specific answer, but to suggest a way of study.

—*Josef Albers*[1]

A timing analysis is a structured method designed to help you achieve a number of important goals.

First and foremost, it will help you find windows of opportunity. A timing analysis will clarify when the moment is favorable to act and when it is not. Next, it will help you predict the risks associated with action and inaction. Everything we do has timing-related risks. Some may not be obvious. We may be unaware of how quickly a situation can change, for example. A timing analysis will bring these risks to light. It will also help you determine the importance of timing in a given situation. Sometimes timing does not matter. In other situations, timing really *is* everything. Because managers are engulfed in what seems like a tidal wave of information, timing issues can get lost. A timing analysis will surface them. It will also help an executive decide how to proceed. Should she move quickly or slowly, perhaps pause before moving ahead, or match the pace of her own actions to the rhythm of external events, speeding up or slowing down as needed? I call these decisions about rate, punctuation, entrainment, and other elements of temporal architecture the choice of *temporal design*.

Done well, a timing analysis should convincingly confirm or challenge conventional wisdom and surface a wider range of options than is first apparent. It will also clarify what is vague or experienced only as an intuition or feeling in the gut.

A timing analysis consists of seven essential steps. I'll summarize each before going into a more detailed explanation of the process.

Step 1: Describe the Situation. Begin by describing the situation before you. Are there timing decisions involved? If so, what is your best guess about how they should be decided? When should you act, and when should you wait?

Step 2: Sketch a Score Diagram. Think about the situation you have described. What are all the things inside and outside your organization that are going on at the same time? Organize these overlapping events like the tracks in a musical score. (More on this later.) The goal is to see how simultaneous events and actions play out together. Use the six lenses from previous chapters to add detail and discover as much as you can about the "score."

Step 3: Probe More Deeply. Use the polyphony lens to examine two kinds of relationships among the tracks: what leads, lags, or is going on at the same time, and how one process or event influences another.

Step 4: Look for Windows of Opportunity. Windows have a number of characteristics, any one of which can be critical for deciding when to act.

Step 5: Identify Timing-Related Risks. What risks do you face? What could happen more quickly or slowly than you anticipate? What could happen out of order or at the wrong time in relation to something else?

Step 6: Evaluate Your Options. Review the analysis a final time
with a critical eye. I will provide a checklist to help you decide
what else should be considered before the analysis is complete.
Step 7: Act. Decide to act or wait based on the results of the timing
analysis.

As you work through these seven steps, keep in mind Einstein's
comment about simplicity—namely, that "everything should be
made as simple as possible, but not simpler." In conducting a
timing analysis, the devil is often in the details. Several steps are
complicated. The road through them has many twists and turns,
and the speed limit is probably no greater than 30 mph. If there is
a lot at stake, then there is good reason to take your time. There
is a lot to see and consider. But once you become familiar with
the methodology, the steps will become second nature. You will
discover shortcuts as well as substeps you can skip.

Keep in mind that a timing analysis is not a formula. It is a way
to probe and examine real situations to find answers to timing-
related questions. It works with "conditions on the ground"—that
is, with the details, uncertainties, and complexities that are present
in the messy world in which we live. Because managers are always
fighting fires, I'll to use an example from firefighting to illustrate
the seven steps.

Now let's consider each step in more detail.

STEP 1: DESCRIBE THE SITUATION

The first step in a timing analysis is descriptive. Describe the issue
before you in your own words. Every profession or discipline has
its own jargon. People in IT, marketing, and strategy each have
their own ways of thinking and talking about events. It is useful to
write down your initial impression so that you can add or adjust
details as you go along. This description should be no longer than
a few pages. Next, ask yourself: *Given what I want to accomplish, what*

timing issues will I face? Perhaps the issue is when to test-market a product, when to exit a failing business, or how to time a series of steps in a complex process. This initial description should focus on the big picture.

For the firefighter, the goal is to save lives and property. The timing question is how to act as quickly as possible in a manner consistent with safety.

Speed is important in many situations, yet we know from experience that there will be other factors to consider, other questions to ask, and decisions to make—for example, what things should be done at the same time, when is a pause required, can a particular step in a process be skipped entirely, and so on. You will discover these choices and options as you conduct the analysis. At the outset, simply begin by recording your current understanding of the situation.

What kinds of timing issues do you face? For each, list the factors that might affect that decision. Why is acting at one time better than acting at another? In the case of firefighting, the factors involved may include the size and location of the fire, the kind of building involved, whether people are trapped inside, the immediate weather forecast, and the like. This list will come in handy when you begin to sketch a score diagram.

STEP 2: SKETCH A SCORE DIAGRAM

We will use the vertical and horizontal structure of a musical score to create a visual representation or sketch of the factors involved in making a timing decision. (If you are not familiar with what a musical score looks like, examine the score from Beethoven included in the Introduction.) The parts played by different instruments are stacked vertically. The result is that when you look at a score, you can see what follows what (which note follows which), and what is going on at the same time (what chords and harmonies are present). The score diagram that you will sketch—no artistic or musical talent required—will be similarly organized. It will have a vertical and a horizontal dimension.

The act of sketching is important. I do not know why children draw, but I suspect one reason is that drawing is our instinctive response to a world we do not yet understand: we master it by giving it visual shape, a shape that we control. Drawing makes the world graspable; it puts it within the reach of our hands, our eyes, and ultimately our mind. It is the same with the patterns of temporal architecture (see the Appendix for a more complete description). We can't image and explore these patterns in our head. They are too complicated. We need to actually sketch or draw them. And although computers are useful for analytics and calculations, there is an awful lot we can learn with nothing more sophisticated than a pencil and the back of an envelope.

List the Relevant Factors Vertically

Begin by giving each independent factor its own horizontal line. You will remember from the polyphony chapter that these lines are called tracks. You can have one set of tracks for whatever is going on inside your organization, another for the actions of competitors, another for changes in government policy, and so on.

Add tracks for everything you think is important. I can't tell you how many tracks to include because every situation is different. This is where your own knowledge and experience come in. Obviously, you can't include a track for every factor or variable, every actor or stakeholder, but it is better to be overly inclusive at this stage than to miss something important. In my experience, most complex situations need at least two dozen tracks to capture what is going on. As a result, most diagrams will be tall.

Describe and Detail the Horizontal Tracks

Next, fill in what you know about each track. Examine them through the six lenses. Ask yourself about

Sequence: What do I know about the order of events? How do these events tend to develop over time?

Temporal punctuation: What are the punctuation marks for each event or action in the sequence? Where are the deadlines, beginnings, endings, holidays, elections, and so on?

Interval and duration: How much time will separate two events? How long will each take or last?

Rate: What is happening quickly or slowly? What is the minimum and maximum speed of the fastest and slowest process?

Shape: What shapes do I see? (Look for vicious cycles, bubbles, hockey sticks, and processes that start slowly and then rapidly accelerate.)

Firefighting: Sketching a Score Diagram

The following is a common sequence of actions that occur after a firefighter arrives at the scene of a burning house or building:[2]

1. *Ventilate the structure.* Firefighters make holes in the structure to allow the hot gases and smoke to escape.
2. *Search and rescue.* While the structure is being ventilated (and often before the first drop of water hits the fire), other firefighters break windows and begin to search inside.
3. *Use water to extinguish the fire.* Turn on the fire hoses.

In the score diagram in Figure 8.1, I have given each of these actions its own horizontal track. I have also added a track for the *fire* to indicate the changes in its intensity over time. Take the time to study the diagram. It's less complicated than it seems. It's simply that you haven't seen a diagram like it before.

Let's look at the diagram through each of the six temporal lenses we discussed in previous chapters. First, firefighting is a situation in which speed is of the essence. Hence the **rate** (indicated in the upper left-hand corner) at which various actions will be taken and events will occur is *prestissimo*, Italian for "really fast."

Figure 8.1 Conventional Firefighting Score Diagram

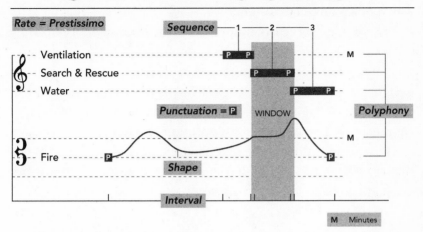

I like to put actions that I have control over in the top section of the diagram, and actions and processes that are part of the context and that I might not have control over lower down. I use the G clef (the S-shaped symbol) for the former, and the alto clef (one half of a figure 8.1) for the latter. Because many things are going on at the same time on different tracks, I have included a label for **polyphony**. I've placed a time line with tick marks at the bottom of the diagram to indicate important **intervals**. I also indicate that the timescale of the diagram is one of minutes (M), rather than hours or days, for example.

Each action has its own track. There is a track for ventilation, another for search and rescue, and a third for the use of water, which is the order in which these activities take place. As a general rule, I give each step or stage in a **sequence** its own track. As you follow each track from left to right, you will find marks of **punctuation**. Every action or condition has a beginning and ending, which can be abrupt or gradual. I use the letter P as a placeholder to remind me that punctuation may be important. Some fires, for example, may take a long time to fully extinguish.

Notice the intensity of the fire as it changes over time (**shape**). The fire will subsequently burn more intensely after firemen ventilate the structure and break windows, which provides the fire with a new source of oxygen.

The shaded vertical column defines the window of opportunity for conducting search-and-rescue operations.

What I have drawn is intended as a sketch. When architects design a building, they begin with a sketch rather than with a detailed set of engineering drawings. We are not after mathematical precision. Later, you can superimpose the normal grid of days, weeks, and months on the diagram, and include measurements that are more precise. But that should be the last step. Remember the mantra: *before precision, pattern.*

STEP 3: PROBE MORE DEEPLY

You now have a basic score diagram that represents a beginning attempt at capturing the essence of the situation you face. The next step is to explore, expand, and refine the diagram using two factors that I discussed in the polyphony chapter: structure and influence. We will begin with structure—the vertical relationships among the tracks.

Explore the Vertical Relationships Among the Tracks
Look at the different tracks in the score diagram and ask yourself:

- What is aligned and not aligned? Does the launch of a product correspond with a spike in demand for it, for example?
- Which tracks lead, lag, or overlap? Are three companies launching virtually identical products at the same time?
- Are there gaps, and do they matter? A company can struggle if there are long gaps between new products.
- Which tracks or parts of tracks are synchronized or out of sync with others? How are the internal systems within the company aligned or out of sync with changes in the market?

- How do the tracks influence one another? Do the contents of one track cause, mask, amplify, or compete with what is going on in another track?

A timing analysis draws your attention to the relationship between the horizontal and vertical dimensions of a situation. In most cases, you will not know at the outset which parts of the score will give you the most information about timing. It could be the realization that one step or stage must follow another, that two processes should not be allowed to overlap, or some other pattern. (Review the polyphony chapter for a more complete discussion of the ways one track can influence another.)

FIREFIGHTING: THE CONVENTIONAL WISDOM OF SEARCH AND RESCUE

As we can see from the score diagram in Figure 8.1, there is a period of time before additional oxygen causes the fire to intensify. Clearly, the longer this brief respite lasts, the better, because it gives firefighters time to find and rescue whoever may be trapped in the building. George K. Healy, a fire battalion chief in Queens, New York, said, "years ago you could break a window and it took the fire several minutes to develop—or tens of minutes."[a] Search-and-rescue specialists built that time into their operations.

a. J. Goldstein, "As Furniture Burns Quicker, Firefighters Reconsider Tactics," *New York Times*, July 2, 2012, A3.

Adjust the Size of the Diagram
Ask yourself:

- Have I included enough tracks and enough detail about sequence, punctuation, and so on within each track?
- Is my diagram "tall" enough?

- Is it also long or wide enough?
- Does it include enough of the known past and probable future to make sense of the situation?

If your answer to any of these questions is no, go back and add tracks and fill in the blanks.

When we don't look far enough into the past or forward into the future, we can be surprised by what happens. For example, everyone believes that good performance should be rewarded over bad performance. But we need to be careful about how we measure "good" and "bad" performance—and what effect that measurement will have on the outcome. For example, a California study of thirty-five thousand physicians who were graded on their performance revealed that some doctors dropped "noncompliant" patients and those with a poor prognosis or a complicated illness. In other words, they dropped patients who would lower their rating.[3] A score diagram that included a track for physicians and separate tracks for different types of patients might have identified the problem before the program was implemented. What is obvious after the fact should have been obvious at the beginning.

When something goes wrong, the proposed solution we hear most often is to tighten control—strengthen oversight or regulation. But that skips a step. The first step is *to better describe the situation to be controlled.* That includes taking into account what can change with the passage of time. To do that, you will need a score diagram that contains enough tracks, and long enough tracks, to capture all the important time-dependent phenomena. Everything we do takes time—happens before, during, or after something else. If we don't consider what doctors are likely to do *before* agreeing to see a patient or what their decisions might be *during* the course of treatment, the results of an intervention or change in policy may come as a surprise.

Ask yourself:

- What might happen in the future that will impact my business?
- What from the past continues to impact the present?
- What else is going on at the present time that I may have overlooked?

The fact that we operate in a global environment means that there are always more factors to consider. Ask yourself what would happen if the diagram you are working with were taller—that is, if it contained more tracks—and how these added tracks could change your decisions about timing.

FIREFIGHTING: THE CONVENTIONAL WISDOM CHANGES

Over time, as plastics have replaced cotton and other natural materials in the home, the situation for firefighters has changed in two ways.

First, "with more plastic in homes, residential fires are now likely to use up all the oxygen … before they consume all flammable materials. The resulting smoky, oxygen-deprived fires appear to be going out. But they are actually waiting for an inrush of fresh air, which can come as firefighters cut through roofs and break windows." The rate at which a fire uses up oxygen in the room before it burns up all of the flammable material (a rate difference issue) leads to an error of temporal punctuation—namely, a process one thinks is over, or almost over, is not.

Second, "plastics, like the polyurethane foam that is used as a filling in many sofas and mattresses, have drastically reduced the time it takes for a fire to heat a room to 1100 degrees, the point at which it will often burst into flames,"[a] leaving firefighters with much less time to search for survivors. The maximum speed of the fastest process has increased dramatically, leaving a smaller window of opportunity for search and rescue.

Figure 8.2 Firefighting Updated Score Diagram

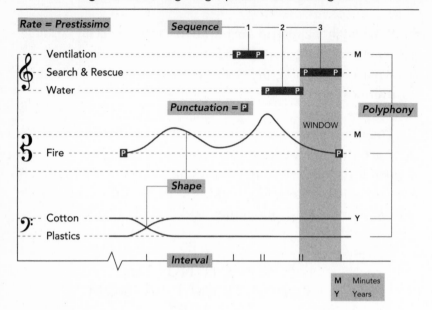

As depicted in Figure 8.2, firefighters are now rethinking conventional wisdom. In some cases, the best strategy is to hose down a fire before proceeding with search and rescue. The timing of this decision needs to be built into the firefighters' protocols.

This diagram is similar to Figure 8.1. The rate is still very fast; time is of the essence. You will, however, note several additions and modifications.

At the bottom of the diagram, next to the bass clef, I've added tracks for changes in flammable materials, guessing that the increase in plastics occurred gradually over a period of time and therefore wasn't noticed.

As a diagram gets taller, I use the G clef for events and processes in the foreground, the alto clef for tracks in the middle ground, and the bass clef for events and processes in the background. This is not a hard-and-fast rule. But it is one way to begin to organize what can become a very complex diagram. For example, the G clef can be used to describe what is happening in your team or group, the alto clef for what is going on in your organization, and the bass clef for what is happening in your industry.

To bring multiple timescales within the same diagram, I use a broken line with the appropriate timescale indicated beside each track (M for minutes and Y for years, in this case).

Adding changes in flammable materials and how they influence fire-fighting strategy results in a larger diagram, one that is taller (has more tracks) and wider (contains tracks that cover a longer time period).

The sequence has also changed, with the application of water now starting before search and rescue, as a result of the change in composition of flammable materials.

A gray column indicates the window of opportunity for conducting search-and-rescue operations. In this example, search and rescue begins and ends when the window for it opens and closes.

a. J. Goldstein, "As Furniture Burns Quicker, Firefighters Reconsider Tactics," *New York Times*, July 2, 2012, A3.

There is a lot to be seen through each timing lens. The firefighting example, simple as it is, illustrates the importance of determining the maximum speed of the fastest process (how quickly the fire can spread), noting the presence of termite tracks (the rate at which plastics replaced cotton), being aware of punctuation (when is the fire really over), and choosing the right sequence (search and rescue followed by water, or vice versa). Were we to look at the firefighting example more closely through each lens, additional issues would be revealed. For example, when I drew lines for ventilation, search and rescue, and the use of water, I didn't know how long each of these processes would last. How long should firefighters wait after drilling a hole in the roof to enter the dwelling? Maybe half a minute one way or another would make all the difference—or perhaps no difference at all.

As you use all the lenses, and add the details that they surface, you may find that the score diagram you are sketching is becoming too big and too complex. There are two strategies for dealing with complexity. The first is an organizing strategy. You can group the tracks. The second is to redraw the diagram using a more macro timescale. I describe both strategies here.

Group the Tracks
I have suggested that you use the G, alto, and bass clefs for tracks that describe the foreground (actions you can take), middle

ground (your immediate context), and background (the more remote context). Usually you have the greatest chance of influencing what is going on in your immediate environment—for example, inside your team or group. Few of us can affect the global economy. So one way to group tracks is according to what you can influence. Another way is to group them by importance. Which tracks are likely to have the greatest impact on the outcome you desire? You can also group tracks by rate or speed, putting the fastest tracks together. Another option is to group by stakeholder. There is no best way to group tracks. In fact, using different groupings will help you not only manage the complexity of the diagram but also gain greater insight into the situation you must manage.

Use Different Timescales

If a diagram becomes overly complicated, and grouping strategies are not sufficient, break off tracks and develop a separate diagram. Conducting a timing analysis is an art, so be prepared to move back and forth between focusing on a detail and working with the larger composition. For example, in the case of firefighting, you could sketch a detailed diagram just for the search-and-rescue portion, assigning a separate track for each individual and what he or she is doing at each moment. You can also redraw the diagram using a more macro timescale. If you have been looking at a business situation using one timescale, consider using another. If you plot sales every hour, you will see one thing. If you look at the pattern of sales month-by-month over the course of a year, you will likely see something else.

■ ■ ■

By this point you may have discovered everything that you need to know or have time for. Yet if you want to extract the maximum amount of information from the score diagram, there is more that can be done.

Modify the Diagram

Sometimes the best way to understand something is to change it. Here are three ways to further explore a score diagram.

Change the Direction or Magnitude of the Forces

Actions are always being pushed or pulled in one direction or another by different forces. Ask yourself: *What happens, for example, when a deadline is removed? How long will it take to finish a project without the pressure to complete it by a specific date?* In the firefighting example, suppose you hear a woman crying out for help just inside the front door of the building. You probably wouldn't wait for water cannons to douse the fire before attempting a rescue. Prescriptive rules about what to do (and when) can be overridden by the force of circumstance.

Change the Alignment of Tracks

Ask yourself: *What are the consequences of changing the alignment, overlap, leads, and lags among the different tracks?* In the firefighting example, when should water come first rather than last, and what impact would that have on the other tracks?

Vary the "Loudness" of Each Track

Try making some tracks louder or softer—that is, more or less important or prominent than others.

I had a conversation with a manager who had recently joined a company to head mergers and acquisitions. But soon after he arrived, a battle over CEO succession left little time or energy to consider mergers or acquisitions. The manager told me that he wondered if he had made a mistake. When there is a firefight going on inside a company, it will tend to consume the resources needed to find and exploit outside opportunities. When firefighters face a real fire, a prime consideration will be the number of people inside the building and their location. If and when that changes, so will their tactics and strategy.

Use the P4 Strategy

Some people think visually, others in terms of numbers or symbols. The score diagram is a visual image. Let me give you another way to think about it. When you sketch a score diagram, you are executing what I call a *P4 strategy*, which represents a movement from *point* to *path* to *polyphony* to *pattern*.

When you face a timing question, ask yourself: *What do I know now, at this* point *in time?* Then think about time-extended *paths*. Ask, *What sequences of events are playing out before me, both inside my group or company and in the larger environment?* The movement from point to path allows you to begin to envision the *horizontal dimension* of the score. Think about what follows what (sequences); where things begin, pause, and end (punctuation); how quickly they might develop (rate); how long they could take (duration); how much time separates the different events you have identified (interval); and what time-extended shapes, such as the rise and fall of the business cycle, are present that might influence your decision. Because we exist in a world of simultaneous events, think about what is likely to be going on at the same time (polyphony). That is the *vertical dimension* of the score. Then look for the *patterns* that are formed as these parallel processes play out together. Asking these questions is the verbal equivalent of sketching a score diagram.

STEP 4: LOOK FOR WINDOWS OF OPPORTUNITY

A timing analysis is designed to help you decide when to act. The gray columns in the firefighter diagrams point to an interval when search-and-rescue operations can be carried out safely. We often talk about windows of opportunity. *When* is the time favorable for what we want to do, and when is it not? The metaphor of a window suggests an interval, often brief. The implication is that if you don't act quickly, you will miss it and the window will have closed. But that is an oversimplification. Windows have other characteristics besides their length or duration. Here is what to look for.

Sign

Is a window of opportunity open $(+)$ or closed $(-)$? Sometimes it is just as important to know when a window is closed as it is to know when it is open. In the firefighting example, it is just as important to know when *not* to enter a building as it is to know when the time is right to do so.

States and Dates

When will a window open? *State rules* give one set of answers to the question. State rules are "whenever" rules. A window is open *whenever* a specified state or condition is present. For example, "Don't fire till you see the whites of their eyes" was a command issued by Colonel William Prescott during the Battle of Bunker Hill. We may not know when that time will occur, but when it does, FIRE!

State rules can refer to any element of temporal architecture. When is the best time to buy stocks? According to some analysts, wait until there are three or four rebounds, essentially an extended W—a shape-based rule. Sometimes the right time to act is just before a deadline (a mark of punctuation), because that is when people are preoccupied and one has the element of surprise. When you have found—or think you have found—a window of opportunity, note which feature(s) of temporal architecture are the reason you believe it is present.

The simplest timing rule is a *date rule*: act at a predetermined time or date. "The best time to do that is right at the end of the fiscal year."

In the firefighting example, all timing rules are likely to be state rules. Firefighters watch the fire, not the clock, to time their actions. In other contexts, such as law or accounting, date rules may predominate.

Length and Height

How long will the window remain open (its length), and to what degree (its height)? The latter indicates how favorable that period of time is for what you want to accomplish. Some windows can be raised only a crack. You may succeed if you act during that time period, but success is far from guaranteed. Other windows can be opened fully, even if they remain so for only a short period of time.

How long, and with what degree of safety, will firefighters be able to continue search-and-rescue operations? The answer depends on the height and length of the window.

Punctuation and Shape

Some windows, no matter their size, pop open and slam shut. Others open and close more gradually. It is always useful to sketch the curve that describes how the window opens and closes. Some windows may open so gradually that you don't even realize that there is a window of opportunity until a competitor takes advantage of it. Others open with a bang: everyone in the neighborhood knows there is an opportunity to be exploited.

Singularity

Is the opening of the window a one-time event (a singularity)? If not, when will it reopen? If you miss an opening, will you have another chance? And if so, when?

If firefighters are forced to exit a building engulfed in flames, when will it be safe to return?

Synchrony

What must be present (synchronous requirements) for the window to open? What must be absent (synchronous risks)? In the case of the latter, what conditions, if they occurred at the same time, would prevent a window from opening or force one already open to close?

In the firefighting example, the fire must be sufficiently contained that search-and-rescue operations can be conducted safety.

Assessing the Cost of an Error

Once you have found a possible window, ask yourself:

- What is the cost of missing it?
- What will happen if I am too early or too late?
- Does how early or how late matter?

To investigate this question, plot a cost-of-error curve (COE), as illustrated in Figure 8.3.

In this example, the cost of being early or late is not the same. The COE curve is not symmetrical. Clearly, you don't want to be too early. But if you are late, it doesn't seem to matter how late you are. The cost is the same: very high. An analysis of a window is not complete until you have plotted a COE curve.

In 2011, a firefighter was very badly burned in a brownstone fire that officials said "fed quickly on home furnishings and inrush

Figure 8.3 Cost-of-Error Curve

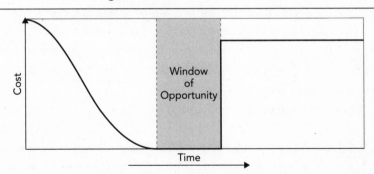

of air through open windows."[4] Yet delay in beginning search-and-rescue operations can cost lives. COE curves will always be on the mind of those fighting fires.

STEP 5: IDENTIFY TIMING-RELATED RISKS

Look at the score diagram you have sketched and ask yourself: *What timing-related risks does it surface?* There will be both element-specific and pattern-level risks.

Use the summaries at the end of each of the lens chapters to look for element-specific risks. For example, in a sequence, the risk is that something may occur out of order. You expect A to be followed by B, but B occurs first. Each element will have its own set of risks.

By pattern-level risks, I mean risks that result from the way two or more elements relate to each other or interact. In the firefighting example, we saw that a change from cotton to plastics affected when search-and-rescue operations should be carried out.

Clearly, the more you know about the risks related to your plans and projects, the better prepared you will be to avoid or manage them.

STEP 6: EVALUATE YOUR OPTIONS

Appraise and evaluate the timing analysis you have conducted. Ask yourself: *Has it surfaced timing issues that I didn't see originally? Has it helped me locate windows of opportunity and understand their characteristics?* Use the checklist here to assess the adequacy and completeness of your analysis.

A good timing analysis should help you

- Find the information you need for you to decide when to act. It should help you put your finger on exactly what matters.

- Decide whether the timing strategy or rule you started with (for example, act immediately) was the right one.
- Challenge or confirm conventional wisdom.
- Surface a wider range of options than were first apparent. Some may suggest creative or innovative solutions.
- Clarify the relationship between *what* you intend to do and *when* you intend to do it.
- Help you decide the importance of timing. Sometimes timing may not matter. Sometimes timing is everything.
- Clarify, confirm, or perhaps even challenge your intuition.

STEP 7: ACT

Act on the basis of what you have discovered: immediately if time is of the essence, later if you have determined that it is better to wait. Sometimes the answer to a timing question is obvious. At other times there is no choice. (Speak now, or forever hold your peace.) Sometimes timing may not matter because you have the power to do what you want anytime. Or perhaps one time is as good as another. There is no substitute for experience and good judgment. But there is one thing of which I am certain: when you conduct a timing analysis, you will discover that you know more about timing than you thought you did. You simply needed to access that knowledge and put it to good use.

Obviously, it is better to conduct a timing analysis before you act, rather than after. But even after the fact, conducting a timing analysis can be helpful. It can be used to defend a decision as timely even if the outcome was less than satisfactory. It can also be used to learn what went wrong and how timing was involved.

■ ■ ■

As you have no doubt observed, a complete timing analysis takes time and, to do well, training. We have all heard the term *analysis paralysis*—too much time analyzing, not enough time doing what needs to be done. A timing analysis, however, can actually speed up decision making. What was previously unknown and uncertain will, as a result of a competent timing analysis, be much better understood. When a situation is clarified, uncertainty becomes risk, and risk can be managed. In the face of uncertainty, we tend to be impulsive and act too soon, or we hesitate and act too late. Conducting a timing analysis improves the odds of getting the timing right the first time, and hence saves the time needed to correct a mistake, which can be considerable.

There is another reason why learning to conduct a timing analysis will save time in the end. What makes a timing analysis powerful is the fact that the same temporal pattern can exist in many different contexts. That means you can transfer what you learn from one context to the next. You don't have to reinvent the wheel. Recall the ketchup-and-Rogaine example I described in the Introduction. Both had to do with marketing and product design opportunities that came from seeing the underlying "sequence of use" for each product. Let me give you another example of the value of seeing the same temporal design in different situations. In this case, the issue is one of asynchronous risk—the risk that what should occur at the same time, doesn't.

Computer encryption. When we turn off our computers, the information stored in the DRAM (dynamic random-access memory) chip is supposed to disappear along with the algorithms (the keys) necessary to encrypt the data in the computer. Researchers at Princeton discovered, however, that "when the chips were chilled using an inexpensive can of air, the data was frozen in place, permitting the researchers to easily read the keys."[5] Essentially, one part of the computer turns off more slowly than the rest. The fact that one can retrieve data after the computer is turned off makes it possible to steal encrypted information.

The lost violin. On May 7, 2008, the Russian violist Philippe Quint got out of a cab at Newark Liberty International Airport.

He walked to the back of the cab, collected his luggage from the trunk, and moved it to the curb. He had already paid his fare. The cabbie closed the side door of the minivan and drove off. Unfortunately, Mr. Quint's $4 million Stradivarius violin was still in the backseat. According to Quint, he did not forget the violin. He left it in the cab for safekeeping while he moved his bags from the trunk to the curb. He intended to retrieve it, but the driver pulled away just as he slammed the trunk. After a number of frantic phone calls, the cab was located, and the violinist and his violin were reunited. A few days later, Mr. Quint returned to Newark Liberty and gave a thank-you concert for the taxi drivers.[6]

When a process is complete, we want everything tied up in a nice knot, no loose ends. If something is turned off, we assume that all components will shut down at the same time. When a cab fare has been paid, we expect the violinist to take his priceless violin with him as he leaves the cab. Asynchronous endings are common, however. Whether you are in charge of managing an exit, closing down a factory, discontinuing a product, or selling an organization, expect different components of the process to have their own pace and to last different amounts of time. When you have the concept of asynchronous endings in mind, you are better prepared to manage the difficulties such loose ends present.

And now, with these two stories, we are truly at the end of this book. There is nothing more that I have time to add. All that's left is the Coda.

coda

Re-Imaging the World

Coda: A concluding passage or section, falling outside the basic structure of a composition, and added in order to obtain or to heighten the impression of finality.

—*The Harvard Dictionary of Music*[1]

Finished, it's finished, nearly finished, it must be nearly finished.

—*Samuel Beckett*[2]

In 1936, Albert Camus wrote in *Notebooks* that "people can think only in images."[3] This is no doubt an overstatement, but images are important. We like to say that the world is more interconnected than it used to be. When we think about globalization, the eponymous image is that of a globe, a spinning sphere, overlaid with a network of interconnections of which the World Wide Web is a prime example. But that image simply traps us in a spider web of infinite complexity. Too much is going on in too many directions for us to make sense of it all. That is why I think a polyphonic score is a useful organizing image. In the past, when the United States was more of an unrivaled power, it could

239

call the tune. Weaker countries had no choice but to *accompany* (be in harmony with) what the United States was doing, or pay the price. That still is true, but to a lesser extent. With the rise China, India, Brazil, and the developing world, the United States becomes one player in a large polyphonic, polyrhythmic score. It is still a major player, but not the only one. Other countries want to decide for themselves what part they should play. They also have their own ideas of what the total composition should look like and how it should be performed and interpreted.

We need to move beyond spheres and networks, boxes and arrows, trees and branches (a common image for hierarchical organizational charts). These images have their uses, but they are limited. They will not help us get the timing right. Instead, I suggest that you imagine the world and the process of globalization in terms of a tall polyphonic musical score in which a large number of processes and events are playing at the same time.

In the musical score shown in Figure C.1, I have placed the beginning section of the national anthems of a small number of countries transposed so that they are in the same key as ''The Star-Spangled Banner,'' namely, D major. Borrowing from Dvořák, I call the resulting score *The New 21st Century World Symphony*.

If you play the national anthems of the United States, Canada, and Mexico at the same time and at the same volume, the U.S. anthem becomes clearly dominant toward the end. Play the French and German anthems together, and the result, to my ear at least, is simply noise. I have not tried other combinations, but when you play all the anthems together, to my surprise—and I take it as a hopeful sign—the result doesn't sound all that bad. It's not something I would want to listen to every day, but it is music, not just chaos or noise. At the very end, the composition sounds off-key for a moment, not quite right. But that's a relatively short interval.

I think there are a number of lessons we can learn from this musical score that are relevant to conducting a timing analysis in any situation.

Figure C.1 The New 21st Century World Symphony

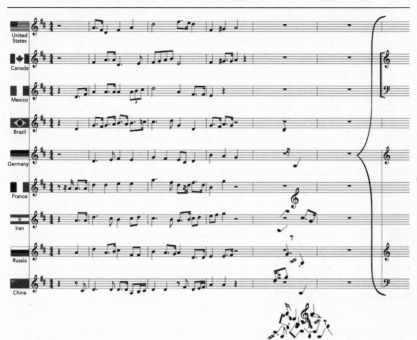

I included only nine out of approximately two hundred countries in the world, and only the first few measures of each country's national anthem. The image we hold of the world, and of the environment in which we act, will be very restricted unless we make efforts to enlarge it.

Mozart, as an example, could keep the whole in mind.

Provided I am not disturbed, my subject enlarges itself, becomes methodized and defined, and the whole, though it be long, stands almost complete and finished in my mind, so that I can survey it, like a fine picture or beautiful statue, at a glance. Nor do I hear in my imagination the parts *successively*, but I hear them, as it were, all at once [*gleich alles zusammen*]. What delight this is I cannot tell! All this inventing, this producing, takes place in a pleasing lively dream. Still the actual hearing of the *tout ensemble* is after all the best.[4]

Because none of us are Mozart, we need to sketch score diagrams that are both tall and wide enough to allow us to see what we need to see.

Actors (players) may change. The USSR no longer exists. I have included Russia to remind us of that fact. This score reminds us to keep track of new actors as well as the demise of old ones (for example, Lehman Brothers) and the conditions that will create or destroy them.

All the anthems were transposed into D major, the key in which the U.S. anthem is played. The key of a piece determines the goal and the field of forces acting on actions (each note and chord) that will move it in a specified direction (the tonic). Each key contains only a subset of possible notes (actions). The idea of a key reminds us that there will always be a contest among actors to determine what should be given priority—for example, short-term profits, long-term competitive advantage, defending an existing market niche, diversifying, and so on.

We sometimes say that the world has become multipolar. The difficulty with this description is that it has little organizing power; all we see are multiple centers competing for influence in a myriad of ways. That is why the musical score is useful as a way to make sense of what is going on. It reminds us to consider vertical relationships, how one course of action may influence, join, control, or compete with another. The score also calls our attention to the distinction between foreground and background, between melody and its accompaniment. What is background today may be foreground tomorrow.

Because we cannot easily imagine the vertical dimension of the world—and find patterns in what is going on at the same time—we shrink the vertical until it becomes a single horizontal *time line*. Then, because we seek speed, we shorten the line until it becomes a *point*. We think about the short run: we want results now. In terms of what I have called the P4 strategy (discussed in Chapter Eight), we have moved from pattern and polyphony to a single time-extended path, and from there, to a single point. In doing so, we have collapsed the vertical and shrunk the horizontal. *The result is that we are living in an architectural ruin.* We need the P4 strategy and the score representation to enlarge and rebuild our image of the world, not, as I said before, to add complexity, but to restore it. And restore it we must, because to act on the basis of an incomplete image or map is to risk making a wrong turn, or worse, going over a cliff we could have seen in time.

Re-imaging the world as a polyphonic, polyrhythmic score shifts how we think about the causes and consequences of events. Most of us spend a considerable amount of time looking "down the road" to the next period of time, the one we call the future. So, naturally, when we think about the consequences of our actions, we think in terms of a line, antecedents to the left, consequences—separated by some amount of time—to the right. Similarly, when we ask about the cause of an event, we typically look back to what came before. When we say that A causes B, we are focusing on the horizontal dimension of the score. We are focused on what comes before (the cause) and what comes after (the effect). That is fine, but we should also be paying attention to what is going on vertically, to what must and must not go on at the same time. That means paying attention to *chords and chord progressions*. Anytime someone offers an explanation or a prediction without saying what is going on *simultaneously* at *successive* points in time, you know that he or she is likely to be wrong, or right only by accident.

It was, in fact, a lucky accident that the "music consultant" I was working with decided to play the U.S., Canadian, and Mexican anthems at the same time, as well as France at the same time as Germany. Because we did not play all possible combinations, we don't know which anthems might go together and which would not. That is true of any complex environment. Do multiple streams of action form a coherent pattern, or does their copresence simply produce chaos?

Each anthem is unique to each country. To what extent must its musical or temporal identity be maintained? The falling notes suggest erosion. The future can be built from recombinations of existing notes (actions) or perhaps from a new source, the large pile of notes at the bottom. Some actors (countries) will have claimed a position in the new world, in the treble clef or the bass clef. Others may not have planned that far ahead, or if they have, they have not made their intentions public. Still others will have already found partners and will be at work creating their own mini-compositions, as indicated by the brackets.

As a score unfolds, different actors (nations, groups, organizations, institutions, or individuals) perform, audition for, or compete for different roles—namely, those of composer, conductor, performer, audience, and critic. Who will create the new score, the new strategy or business model? Who will take time-tested products and services and bring them up-to-date in the same way that a conductor reinterprets a classic for modern ears? Who will become skilled in executing the steps needed to implement a plan, program, or process? Who will perform its steps with perfection? Who will attend to and value what is produced? Finally, who will judge and critique what has been carried out and accomplished?

One reason to think about *business environments as musical scores* is Jacques Attali's provocative suggestion that

> music is prophecy. Its styles and economic organization are ahead of the rest of society because it explores, much faster than material reality can, the entire range of possibilities in a given code. It makes audible the new world that will gradually become visible, that will impose itself and regulate the order of things; it is not only the image of things, but ... the herald of the future.[5]

He concludes, "Thus ... if it is true that *the political organization of the twentieth century is rooted in the political thought of the nineteenth, the latter is almost entirely present in embryonic form in the music of the eighteenth century.*"[6]

If Attali's comments seem extreme or far-fetched, consider the music of Charles Ives. His fourth symphony, written between 1908 and 1916, required two conductors because the rhythm was so complex.[7] As described by Lawrence Kramer, typical Ivesian techniques included "the superimposition (layering) of diverse musical styles and processes, the withholding of goal-directed harmonic motion, the fragmentation of material, and the drastic complication of texture."[8] I would suggest that here we are, a century later, right in the middle of an Ivesian score—one that needs a new generation of composers, performers, and analysts to make sense of it. Radically new music is always difficult to listen to—to say nothing of the skills needed to lead it.

Finally, the *New 21st Century World* score reminds us that the skills needed to address issues of timing are not ones of decisiveness, calculation, or even judgment. These are virtues, of course. But the more relevant skill is the ability to envision, find, and work with the music-like patterns that run through and define the modern business environment. If we treat time as a date on a calendar—that is, if we *separate* it from the actions or events that take place at those moments, which is the essence of scheduling—we will be forever mystified by *when* things happen. We can't solve for t unless T is part of the equation, which means that we can't decide what time (t) to act unless our description of the context of action includes all six elements of temporal architecture (T)—all of the sequences, rates, durations, beginnings, endings, etc., that describe the dynamics of the world around us. The image of a score reminds us to consider time as a *pattern* and a *process* and not simply as a *line* or *number*, to think of time as a *constituent* and not simply a *container* for our actions.

And we need a reminder. In the *Bhagavad Gita*, the Blessed Lord said to Arjuna:

> ... for embodied beings,
>
> the Unmanifest is obscure.[9]

Time is intangible. We cannot see, hear, smell, touch, or taste it. We may measure it, but we are not at all certain—at least not yet—what time itself consists of. Time is hidden and mysterious, and therefore easy to overlook.

Over time, the substantive issues that business leaders will face will change. The map of world will be altered; companies, business models, nation-states will come and go. The need to make the right decisions *at the right time* will remain. We will always face the question of timing: is it too early for a particular action, or is it already too late? How should I proceed, quickly or slowly, and what risks will I encounter along the way? In this book, I have tried to show that there is much more that we can know about such issues than meets the eye or is found in contemporary practice. Skill in matters of timing can be acquired and can become a continuing source of knowledge and competitive advantage.

So it is now time to close the book, turn off the screen, and begin the work that needs to be done. Because, as Hillel said, if not now, WHEN?

appendix

Temporal Architecture
Concept and Field of Inquiry

Temporal architecture is the art and science of designing, creating, analyzing, and using the music-like patterns that form when multiple actions and processes are aligned, synchronized, superimposed, or otherwise related to each other in time. The life span of these patterns, which have the vertical and horizontal structure of a musical score, can vary from seconds to years. Temporal architecture includes the study of the *functions* or *purposes* that these patterns serve, the *qualities* and *meanings* they express, the *emotions* they provoke, the *intentions* they realize or resist, and perhaps most important for the practical actor, the *actions that they make possible or prohibit.* In contrast to spatial architecture and like the structures of the human brain and body, the designs of temporal architecture are rarely visible on the surface. They are not part of what we usually see. They are not part of what we usually think about when we plan our actions. As a general rule, we include only fragments of these designs in our descriptions of the world.

The field of temporal architecture is related to that of spatial architecture. Vitruvius defined the classic functions of spatial architecture as *firmitatus, utilitatis,* and *venustatis.* Firmitatus is structure—buildings must stand up. Utilitatis means that buildings must serve a useful purpose; venustatis, that buildings should be beautiful. They should have a pleasing appearance. The patterns of temporal architecture serve similar functions. They must support or house different actions, events, and activities. They must last long enough to do so. They should also feel right. The right temporal pattern will have an esthetic quality as well as an instrumental use.

Goethe famously referred to traditional architecture as "frozen music." That phrase also captures the patterns of temporal architecture. The difference is that rather than being literally set in stone—that is, frozen, as is the case with traditional architecture—the patterns of temporal architecture describe a process that, like music, develops and changes over time. If we "unfreeze" music and let it play, then music is time made audible,[1] capturing the twin features of human temporal experience: the possibility of simultaneity and the requirement of succession.

notes

Preface

1. E. Brann, *What, Then, Is Time?* (Lanham, MD: Rowman & Littlefield, 1999); J. T. Fraser, *Time and Time Again: Reports from a Boundary of the Universe* (Boston: Brill, 2007).

   For a summary of research on time within management, see *Academy of Management Review* 26, no. 4 (October 2001). There is of course a vast literature dealing with time, which I will not attempt to reference. The best short review of philosophical approaches that I have found is Brann's *What, Then, Is Time?* For those interested in the interdisciplinary study of time, none can surpass the work of J. T. Fraser. See his *Time and Time Again* for a series of essays summarizing some of his work. I also call your attention to the work of the International Society for the Study of Time, which has triannual conferences and an edited book series.

Introduction

1. Dan Gilbert makes a similar point about how much we leave out. See D. T. Gilbert and T. D. Wilson, "Prospection: Experiencing the Future," *Science* 317, no. 5843 (September 7, 2007): 1351–1354.

2. For a history and discussion of the term *kairos*, which refers to the right time or moment, see J. Bartunek and R. Necochea,

249

"Old Insights and New Times: Kairos, Inca Cosmology, and Their Contributions to Contemporary Management Inquiry," *Journal of Management Inquiry* 9, no. 2 (2000): 103–113.

3. L. Bernstein, *The Joy of Music* (New York: Amadeus Press, 2004), 160.

4. M. B. Lieberman and D. B. Montgomery, "First-Mover Advantages," *Strategic Management Journal* 9 (Summer 1988): 41–58; M. E. Porter, *Competitive Strategy* (New York: Free Press, 1980).

5. J. Glover, *Humanity: A Moral History of the Twentieth Century* (New Haven, CT: Yale University Press, 2000), 242.

6. M. Ingebretsen, *Why Companies Fail: The Ten Big Reasons Businesses Crumble and How to Keep Yours Strong and Solid* (New York: Crown Business, 2003), xi.

7. A. Ballmer, "Openers: Corner Office," *New York Times*, May 17, 2009, B2.

8. G. Mitchell, *Making Peace* (New York: Knopf, 1999), 173.

9. Beethoven, Ludwig van, 1770–1827, Symphonies, no. 5, op. 67, C minor, (New York: Kassel, Bärenreiter, 1999).

10. K. E. Weick, "Improvisation as a Mindset for Organizational Analysis," *Organizational Science* 9, no. 5 (1998): 543–555. Management scholars such as Weick have discussed organizational action as improvisational jazz. My focus is different, but related. I am interested in describing the environment for organizational action and in using the music-like patterns that are present in the environment as a source of information about risk and windows of opportunity. It is precisely because we can't describe the structure of a musical score in mathematical terms that we can't model our world mathematically. We can describe the resultant—the sound of the symphony in terms of waves and wavelets—but we can't describe the score itself. That is one reason models of risk fail: they are based on incomplete qualitative data.

11. P. Brook, *The Empty Space* (New York: Simon & Schuster, 1968), 125–126.

Chapter One

1. "John Archibald Wheeler," TastefulWords.com/, http://quotations .tastefulwords.com/john-archibald-wheeler/.

2. D. Owen, "The Inventor's Dilemma," *New Yorker*, May 17, 2010, 42.

3. Ibid.

4. L. Story and D. Barboza, "The Recalls' Aftershocks," *New York Times*, December 22, 2007, B1, B9.

5. *Pepper . . . and Salt*, *Wall Street Journal*, August 27, 1999, p. A9. Most of us think of "salt and pepper" as the usual order for this expression. For some reason I haven't been able to why discover the cartoon is titled with this sequence inverted.

6. K. Gesswein and S. Fealy, "Vows," *New York Times*, January 23, 2000, 38.

7. American Society of Clinical Oncology, "Progress Against Stomach Cancer" (2012), http://www.cancerprogress.net/downloads/timelines/progress_against_stomach_cancer_timeline.pdf.

8. J. P. Newport, "Why Scientists Love to Study Golf," *Wall Street Journal*, March 24–25, 2012, A16.

9. "Inventive Warfare," *Economist*, August 20, 2011, 57–58.

10. J. Clements, "Don't Get Hit by the Pitch: How Advisors Manipulate You," *Wall Street Journal*, January 3, 2007, D1.

Chapter Two

1. J. Becker and M. Luo, "In Tucson, Guns Have a Broad Constituency," *New York Times*, January 10, 2011, http://www.nytimes.com/2011/01/11/us/11guns.html.

2. J. Markoff, "Slogging up PC Hill at I.B.M.," *New York Times*, May 10, 1992, http://www.nytimes.com/1992/05/10/business/slogging-up-pc-hill-at-ibm.html?pagewanted=all&src=pm.

3. B. O'Brian, "You Must Remember This: A Slide Is Still a Slide," *Wall Street Journal*, March 5, 2001, R1.

4. L. Greenhouse, "Tactic of Delayed Miranda Warning Is Barred," *New York Times*, June 29, 2004, A17.

5. S. Albert and G. Bell, "Timing and Music," *Academy of Management Review* 27, no. 4 (2002): 574–593. This analysis follows closely and in parts is identical.

6. G. Morgenson, "The Markets: Market Place—Mixed Signals from the Fed; If the Water's Fine, Why Are Those Sharks Still Circling?" *New York Times*, http://www.nytimes.com/1998/10/16/business

/markets-market-place-mixed-signals-fed-if-water-s-fine-why-are-those-sharks.html.

7. "I Think It's Time We Broke for Lunch ... Court Rulings Depend Partly on When the Judge Last Had a Snack," *Economist*, April 16, 2011, 87.

8. G. Bowley, "Loan Sale of 4.1 Billion in Contracts Led to 'Flash Crash' in May," *New York Times*, October 2, 2010, B1.

9. T. Lauricella, "Bond Funds Fall Victim to Timing: Thinking Worst Was Over, Top Performers Now Lag Behind," *Wall Street Journal*, November 17–18, 2007, B1.

10. D. Gross, "A Phantom Rebound in the Housing Market," *New York Times*, January 7, 2007, C5.

11. M. R. Gordon, "War, Meet the 2008 Campaign," *New York Times*, January 20, 2008, A4.

12. L. Tamura, "Who Really Runs Yellow Lights?" *Washington Post*, in the *Star Tribune*, June 30, 2010, A4.

13. Some of these questions are based on analysis in B. M. Staw and J. Ross, "Behavior in Escalation Situations," in *Research in Organizational Behavior*, ed. Barry M. Staw and Larry L. Cummings (Greenwich, CT: JAI Press, 1987), 9:39–78.

14. Ibid.

15. For a discussion of the relationship between time and organizational culture, see E. H. Schein, *Organizational Culture and Leadership* (San Francisco: Jossey-Bass, 2004); 151–163N. For a discussion of how the future is viewed differently in different cultures, see Ashkanasy, V. Gupta, M. S. Mayfield, and E. Trevor-Roberts, "Future Orientation," in *Culture, Leadership, and Organizations: The GLOBE Study of 62 Societies*, ed. R. J. House, P. J. Hanges, M. Javidan, P. W. Dorfman, and V. Gupta (Thousand Oaks, CA: Sage, 2004), 282–342.

16. Quoted in W. W. Lowrance, *Modern Science and Human Values* (New York: Oxford University Press, 1986), 168.

17. Peter Leo, "Channeling Man's Basic Instinct," *Pittsburgh Post Gazette*, August 25 1994, http://global.factiva.com ezp-prodl.hul.harvard.edu/hp/printsavews.aspx.

18. L. Ellison, "The America's Cup Comes to Europe," *Economist*, November 16, 2006, http://www.economist.com/node/8132643.

19. S. Shellenbarger, "Time-Zoned: Working Around the Round-the-Clock Workday," *Wall Street Journal*, February 15, 2007, D1.

20. R. Walker, "Pointed Copy: The Ginsu Knife," *New York Times Magazine*, December 31, 2006, 18, http://www.nytimes.com/2006/12/31/magazine/31wwln_consumed.t.html?n=Top%2fFeatures%2fMagazine%2fColumns%2fConsumed&_r=0.

Chapter Three

1. I. Calvino, *Six Memos for the Next Millennium* (Cambridge: Harvard University Press, 1998), 54.

2. S. Mydans, "Australians Enter East Timor in Show of Force," *New York Times*, September 29, 1999, A7.

3. R. Gulati, M. Sytch, and P. Mehrotra, "Preparing for the Exit," *Wall Street Journal*, March 3, 2007, R11. Reprinted with permission of Dow Jones & Company, Inc.

4. G. Kolata, "Researchers Dispute Benefits of CT Scans for Lung Cancer," *New York Times*, March 7, 2007, A18.

5. Ibid.

6. C. Dawson, "Japan Plant Had Earlier Alert," *Wall Street Journal*, June 15, 2011, A11.

7. R. L. Rose, "Work Week: A Special News Report About Life on the Job—and Trends Taking Shape There," *Wall Street Journal*, December 6, 1994, A1.

8. Quoted in "Commencements: Change the World and Godspeed," *Time*, June 12, 1995, 82.

9. A. Alter, "What Don DeLillo's Books Tell Him," *Wall Street Journal*, January 30–31, 2010, W5.

10. J. P. Richter, *The Notebooks of Leonardo da Vinci* (New York: Dover 1970), 296.

11. J. Steinhauer, "Sometimes a Day in Congress Takes Seconds, Gavel to Gavel," *New York Times*, August 6, 2011, A12.

12. "A 120-Year Lease on Life Outlasts Apartment Heir," *New York Times*, December 29, 1995, A8. Used with permission of The Associated Press, copyright © 2013. All rights reserved.

13. J. E. Garten, "A Crisis Without a Reform," *New York Times*, August 18, 1999, http://www.nytimes.com/1999/08/18/opinion/a-crisis-without-a-reform.html.

14. S. Shane, "The Complicated Power of the Vote to Nowhere," *New York Times*, April 1, 2007, D4.

15. E. Nagourney, "Undue Optimism When Death Is Near," New York Times, February 29, 2000, D8.

16. A discussion of the empty interval can be found in S. Zaheer, S. Albert, and A. Zaheer, "Time Scales and Organizational Theory," *Academy of Management Review* 24, no. 4 (1999): 725–741.

17. D. Finn, *How to Look at Everything* (New York: Abrams, 2000), 95.

18. D. Landes, *Revolution in Time: Clocks and the Making of the Modern World* (Cambridge, MA: Harvard University Press, 1983), 348–349.

19. B. Hubbard Jr., *A Theory for Practice: Architecture in Three Discourses* (Cambridge, MA: MIT Press, 1996), 164.

20. R. Wright, E. de Sabata, and G. Segreti, "Alarm Delay 'Critical' Says Concordia Probe," *Financial Times*, May 18, 2012, http://www.ft.com/intl/cms/s/0/0c0cbd0e-a0f7-11e1-aac1-00144feabdc0.html#axzz2P96YG0Fy.

21. J. McPhee, "Checkpoints," *New Yorker*, February 9, 2009, 59.

22. J. Bailey, "Chief 'Mortified' by JetBlue Crisis," *New York Times*, February 19, 2007, A1.

23. P. Greer, 1970, cited in J. G. Miller, *Living Systems* (New York: McGraw-Hill, 1978), 163.

24. S. Adams, *Dilbert, Minneapolis Star and Tribune*, October 16, 2005, Comics, 1.

25. J. Longman, "Lilliputians Gaining Stature at Global Extravaganza," *New York Times*, June 17, 2002, D2.

26. G. Morgenson, "When Bond Ratings Get Stale," *New York Times*, October 11, 2009. B1.

27. J. Wilgoren, "President Stuns Brown U. by Leaving to Be Vanderbilt Chancellor," *New York Times*, February 8, 2000, A18.

28. B. Pennington and J. Curry, "Andro Hangs in Quiet Limbo," *New York Times*, July 11, 1999, D4.

29. T. McGinty, K. Kelly, and K. Scannell, "Debt 'Masking' Under Fire," *Wall Street Journal,* April 21, 2010, A1.

30. A. K. Naj, "Whistle-Blower at GE to Get $11.5 Million," *Wall Street Journal,* April 26, 1993, A3.

31. M. Jay, "The Downside of Cohabiting Before Marriage," *New York Times,* April 15, 2012, SR4.

32. V. Bernstein, "No Cutting Corners as NASCAR Seeks a Clean Start," *New York Times,* February 18, 2007, http://www.nytimes.com/2007 /02/18/sports/othersports/18nascar.html.

33. P. Dvorak, "Businesses Take a Page from Design Firms," *Wall Street Journal,* November 10, 2008, B4.

34. I. Molotsky, "Winters Warms Up for Humor Prize," *New York Times,* October 21, 1999, A14.

35. C. Berg, "The Real Reason for the Tragedy of the Titanic," *Wall Street Journal,* April 13, 2012, A13.

Chapter Four

1. L. Neri, L. Cooke, and T. de Duve, *Roni Horn* (London: Phaidon, 2000), 18.

2. M. Ali, transcribed from "Muhhamad [*sic*] Ali's Greatest Speech," YouTube, http://www.youtube.com/watch?v=LxLokrATgIw.

3. G. Kolata, "New AIDS Findings on Why Drugs Fail," *New York Times,* January 12, 1995, A1.

4. J. Grant, "Wired Offices, Same Workers," *New York Times,* May 1, 2000, A27.

5. G. Kolata, "Study Finds That Fat Cells Die and Are Replaced," *New York Times,* May 5, 2008, http://www.nytimes.com/2008/05/05 /health/research/05fat.html.

6. Ibid.

7. R. Ludlum, *The Cry of the Halidon* (New York: Bantam Books, 1996), ix.

8. G. Ip, "Tough Equations," *Wall Street Journal,* May 16, 2001, A1, A10.

9. T. Gabriel, "Roll Film! Action! Cut! Edit, Edit, Edit," *New York Times,* May 5, 1997, C1, C13.

10. A. Zimbalist, "Stamping Out Steroids Takes Time," *New York Times*, March 6, 2005, http://www.nytimes.com/2005/03/06/sports /baseball/06zimbalist.html.

11. A. R. Sorkin, "A 'Bonfire' Returns as Heartburn," *New York Times*, June 24, 2008, C5.

12. Relating to a mirror, a reflector, or a reflection.

13. I. Calvino, *If On a Winter's Night a Traveler* (New York: Knopf, 1993), 162.

14. W. Tapply, *Client Privilege* (New York: Delacorte Press, 1990), 73–74.

15. G. Stalk and T. Hout, *Competing Against Time* (New York: Free Press, 1990), 58–59.

16. J. Maeda, *The Law of Simplicity* (Cambridge, MA: MIT Press, 2006), 27–28.

17. S. Kern, *The Culture of Time and Space, 1880–1918* (Cambridge, MA: Harvard University Press, 1983), 275–276.

18. Ibid.

19. "The Hollow Promise of Internet Banking," *Economist*, November 11, 2000, 91.

20. B. Bahree and K. Johnson, "Iraqi Shortfall Means Oil Prices Could Stay High This Year," *Wall Street Journal*, June 27, 2003, C10.

21. J. E. Hilsenrath, "Why For Many This Recovery Feels More Like a Recession," *Wall Street Journal*, May 29, 2003, A1, A14.

22. N. Pachetti, "Crude Economics," *New York Times Magazine*, April 23, 2000, 36.

23. Crystal Classics, n.d., http://www.crystalclassics.com/riedel /riedelhistory.htm.

24. Merleau-Ponty, *L'Œil et l'Esprit*, quoted in J.-P. Montier, *Henri Cartier-Bresson and the Artless Art* (Boston: Little., Brown, 1996), 308. I have slightly modified the English translation to make the quotation a little more readable.

Chapter Five

1. G. Anders and A. Murray, "Behind H-P Chairman's Fall, Clash with a Powerful Director," *Wall Street Journal*, October 9, 2006, A14.

2. P. James, *The Documents of 20th Century Art: Henry Moore on Sculpture* (New York: Viking Press, 1971), 67.

3. Ibid.

4. E. Eakin, "Penetrating the Mind by Metaphor," *New York Times*, February 23, 2002, A19.

5. M. Gimein, "Is a Hedge Fund Shakeout Coming Soon? This Insider Thinks So," *New York Times*, September 4, 2005, B5.

6. R. Kurzweil, *The Singularity Is Near: When Humans Transcend Biology* (New York: Penguin Books, 2006), 8.

7. G. Soros, *The New Paradigm for Financial Markets* (New York: PublicAffairs, 2008), xviii–xix.

8. B. Childs, *Time and Music: A Composer's View* (Seattle: University of Washington Press, 1977).

9. J. Angwin, "Consumer Adoption Rate Slows in Replay of TV's History: Bad News for Online Firms," *Wall Street Journal*, July 16, 2001, B8.

10. M. Oliver, "Flare," in *The Leaf and the Cloud* (Cambridge, MA: Da Capo Press, 2000), 1.

11. D. A. Redelmeier and D. Kahneman, "Patients' Memories of Painful Treatments: Real-Time and Retrospective Evaluations of Two Minimally Invasive Procedures," *Pain* 66, no. 1 (1996): 3–8.

12. J. C. Miller, *Fatigue* (New York: McGraw-Hill, 2001), 46.

13. M. Bloom, "Girls' Cross-Country Taking a Heavy Toll, Study Shows," *New York Times*, December 4, 1993, http://www.nytimes.com/1993/12/04/sports/track-field-girls-cross-country-taking-a-heavy-toll-study-shows.html.

14. J. Mouawad, "Volatile Swings in the Price of Oil Hobble Forecasting," *New York Times*, July 6, 2009, A3.

15. K. Brown, "Leaner Budgets at Corporations Are Bad Omen," *New York Times*, July 16, 2001, C2.

16. Soros, *New Paradigm*, 68.

17. "The Trade Talks That Never Conclude," *Economist*, August 2, 2008, 71.

18. Quoted in A. Delbanco, *Required Reading: Why Our American Classics Matter Now* (New York: Farrar, Straus & Giroux, 1997), 116.

19. M. Corkery and J. R. Hagerty, "Outlook: Continuing Vicious Cycle of Pain in Housing and Finance Ensnares Market," *Wall Street Journal*, July 14, 2008, A2.

20. B. Mutzabaugh, "Brazil's Embraer Jets Are Sized Just Right," *Florida Today*, July 20, 2012. Available at http://www.floridatoday.com /article/20120722/BUSINESS/307220011/Brazil-s-Embraer-jets-sized-just-right.

21. A. Zuger, "Nighttime, and Fevers Are Rising," *New York Times*, September 28, 2004, D6.

22. T. Parker-Pope, "Why Curing Your Cancer May Not Be the Best Idea," *Wall Street Journal*, February 11, 2003, R1.

23. L. Sterne, *Tristram Shandy*, ed. H. Anderson (New York: Norton, 1980), vii. Originally published in nine volumes, 1759, 1761, 1762, 1765, 1767.

Chapter Six

1.   Quoted in E. W. Soja, *Post Modern Geographies: The Reassertion of Space in Critical Social Theory* (London: Verson, 1989), 138.

2.   A. Copland, *What to Listen for in Music* (New York: Penguin Books, 1953), 105, 106, 107–108.

3.   R. Smith, *The Utility of Force: The Art of War in the Modern World* (New York: Knopf, 2007), 19.

4.   A. T. Board, "34 Months and Still No Divorce," *New York Times*, August 3, 1996, A15.

5.   Ibid.

6.   R. Dove, "Fourth Juror," *in American Smooth: Poems* (New York: Norton, 2004), 76. Copyright © 2004 by Rita Dove. Used by permission of W.W. Norton & Company, Inc.

7.   J. Pierson, "Stand Up and Listen: Your Chair May Harm Your Health," *New York Times*, September 12, 1995, B1.

8.   W. Carley, "Mystery in the Sky: Jet's Near-Crash Shows 747s May Be at Risk of Autopilot Failure," *Wall Street Journal*, April 26, 1993, A1.

9.   D. Rodrik, "Elusive 'Giffen Behavior' Spotted in Chinese Homes," *Wall Street Journal*, July 17, 2007, B9.

10. "Panel Says Penn Police Overreacted," *New York Times*, July 28, 1993, B7.

11. W. Connor, "Why Were We Surprised?" *American Scholar* 60, no. 2 (Spring 1991), 177.

12. J. Flint, "NBC Ratings: Olympic-Sized Anticlimax," *Wall Street Journal*, September 22, 2000, B6.

13. B. Carter, "NBC Banks on Olympics as Springboard for New Shows," *New York Times*, August 13, 2012, B1.

14. J. Hoppin, "Tons of Rock, Sand Piled at Point Where Bridge Broke," *Pioneer Press*, March 18, 2008, A1.

15. A. Scardino, "The Market Turmoil: Past Lessons, Present Advice; Did '29 Crash Spark the Depression?" *New York Times*, October 21, 1987, http://www.nytimes.com/1987/10/21/business/the-market -turmoil-past-lessons-present-advice-did-29-crash-spark-the- depression.html.

16. R. H. Thaler and S. Benartzi, *Save More Tomorrow: Using Behavioral Economics to Increase Employee Saving*, November 2000, http://www .cepr.org/meets/wkcn/3/3509/papers/thaler_save_more_ tomorrow.pdf.

17. P. Brook, *Threads of Time* (Washington, DC: Counterpoint, 1998), 63.

18. J. Scott, "Spring Ahead, Sleep Behind," *New York Times*, April 2, 1995, A37.

19. D. Goldner, "Ahead of the Curve," *Wall Street Journal*, May 22, 1995, R19.

20. S. Carey, "Chaos in Jet After It Hit River," *Wall Street Journal*, February 9, 2009, A6.

21. Quoted in A. Koestler, *The Art of Creation: A Study of the Conscious and Unconscious in Science and Art* (New York: Dell, 1964), 175.

22. "The Year in Ideas: The Ambulance-Homicide Theory," *New York Times Magazine*, December 15, 2002, 66.

23. D. Ellsberg, *Secrets: A Memoir of Vietnam and the Pentagon Papers* (New York: Viking Press, 2002), 141–142.

24. J. Darnton, "But How Two Irish Enemies Got the Ball Rolling," *New York Times*, September 5, 1994, A1, A4.

25. There is a large literature on entrainment. See D. Ancona, and C.-I. Chong, "Entrainment: Pace, Cycle, and Rhythm in Organizational Behavior," in *Research in Organizational Behavior*, ed. B. Staw and L. Cummings (Greenwich, CT: JAI Press, 1996) 18:251–284.

    Some writers suggest that organizations should try to synchronize the internal rhythms of their organization with those in their environment. My approach is slightly different. The first task is to find all the rhythms that matter. Given Copland's Constraint, that is not an easy matter. Then one has to understand their interaction or interrelationship, including how and when the rhythms might change. Sometimes it is best to be in sync with an environmental rhythm; sometimes it is best to be out of sync.

26. F. Schwartz, *Blind Spots: Critical Theory in the History of Art in 20th Century Germany* (New Haven, CT: Yale University Press, 2005), 130.

27. From Lindsay, Kenneth C. and Peter Gergo. *Kandinsky, Complete Writings on Art.* © 1982 Gale, a part of Cengage Learning, Inc. Reproduced by permission. www.cengage.com/permissions

28. F. Norris, "Buried in Details, a Warning to Investors," *New York Times*, August 2, 2012, http://www.nytimes.com/2012/08/03/business/a-wells-fargo-security-goes-wrong-for-investors.html?pagewanted=all.

29. C. Dean, "Engineering and the Art of the Fail," review of *To Forgive Design: Understanding Failure*, by Henry Petroski, *New York Times*, July 13, 2012, C25.

30. T. Friedman, "Two Worlds Cracking Up," *New York Times*, June 12, 2012, http://www.nytimes.com/2012/06/13/opinion/friedman-two-worlds-cracking-up.html.

31. T. S. Bernard, "The Best Time to Buy and Sell College Textbooks," *Bucks* (blog), August 8, 2012, http://bucks.blogs.nytimes.com/2012/08/08/the-best-time-to-buy-and-sell-college-textbooks/.

32. S. Blakeslee, "A Rare Victory in Fighting Phantom Limb Pain," *New York Times*, March 28, 1995, B12.

33. J. L. Lunsford, "Gradual Ascent: Burned by Last Boom, Boeing Curbs Its Pace; It Uses New Restraint to Juggle Jet Orders; Avoiding 'Bunny Holes,'" *Wall Street Journal*, March 26, 2007, A1.

34. Ibid, A13.

35. "Joseph and the Amazing Technicalities: Adjusting Banking Regulation for the Economic Cycle," *Economist*, April 26, 2008, 18.

36. "And Now Here Is the Health Forecast: Understanding the Link Between Illness and Temperature Should Help Hospitals," *Economist*, August 1, 2002, http://www.economist.com/node/1259077.

37. A. Stone, "Why Waiting Is Torture," *New York Times*, August 18, 2012, SR12.

Chapter Seven

1. "Mahatma Gandhi Quotes," *BrainyQuote*, http://www.brainyquote
.com/quotes/authors/m/mahatma_gandhi.html#8K8lItl36
cQKsbQR.99.

2. S. Albert, "The Timing of Dissent," *Leader to Leader*, Fall 2001, no. 22, 34. The analysis in this chapter follows closely from the *Leader to Leader* article. The dialogue is based on my notes taken from a 16mm black-and-white film on group process that is no longer available. I believe the distributor was McGraw-Hill, but I cannot be sure. The title might have been *Victims of Group Think*.

3. *Robert's Rules of Order Newly Revised*, 11th ed. (New York: De Capo Press, 2011).

Chapter Eight

1. J. Albers, *Interaction of Color* (New Haven, CT: Yale University, 2006), 2. Originally published 1963.

2. J. Goldstein, "As Furniture Burns Quicker, Firefighters Reconsider Tactics," *New York Times*, July 2, 2012, A1.

3. J. Groopman and P. Hartzband, "Why Quality of Care is Dangerous," *Wall Street Journal*, April 8, 2009, A13.

4. Goldstein, "As Furniture Burns Quicker," A3.

5. J. Markoff, "Researchers Find Way to Steal Encrypted Data," *New York Times*, February 22, 2008, C1, C6.

6. D. J. Wakin, "Time to Tie a String Around That Strad," *New York Times*, May 11, 2008, A6.

Coda

1. W. Apel and R. T. Daniel, *The Harvard Brief Dictionary of Music* (New York: Pocket Books, 1960), 62.

2. S. Beckett, *Endgame and Act Without Words* (New York: Grove Press, 1958), 1.

3. A. Camus, *Notebooks 1935–1942* (New York: Knopf, 1963), 10.

4. From a letter attributed to Mozart in E. Brann, *The World of the Imagination: Sum and Substance* (Savage, MD: Rowman & Littlefield, 1991), 321.

5. J. Attali, *Noise: The Political Economy of Music* (Manchester, UK: Manchester University Press, 1985), 11.

6. Ibid, 4.

7. M. Hall, *Leaving Home: A Conducted Tour of the 20th Century Music with Simon Rattle* (London: Faber & Faber, 1996), 68.

8. L. Kramer, *Classical Music and Postmodern Knowledge* (Berkeley: University of California Press, 1995), 176.

9. S. Mitchell, trans., *Bhagavad Gita: A New Translation* (New York: Three Rivers Press, 2000), 145.

Appendix

1. S. K. Langer, *Feeling and Form* (New York: Charles Scribner's Sons, 1953), 110. In *Feeling and Form,* Langer said that "*music makes time audible, and its form and continuity sensible.*" (Italics are in the original.)

acknowledgments

Dozens of individuals have helped me make this book a reality. A number of colleagues took the time to read and comment on numerous chapters. I thank Professor Edgar Schein of MIT for several lengthy discussions and for his overall encouragement. My friend and colleague Professor Marc Anderson was very helpful as I developed the Timing of Dissent case. He also read parts of the manuscript with an eye toward improving its presentation. I thank Dean Sri Zaheer and Professors Aks Zaheer and Geoff Bell, of the University of Minnesota, with whom I coauthored articles on time and timing. Geoff helped articulate the relationship between timing and music. I thank Ann Waltner, the director of the Institute for Advanced Studies at the University of Minnesota, for a semester-long fellowship that allowed me to devote myself full-time to writing. I am grateful to Dean Thomas Fisher of the School of Design at the University of Minnesota for co-teaching an honors seminar focusing on temporal and spatial design. The opportunity to consider these two realms side by side was of great value.

I also thank Professors Ellen Langer and Herbert Kelman of the Department of Psychology at Harvard for arranging visiting scholar posts during two sabbaticals, and Professor Deborah Ancona for making it possible for me to be a visiting professor at the Sloan School at MIT, where I spent a wonderful and productive year.

I am grateful to Professor Dan Gilbert of Harvard University for suggesting the title *When*. I only wish that *When* had been ready earlier. Some things take longer than one thinks. It is no small irony that a book on timing happens to be late!

The office staff of the Strategy and Entrepreneurship Department at the University of Minnesota, Julie Cutting, Noelle French, and Kate Nelson, were always ready to lend a hand. They are the best office staff that one could ever hope for.

I also thank Professor Thomaz Wood of Fundação Getúlio Vargas in São Paulo, Brazil, and Professor Bertrand Moingeon of HEC in France for inviting me to talk about my work.

In addition, the International Society for the Study of Time, founded by the late J. T. Fraser, has been an intellectual home for more than twenty years.

I have worked with a number of companies and executives over the course of writing this book. I thank in particular Alex Cirillo of 3M for our monthly breakfasts. The discussion of each chapter greatly contributed to its clarity and usefulness in a business setting. I am grateful to Roger Raigna for his friendship and for an opportunity to consult with his company. Three executives were very helpful in developing my understanding of timing in different business settings: Jim Van Houten, former CEO of MSI Insurance; Dennis R. Costello, managing partner of Braemar Energy Ventures and former chief investment officer for North America at Advent International; and Michael Colson, VP of research and business development at Medtronic.

Mariam Kocharian was a wonderful research assistant, and as my music consultant she was instrumental in helping envision and play the *New 21st Century World Symphony*. I thank Natalie Roberts for creating the early drafts of some of the figures, and Erin Mason of First Street Design for the fine way she executed the graphics in this book and for her design suggestions. I am grateful for the feedback and support of this project provided by Amjad Habouch, a consultant and former student.

Without my current editor and collaborator, Jacqueline Murphy of Cottage Literary, this book would never have seen the light of day. From my perspective, our work together has been an ideal editorial collaboration. Her ability to simplify complex ideas and identify the best structure is unparalleled. Jacque is also my literary agent, and I am grateful that she was able to connect me with the excellent people at Jossey-Bass/Wiley.

I thank Genoveva Llosa, senior editor at Jossey-Bass, for being a strong advocate for the book and for encouraging me all along the way. I also acknowledge Clancy Drake and John Maas of Jossey-Bass. Clancy offered in-depth editorial advice that served to strengthen the book. John has been extremely supportive and ever helpful. Michele Jones did a superb job of copyediting.

I thank Janet Coleman for her editorial help and hospitality in the early days, when this book was more a gleam in my eye than anything else. Our discussions over lunch, dinner, and around the clock helped corral and shape the ideas at the core of book.

I also thank Erin Wigg for her help in coding and managing the database on which this book is based, and for responding to my many requests regarding bibliographical information. She has probably now memorized the location of every one of the three thousand books in my home library. I also acknowledge the assistance of Joe Scott and Clayton McClintock for their help in copyediting and to Alan Fine for his comments and feedback on the cover.

Jack Galloway was my editor during the early drafts. My work with Jack became a master class in the art of writing; this is still a work in progress. Jack's passionate defense of the legitimate needs of the reader, and his deep belief in the value of this book helped make the book possible. When I think of our long discussions, the "out-of-category climbs," the struggle to find the right language for a particular section, I find myself thinking back to a few lines by the poet Czeslaw Milosz:

> To find my home in one sentence, concise, as if hammered in metal. . . An unnamed need for order, for rhythm, for form, which three words are opposed to chaos and nothingness.[†]

I also thank Lucy McCauley, editor and filmmaker, for her support of this project, as well as Joan Poritsky and Jacque Wiersma for their support and advice over the years. John Bryson and Barbara Crosby have been dear friends for decades. Their professional accomplishments have served as a model and inspiration to me. I also remember fondly the many dinners my wife and I had with Alan and Carol Bensman, when we talked about the ideas in this book.

I am particularly fortunate to have a wonderful family in Brazil. Clarice and José Abuleac and Suely and Thomas Hirschbruch have provided warmth, companionship, and laughter, and have been supportive of this work for many years. My late in-laws, Bernardo and Ella Daskal, provided love and a home away from home. I continue to miss them. I also thank Lucia Vicente for always asking, "How's the book coming?"

Thank you to my sister, Myra Albert, for her interest in my work and for insightful feedback on the cover. I also thank Robert and Kathy Mintz and Ginny and Steve Freid for their interest and enthusiasm for this project over the years.

Finally, I find myself at a loss for words in expressing my gratitude to my wife, Rosita, for a lifetime of love and support.

[†]*Unattainable Earth* by Czeslaw Milosz and translated by Robert Hass. Copyright © 1986 by Czeslaw Milosz and Robert Hass. Reprinted by permission of HarperCollins Publishers.

about the author

Stuart Albert is one of the foremost timing experts in the world. He has developed a practical, research-based method for managing timing in business, and his patent on the interpretation of movement in time was featured in the *New York Times*. He is on the faculty of the Carlson School of Management at the University of Minnesota, and has been a visiting scholar at Harvard and MIT. Albert's theory of temporal comparison continues to be cited and to stimulate work thirty years after it was published, and he has developed a new time-sensitive format for business cases that will help executives plan and implement better timing strategies.

This book is the product of more than ten thousand hours of research and writing by Albert over the course of twenty years. During that time, he has written numerous articles on timing and has worked with a small group of companies as clients and collaborators, helping them craft successful timing strategies and learn from past timing mistakes.

Albert is a member of the Academy of Management and the International Society for the Study of Time, the premier organization in the world for the interdisciplinary study of time. He has published in top academic and applied journals in management and psychology and has presented his work on timing at conferences and seminars in Paris, Stockholm, and São Paulo, as well as at universities and executive workshops in the United States. He divides his time among Minneapolis, Minnesota; Cambridge, Massachusetts; and São Paulo, Brazil. For more information, please visit http://www.stuartalbert.com.

index